THE NOAH PLAN®
READING
CURRICULUM GUIDE

THE PRINCIPLE APPROACH®

KINDERGARTEN THROUGH TWELFTH GRADE

Martha Barnes Shirley

*Why . . . should not the Bible regain the place it once held as a school book?
Its morals are pure, its examples captivating and noble. The reverence for
the sacred book that is thus early impressed lasts long; and probably, if not
impressed in infancy, never takes firm hold of the mind. One consideration
more is important. In no book is there so good English, so pure and so
elegant; and by teaching all the same book they will speak alike, and
the Bible will justly remain the standard of language as well as of faith.*

(Fisher Ames, 1801)

FOUNDATION FOR AMERICAN CHRISTIAN EDUCATION
CHESAPEAKE, VIRGINIA

THE NOAH PLAN®
READING CURRICULUM GUIDE
THE PRINCIPLE APPROACH®
KINDERGARTEN THROUGH TWELFTH GRADE

Martha Barnes Shirley

Acknowledgment
In loving memory of my parents,
Ada Jane and Clarence Solomon Barnes

SECOND EDITION
COPYRIGHT © JULY 2005
FOUNDATION FOR AMERICAN CHRISTIAN EDUCATION
ISBN 0-912498-37-4

FIRST EDITION
COPYRIGHT © SEPTEMBER 1997

Graphic Design,
Desta Garrett

Copyediting,
Sarah Huston

All Scripture references are taken from either the King James Version or
the New International Version of the Bible unless otherwise noted.

Cover Art:
Orchard Window by Daniel Garber
Platinum print on paper mounted on cardboard
H. 7.75 x 7.25 inches
James A. Michener Art Museum, Michener Art Endowment Challenge
Gift of John Garber

PUBLISHED BY

The Foundation for
American Christian Education
P.O. BOX 9588, CHESAPEAKE, VIRGINIA 23321
Ordering and catalogue
800-352-3223 • www.face.net

PREFACE

Whoso loveth instruction loveth knowledge.
(Proverbs 12:1a)

To be instructed by the Holy Spirit is the highest and only permanent means of learning and gaining knowledge. The writer of this *Noah Plan® Reading Curriculum Guide*, Martha Shirley, is a true teacher (one who loves learning), who gives here a truly valuable package—the instruction and means of teaching children to read using the Bible.

This new revised edition of *The Noah Plan Reading Curriculum Guide* has the added value of several more years of road testing by many teachers and homeschoolers as Martha continued to work in the classroom, instruct teachers, conduct training, and research her subject thoroughly. The revision includes the refinement of the overviews and curriculum charts to be used hand in hand with *The Noah Plan* Bible curriculum overviews. As shown in *The Noah Plan Lessons* series, the teaching of Bible and the teaching of reading are a naturally paired unit in the curriculum. This revision gives many recently developed tools for teaching reading using the Bible. It also offers sample student work.

The teacher who loves learning is always searching for new and better ways of instructing and new and fresh insight into the subject. Here, in *The Noah Plan Reading Curriculum Guide*, you will find the latest and best tools of fulfilling the Lord's commission to teach truth to children that "these words . . . shall be in [their] hearts." (Deuteronomy 6:6)

Carole Adams
Chesapeake, Virginia
2005

PREFACE TO THE FIRST EDITION

Noah Webster
(1758–1843)

It might be said that Noah's books were an ark
in which the American Christian spirit
rode the deluge of rising anti-Christian and anti-republican waters
which threatened so often to inundate the nation.

(Rosalie J. Slater, "Noah Webster: Founding Father of American Scholarship and Education" in
Noah Webster's *American Dictionary of the English Language*, Facsimile 1828.
San Francisco: Foundation for American Christian Education, 1967, 13b)

The Noah Plan was named in response to the inspiration of this quote by Rosalie Slater. It is appropriate that she would inspire the name for the first publication of a complete Principle Approach® educational program. Her inspiration was the driving force in the development of the curriculum for all the years of research and writing by StoneBridge School teachers. Rosalie Slater's love of the Word of God, of Christ, His Story, and of the great classical literature, the repository of the grand ideals inspired by them, is like the little bird in one of her favorite James Russell Lowell poems who "lets his illumined being o'errun." And we at StoneBridge were the glad and privileged recipients of this treasure.

Carole Adams
Chesapeake, Virginia
1997

Teacher reading the Bible aloud to student, kindergarten

THE NOAH PLAN® © 2005 • FOUNDATION FOR AMERICAN CHRISTIAN EDUCATION

FOREWORD

This 2005 revision of *The Noah Plan® Reading Curriculum Guide* has given me an opportunity to review, to re-examine, and to revisit reading within the context of Principle Approach® education. Thank you to all of you who purchased the 1997 edition. As the number of copies dwindled in the warehouse, the editors decided rather than reprint from the existing proofs, I would incorporate the new research, revised methods, and my classroom teaching experiences into a new revision. One of the major changes of this 2005 edition is the coordination of the Bible as Reader Program (BAR) schedule for reading the books of the Bible with *The Noah Plan* Bible overview topics. It was determined that a student would benefit from the reinforcement and expansion of the Bible topics and the Biblical principles and leading ideas introduced during the morning Bible class. Bible is taught daily to provide inspiration and encourage changed hearts, while the BAR class focuses on direct instruction of reading and higher-order thinking skills using the same Biblical text.

A review of the most recent scientific research in reading instruction has identified effective practices that can help teachers and parents with methods and approaches that work well and will result in reading improvement. To help assist you, I have summarized the findings of the 2000 National Reading Panel report in the areas of phonemic awareness, fluency, vocabulary, and comprehension.

As I re-examined the first step in the whole program for teaching reading—phonetic instruction—I saw the need for providing phonemic awareness (an awareness of the sounds that make up spoken words) activities to beginning readers with phonics instruction.

Using the suggestions of the newly revised Spalding manual, *The Writing Road to Reading®*, Fifth Revised Edition, I have included the steps of connecting reading and writing, identifying the elements in paragraphs—text structure and using the concept of mental actions to comprehend print. Students need to continually check their understanding and make connections with what they already know with the text they are reading.

After brainstorming with the editor of the second edition, Carole Adams, we felt the presentation of the skills and methods would be more useful in chart form. The Strategic Reading Process now has skilled readers responses to the before, during, and after reading stages. The methods and strategies for teaching Bible as Reader Program have been organized under the five headings: (1) vocabulary, (2) comprehension and interpretation, (3) reading and writing, (4) remediation/enrichment, and (5) evaluation. This structure will guide you as you plan lessons and develop reason questions for higher-level thinking.

Revisiting the foundations for reading gave me new insights into the principles for using the Bible as a reader. The Biblical foundations and the principles have been customized for learning to read using the Bible. The first principle states that reading the Bible prepares a Biblical character in children. Students hear the Word of God daily until they can read for themselves from the *Early Reader's Bible*, equipping them with truth for the practice of Christian liberty.

A special thank you is extended to the classroom teachers at StoneBridge School who invited me into their classrooms to demonstrate the techniques and methods, to instruct their students, and to benefit from their observations and critiques. Connecting with the students was encouraging and refining. I found out what worked and what needed improvement. I was challenged to write this revision by those experiences.

The primary purpose of the guide is unchanged from the first edition—the goal of returning to the Bible as the first book of instruction—a return to the Biblical model.

Martha Barnes Shirley

Martha Barnes Shirley, M.S.Ed.
2005

Principle Approach Model of Education

This diagram shows the components of the Principle Approach Model of Education—a philosophy, methodology, and curriculum that produce particular results and are governed by the Spirit of Christ.

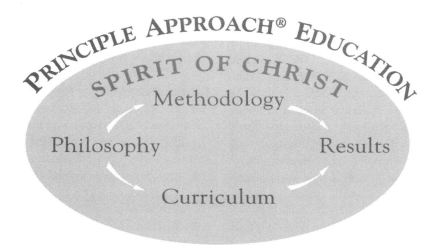

Bible as Reader lesson, first grade

THE NOAH PLAN® © 2005 • FOUNDATION FOR AMERICAN CHRISTIAN EDUCATION

Key

Abbreviations

The following are abbreviations used throughout this guide for books published by the Foundation for American Christian Education (the Foundation):

B & C	*The Bible and the Constitution of the United States of America*, Verna M. Hall and Rosalie J. Slater
C & P	*The Christian History of the American Revolution: Consider and Ponder*, compiled by Verna M. Hall
CHOC I	*The Christian History of the Constitution of the United States of America*, Vol. I: *Christian Self-Government*, compiled by Verna M. Hall
CHOC II	*The Christian History of the Constitution of the United States of America*, Vol. II: *Christian Self-Government with Union*, compiled by Verna M. Hall
NPEG	*The Noah Plan® English Language Curriculum Guide*, Carole G. Adams
NPLG	*The Noah Plan Literature Curriculum Guide*, Rosalie J. Slater
NPRG	*The Noah Plan Reading Curriculum Guide*, Martha Shirley
NPSDS	*The Noah Plan Self-Directed Study in the Principle Approach®*, Carole G. Adams and Elizabeth L. Youmans
Rudiments	*Rudiments of America's Christian History and Government: Student Handbook*, Rosalie J. Slater and Verna M. Hall
T & L	*Teaching and Learning America's Christian History: The Principle Approach*, Rosalie J. Slater
Webster's 1828 Dictionary	*An American Dictionary of the English Language*, Noah Webster. Facsimile 1828 edition

The following are abbreviations for other recommended resources:

Dickson Bible	New Analytical Bible and Dictionary of the Bible, KJV. Dickson, John A., Editor. World Bible Publishers
KJV	King James Version of the Bible
Matthew Henry's Commentary	*Commentary on the Whole Bible*, Matthew Henry
NIV	New International Version of the Bible
NIrV	New International Reader's Version, Kid's Study Bible, Zondervan
Spalding	Spalding Education International
Strong's Concordance	*Exhaustive Concordance of the Bible*, James Strong
SRA	Science Research Associates
WRTR	*The Writing Road to Reading*, Spalding

Trademarked and Registered Resources and Phrases

The Chain of Christianity®   The Principle Approach®

The Noah Plan®   The Spalding Method®

Table of Contents

HOW TO USE THIS GUIDE

This guide directs and points you, the teacher, along a path or course for developing a reading program using the Bible as a primary reader based upon the philosophy of American Christian education, the Principle Approach®.

Goals

1. Establish the foundations for teaching reading

This guide presents the Biblical origins and purposes for reading instruction and for reading the Bible. It gives you a historical perspective of the influence of the Bible on the history of America. It demonstrates God's providence in the teaching and learning of reading through the Christian History of Reading Timeline. *Reading* is defined using Webster's 1828 *Dictionary* and the principles and leading ideas of reading the Bible are identified.

2. Present the whole program for teaching reading in the Principle Approach

What makes reading instruction in the Principle Approach distinctive? It begins with a wholistic view of reading and ends with Christian character. You will view the components of the Bible as Reader model. Then examine grade level curriculum charts with teacher objectives and resources, student performance goals, and reading skills—vocabulary development, comprehension and interpretation, and reasoning and writing—charted for kindergarten through eighth grade.

A high school reading program parallels the academic subjects, offering a forum to discuss and debate books selected for their value in giving breath and depth to the curriculum. The program relates twelve leading ideas to all the subjects of the curriculum and to books, writing, theater, dance, art, and music.

3. Teach reading methods

This guide will also show you how to develop purposeful and active readers. The Strategic Reading Method asks the student to analyze and plan before reading, monitor and regulate his comprehension during reading, and evaluate and react after reading.

The methods presented are a combination of tried and true methods: paraphrasing from Scripture (used in colonial America) and SQ3R, the study skill for recall and test taking. The older methods are grouped with newer scientific methods and activities developed from recent research. For example, this new edition includes Readers Theatre for oral reading practice and graphic organizers to illustrate concepts. You will review the latest research in the areas of phonemic awareness, vocabulary, comprehension, and fluency. You will answer the questions, Why is this instruction important? When should it begin? Which methods of instruction are most effective? What materials should I use? The reading/writing connection is included as a best practice in teaching reading.

Uses for This Guide

1. As a plan book

This guide will direct you as you prepare to teach reading to each child, enabling him to reach the fullest expression of his value in Christ through a Biblical Principle Approach to reading instruction. You will learn the foundations of reading through a word study and develop principles that you will record in your teacher notebook. There are suggestions for setting up your reading notebooks in chapter four. As you prepare quarterly overviews, use the chart of quarterly topics in chapter one.

2. For model lessons

If you need examples to help you write your lessons, check in chapter one for model lesson plans that detail the six steps that you use for chapters or sections of the Bible text. Completion of the steps will take one to three days. Pacing of the steps will vary according to the age and ability of your child or group, length of the selection, and the number and difficulty of the skills you have selected for teaching or reinforcement.

3. As a reference

There is a glossary of specialized terms used for reading and writing. There is also a list of books and resources you will use as you teach reading.

4. For reading tools or strategies

This guide also gives you the "how to" for reading strategies and methods for direct instruction in reading. There are model forms and graphic organizers that have been completed by students to demonstrate the results you can expect from using the teaching and learning tools. Blank forms for duplication are found in the Appendix.

Book Organization

In this guide you will see four different kinds of direction.

1. Curriculum charts to direct your lesson planning

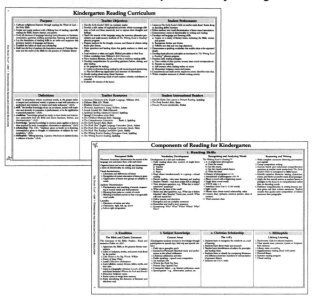

2. Christian History Reading Timeline to give you the providential view of reading

Eternity Past

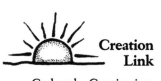

Creation Link

God spoke Creation into existence. Man was created in the image of God with the gift of language. (Genesis 1:2)

"In the beginning was the Word and the Word was with God and the Word was God." (John 1:1)

3. Bible course overview topics coordinated with the Bible as Reader program to integrate Biblical Principles and Bible reading text

Overview of Quarterly Topics for Kindergarten through Eighth Grade

	First Quarter	Second Quarter	Third Quarter	Fourth Quarter
Grades K–4th	The Immediacy of Christ	Old Testament History	The Wisdom Literature & Prophets	New Testament History
Grade 5	Old Testament Survey: Foundations	Old Testament Survey: Taking the Land	Old Testament Survey: Establishing the Kingdom	Old Testament Survey: Destruction, Exile, and Return
Grade 6	New Testament Survey: The Gospels	New Testament Survey: The Acts of the Holy Spirit	New Testament Survey: The Epistles	New Testament Survey: The Apocalypse
Grade 7	Christian Youth Leadership: Youth in Scripture	Christian Youth Leadership: Christian Leadership	Christian Youth Leadership: Old Testament Portraits	Christian Youth Leadership: New Testament Portraits
Grade 8	Christian Doctrine and Creeds: God & Creation	Christian Doctrine and Creeds: Person & Work of Christ, Apostles' Creed	Christian Doctrine and Creeds: Holy Spirit	Christian Doctrine and Creeds: The Church & Last Things Nicene Creed

4. Methods for teaching reading to direct you as a teacher of reading to build students' skills efficiently and effectively

1. Vocabulary		
Concept/ Definition map*	Multiple meanings	Vocabulary word analysis*
Context clues	Phonemic awareness	Word map*
Dictionary	Three word parts	Word webs
Figurative language	Venn diagram*	Word wheels

2. Comprehension & Interpretation		
Cause and effect organizer*	Picture graph	Sequence chain*
Character chart—"People Who Impacted History"*	Questioning strategies	Story circle
	• Levels of questions • Think Aloud	Story map*
Cyclical organizer	• QAR • Reciprocal teaching* **	T-chart*
Five mental actions	• Bloom's Taxonomy	Timeline
K-W-L chart*	SQ3R	Venn diagram*

3. Reading & Writing	
Paraphrasing from Scripture	Story map composition
Reason, relate, and record questions	Writing process in three types of passage structures

4. Remediation & Enrichment	
Choral Reading	Oral reading*
Fluency Instruction	Readers theatre**
• Teacher model • Partner	Supplementary reading—home reading
• Student-adult • Parent/home	Word wheels
• Choral	

5. Evaluation	
Student profile*	Reading inventory

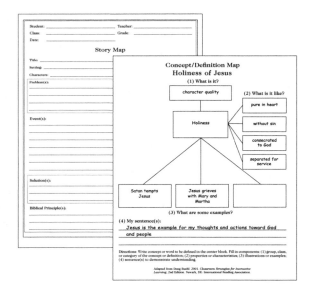

Old Testament History cont.

II. Noah and the Flood

A. The people did not obey God.

   1. God saw evil and cruelty everywhere.

   2. God decided to destroy all the earth with a great flood.

B. Only Noah and his family were saved because Noah was a Godly man.

C. A rainbow is a reminder of God's promise that He will never flood the earth again.

Laura R., 3rd Grade

Scientific Research on Reading and Its Implications for Reading Instruction

Research, *n.* Diligent inquiry or examination in seeking facts or principles;
v. to search or examine with continued care; to seek diligently for the truth.

A review of research in reading instruction and the identification of methods that consistently relate to reading success is the subject of the National Reading Panel Report issued in 2000. The facts coupled with this author's classroom experiences and personal research were used to develop the following reading instruction supplements in the areas of phonemic awareness, fluency, vocabulary, comprehension, and the reading and writing connection. The terminology and the methods and practices will be helpful in writing and implementing your weekly plans for reading instruction. Biblical principles and leading ideas introduce each topic. Each supplement defines the terms, discusses the topic's value, when instruction should begin, effective methods, and suggests materials.

PHONEMIC AWARENESS INSTRUCTION

PRINCIPLE AND LEADING IDEAS
God's Principle of Individuality:
- *Individual sounds (phonemes) make up spoken language*
- *The sounds of speech (phonemes) are distinct from their meaning*

Fact: Current research in beginning reading instruction has shown that phonemic awareness is a powerful predictor of success in learning to read. "Adams (1990) tells us that children who cannot hear and manipulate the sounds in spoken words have an extremely difficult time learning how to decode; at least one out of five children depend critically on explicit instruction in phonemic awareness skills." (White 1998, 10)

What is phonemic awareness? Phonemic awareness is the ability to notice, think about, and work with the individual sounds in spoken words. Before a child learns to read print, he needs to become aware of how the sounds in words work. He must understand that words are made up of speech sounds, or *phonemes*. A child who (1) can easily recognize words that begin alike, (2) can isolate the first or last sound in a word, or (3) combine or blend the separate sounds in a word to say the word will have an easier time learning to read and spell than a child who has few or none of these skills.

Phonemic awareness is not phonics. Phonemic awareness is working with spoken language to make words while phonics is understanding the relationship between letters and sounds in written language.

Why is phonemic awareness important? "Phoneme awareness is a prerequisite to learning phonics. Understanding that syllables are composed of speech sounds is critical for learning to read an alphabetic-phonic language because it is these specific speech sounds (phonemes) that letters represent. Without phonemic awareness, phonics would make no sense. Without an understanding of phonics, word recognition and spelling would depend on rote learning." (White 1998, 10)

Phonemic awareness skills include the following:
- Hearing the separate words within a sentence
- Hearing the number of syllables within a word
- Recognition and creation of rhymes
- Listening for words that begin with the same sounds
- Blending of phonemes into words or syllables
- Substitution of phonemes within syllables/words
- Identification of beginning, middle, and final phonemes in words
- Segmentation of words/syllables into phonemes

The beginning activities for phonemic awareness do not involve written letters (graphemes) or words and are therefore exclusive of phonics. White reminds us that later instruction and practice on phoneme awareness and phonics are complementary. *The most effective programs combine phonemic awareness and letter-sound relationships or beginning phonics.* "New words are always learned by studying the phonetic sounds of the spoken word. This distinguishes The Spalding Method® from most other phonetic methods," *(Spalding 2003, 43).*

When should instruction begin? Instruction is helpful to all students learning to read—preschoolers, kindergartners, first graders who are just starting to read and older, less able readers.

Which methods of instruction are most effective? In the beginning, activities in blending and segmenting words are most effective. Learning to blend phonemes with letters helps children read words. Learning to segment sound with letters helps them spell words. When a student is taught to manipulate phonemes by using the letters of the alphabet, instruction is most effective.

What materials are suggested?

- Alphabet letters (Choose foam or magnetic lower case letters that can be purchased in a toy store or a teacher store.)

- *Put Reading First: The Research Building Blocks for Teaching Children to Read,* Bonnie B. Armbruster, Fran Lehr, and Jean Osborn. September 2001. Copies available from National Institute for Literacy at ED Pubs, PO Box 1398, Jessup, MD 20794-1398. Phone 1-800-228-8813; Fax 301-430-1244. To download, go to the National Institute for Literacy Web site at www.nifl.gov or send e-mail to EdPubOrders@aspensys.com.

- *Phonemic Awareness in Young Children: A Classroom Curriculum,* Marilyn Jager Adams, Barbara R. Foorman, Ingvar Lundberg, and Terri Beeler, 1998. Baltimore, MD: Paul H. Brookes Publishing Co.

- *The Writing Road to Reading: The Spalding Method® for Teaching Speech, Spelling, Writing, and Reading,* Fifth Revised Edition (2003)

References:

Adams, Marilyn Jager. 2000. *Beginning To Read: Thinking and Learning about Print,* Cambridge, MA: The MIT Press.

National Reading Panel. December 2000. *Teaching Children to Read: An Evidence-Based Assessment of the Scientific Research Literature on Reading and Its Implications for Reading Instruction.* National Institute for Literacy, U.S. Deptartment of Health and Human Services. NIH Pub. No. 00-4754.

Spalding, Romalda. 2003. *The Writing Road to Reading: The Spalding Method® for Teaching Speech, Spelling, Writing, and Reading,* Fifth Edition. Phoenix, AZ: Spalding Education International.

White, Nancy. June 1998. "Phonemic Awareness and Phonics: What Are They? How Do They Differ?" *The Virginia Branch Newsletter.* International Dsylexia Association.

FLUENCY INSTRUCTION

PRINCIPLE AND LEADING IDEAS

Conscience Is the Most Sacred of All Property:
- *Individual sounds (phonemes) make up spoken language*
- *The sounds of speech (phonemes) are distinct from their meaning*

The Principle of Christian Self-Government:
- *There is order in language, in sentences, and in words*
- *Rules of propriety govern the way language works*
- *My command of English helps me be self-governed in all areas of my life*

Fact: Repeated and monitored oral reading improves reading fluency and overall reading achievement.

What are the ways of teaching and learning fluency? Activities for repeated oral reading practice include student-adult reading, choral reading, tape-assisted reading, partner reading and Readers Theatre. (Armbruster 2001, 27–29)

- Student-adult reading. The student reads one-on-one with an adult. The adult reads first, providing a model of fluent reading. Then the student reads and rereads with the adult helping with word recognition until the reading is fluent. This usually takes three to four rereadings.
- Choral reading. Students read as a group with an adult leader. First fluent reading is modeled and then students read along, as they are able. The rereading may be spaced over different days to allow the student to read the text independently.
- Tape-assisted reading. The student reads along with a taped recording or as an echo to an audio-taped model. Again, the reading continues until the student can read without the tape.
- Partner reading.
  - The teacher reads the new passage to the class while the students read the passage silently. She may note new words and concepts in the passage.
  - The students work in pairs and take turns reading the passage to each other.
  - One of the pair takes the role of "student" and reads the passage orally. The "teacher" listens while looking at the words in the story. Both are getting practice with the story.
  - Reverse roles.
  - Read the story a total of four times. Partnering can be with a more fluent partner or a partner of equal ability.
- Readers Theatre. Students read from scripts that have been developed from their reading book, preferably those rich in dialogue. No costumes are used, rather students portray the characters with their voices. There is opportunity for many repeated readings as the students rehearse for the performance.

Why is fluency important? "More fluent readers focus their attention on making connections among ideas in a text and between these ideas and their background knowledge." (Armbruster 2001, 22) They are able to focus on comprehension. "Fluent readers recognize words and comprehend at the same time. Less fluent readers, however, must focus their attention on figuring out the words, leaving them little attention for understanding the text." (Armbruster 2001, 22)

When should instruction begin?
Instruction should begin when the student is asked to read orally material he has not practiced and makes more than ten percent recognition errors. A second consideration is if the student does not read with expression, and lastly, if the student's comprehension is poor.

Which methods of instruction are most effective?

A teacher or parent can help his student or child by first modeling fluent reading and then having the student or child reread the text on his own. A second help is have the student repeatedly read passages aloud as you offer guidance. (Armbruster 2001, 26) The reading passages should be at the student's independent reading level and between 50–200 words in length. Use a variety of reading material. Choose stories found in the students' basal readers, Bible readers, or library books. Poetry is also recommended because of the rhythm, rhyme, and meaning, making practice easy and fun.

Research recommends that each passage be read about four times. The number four seems appropriate since the Bible gives us four readings of the life of Christ in Matthew, Mark, Luke, and John.

What materials are suggested?

- Poetry books
- Readers at independent reading level
- *The Writing Road to Reading: The Spalding Method® for Teaching Speech, Spelling, Writing, and Reading*, Fifth Edition, Romalda Spalding. Phoenix, AZ: Spalding Education International, 2003

Reference:

Armbruster, Bonnie B., Fran Lehr, and Jean Osborn. September 2001. *Put Reading First: The Research Building Blocks for Teaching Children to Read.* Copies available from National Institute for Literacy at ED Pubs, PO Box 1398, Jessup, MD 20794-1398. Phone 1-800-228-8813; Fax 301-430-1244. To download go to the National Institute for Literacy Web site at www.nifl.gov.

VOCABULARY INSTRUCTION

PRINCIPLE AND LEADING IDEAS

The Principle of Christian Self-Government:

- *There is order in language, in sentences, and in words*
- *Rules of propriety govern the way language works*
- *My command of English helps me be self-governed in all areas of my life*

Conscience Is the Most Sacred of All Property:

- *God gave me a property in my ability to speak, read, and write*
- *Exercising my gifts makes me a good steward, accountable to God*
- *I use my gift of language to serve God's glory and to keep a good conscience*

Fact: What does research tell us about vocabulary instruction? Research reveals that (1) most vocabulary is learned indirectly, and (2) some vocabulary must be taught directly.

What are the ways of teaching and learning vocabulary? "Children learn the meanings of most words indirectly, through everyday experiences with oral and written language." (Armbruster 2001, 35) The quality and quantity of their conversations with others and adults will have an impact on the word meanings they learn. Secondly, when reading aloud to children make clear the meanings of unfamiliar words and at the end of the passage engage the child in conversation about the passage. Help make connections to previous learning and experience. The third way children learn indirectly is by reading extensively on their own. "The more children read on their own, the more words they encounter and the more word meanings they learn." (Armbruster 2001, 35) God's Word instructs parents to "teach them [God's Word] to your children, talking about them when you sit at home and when you walk along the road, when you lie down and when you get up." (Deuteronomy 11:19)

Indirect or informal instruction should be balanced with direct instruction, especially to learn difficult words and concepts not part of a young child's everyday conversation and experience. "Direct instruction of vocabulary relevant to a given text leads to a better reading comprehension." (Armbruster 2001, 36) Recently when I was teaching the story of Gideon to second graders, it was necessary to check their understanding of the setting—Gideon was threshing wheat in a winepress. Not your typical work in a winepress! Direct instruction should also include teaching students word-learning strategies. We used the dictionary to check the meaning of threshing. We looked at the word *winepress* to figure out the meaning by looking at the word parts—and then we used the context to determine why Gideon would be in a winepress threshing wheat rather than in a field—he needed protection from the marauding Midianites.

Why is vocabulary important? Teaching beginning readers through their oral vocabulary helps them make sense of the words they see in print. As Christians we desire our children to make sense of the Bible and its truths. We extend the oral vocabulary and reading vocabulary through indirect and direct instruction. The reader must know what most of the words mean before he can understand what he is reading. Clarifying and enriching the meaning of known words enables a higher level of thinking and comprehending.

When should instruction begin? Instruction begins by reading aloud to children early and often. The single most important activity for building the knowledge required for eventual success in reading is reading aloud to children. This is especially so during the preschool years. (Anderson 1984) Once the child is able to read himself, switch to having the child read for 15 minutes, followed by the parent or adult reading to the child for 15 minutes. Regular practice of easy readers develops the child's decoding ability. It is important for the parent or teacher to continue reading from books above the child's reading level in order to expand his background knowledge and enjoyment of literature. (Hall and Moats 1999)

Which methods of instruction are most effective? Vocabulary can be developed (1) indirectly, when the student engages in daily oral language, listens to adults read to him, and reads extensively on his own; and (2) directly, when a student is explicitly taught both individual words and word learning strategies. (Armbruster 2001)

What materials are suggested?

- Bible on student's reading level
- *Classroom Strategies for Interactive Learning,* 2nd Ed., by Doug Buehl. Newark, DE: International Reading Association, 2001
- *Help for Struggling Readers: Strategies for Grades 3–8,* by Michael C. McKenna. New York: The Guilford Press, 2002
- Literature classics from private or public libraries
- *A Family Program for Reading Aloud,* Second Edition, by Rosalie June Slater. San Francisco: Foundation for American Christian Education, 1991
- *Reader's Handbook,* by Laura Robb. Wilmington, MA: Houghton Mifflin Co., 2004
- *The Reading Teacher's Book of Lists,* 4th Ed., by Edward Bernard Fry, Jacqueline E. Kress and Dona Lee Fountoukidis. Upper Saddle River, NJ: Pearson Education, 2000
- *Writing Road to Reading: The Spalding Method® for Teaching Speech, Spelling, Writing, and Reading,* Fifth Edition. by Romalda Spalding. Phoenix, AZ: Spalding Education International, 2003

References:

Andersen, Richard C., Elfrieda H. Hiebert, Judith A. Scott, and Ian A. G. Wilkinson. 1984. *Becoming a Nation of Readers: The Report of the Commission on Reading,* Champaign, IL: Center for the Study of Reading, University of Illinois at Urbana-Champaign, National Institute of Education, U.S. Department of Education.

Armbruster, Bonnie B., Fran Lehr, and Jean Osborn. September 2001. *Put Reading First: The Research Building Blocks for Teaching Children to Read.* Copies available from National Institute for Literacy at ED Pubs, PO Box 1398, Jessup, MD 20794-1398. Phone 1-800-228-8813; Fax 301-430-1244. To download go to the National Institute for Literacy Web site at www.nifl.gov.

Hall, Susan L. and Moats, Louisa C. 1999. *Straight Talk about Reading,* Chicago, IL: Contemporary Books.

COMPREHENSION

PRINCIPLE AND LEADING IDEAS

God gave man the ability to learn to read and to reason:

- *Understanding the process of learning helps my ability to learn*
- *Reformatting and categorizing information into new forms promotes flexible thinking*
- *Mastering reading strategies encourages independent learning*

Fact: Research has shown that instruction in comprehension can help students understand what they read, remember what they read, and communicate with others (Armbruster 2001, 49). Good readers need to have a purpose for reading and they need to be actively involved in the process.

What are the ways of teaching and learning comprehension? Six strategies have been identified to have a firm scientific basis for improving comprehension.

1. Monitoring comprehension
   a. The student is taught to think about his thinking (metacognition) and take control over his understanding of the text. Before reading, he clarifies his understanding by checking words or concepts that are not clear. He previews the text and predicts what may happen.
   b. During reading, the student monitors his understanding and adjusts his speed to the difficulty of the text.
   c. After reading, he summarizes, checks his understanding, and reformats the information into new forms like lists, outlines, or paraphrases.
2. Using graphic and semantic organizers
   a. Graphic organizers picture concepts and interrelationships between words and ideas. They may be called *maps, webs, graphs, charts, frames,* or *clusters. Semantic organizers* are graphic organizers that look somewhat like a spider web. Lines connect a central concept to a variety of related ideas and events. (Ibid., 50)
   b. Organizers help a student to focus on what he is reading, to visually represent relationships, and to assist in writing a summary of his reading and thinking.
3. Answering questions
   a. Research shows that teacher questioning strongly supports and advances students' learning. In Principle Approach® teaching, the teacher guides the student's thinking with leading questions calling upon reflective learning.
4. Generating questions
   a. "Teaching students to ask their own questions improves their active processing of text and their comprehension." (Ibid., 50)
5. Recognizing story structure
   a. "Story structure refers to the way the content and events of a story are organized into a plot." (Ibid., 50)
   b. *Story maps* are graphic organizers used to detail the parts of a narrative and the events of the story. In Principle Approach teaching, the student also defines the Biblical principle or foundational premise. What is God's Word teaching us?
6. Summarizing
   a. Summarizing helps a student to synthesize the important ideas in the text and to remember what he has read.

Why is comprehension important? "Comprehension is the reason for reading. If readers can read the words but do not understand what they are reading they are not really reading." (Ibid., 48)

When should instruction begin? Instruction begins with parents and teacher reading aloud to a child and guiding his thinking from the beginning, rather than waiting until the child is decoding on his own. Instruction at all grade levels needs to emphasize the idea that reading is a process of making sense out of text, or constructing meaning.

Which methods of instruction are most effective? "Effective comprehension strategy instruction is explicit, or direct. Research shows that explicit teaching techniques are particularly effective for comprehension strategy instruction. In explicit instruction, teachers tell readers why and when they should use strategies, what strategies to use, and how to apply them. The steps of explicit instruction typically include direct explanation, teacher modeling ('thinking aloud'), guided practice, and application." (Armbruster 2001, 53)

- "Direct explanation. The teacher explains to the student why the strategy helps comprehension and when to apply the strategy.
- Modeling. The teacher models, or demonstrates, how to apply the strategy, usually by 'thinking aloud' while reading the text that the students are using.
- Guided practice. The teacher guides and assists students as they learn how and when to apply the strategy.
- Application. The teacher helps students practice the strategy until they can apply it independently." (Ibid.)

"Effective comprehension strategy instruction can be accomplished through cooperative learning. Students working as partners or in small groups with clearly defined tasks help each other to learn and apply comprehension strategies. Teachers monitor the progress of students." (Ibid., 54)

"Effective instruction helps readers use comprehension strategies flexibly and in combination. . . . Multiple-strategy instruction teaches students how to use strategies flexibly as they are needed to assist their comprehension. There is one example of multiple-strategy called 'reciprocal teaching,' the teacher and students work together so that the students learn four comprehension strategies:

- asking questions about the text they are reading
- summarizing parts of the text
- clarifying words and sentences they don't understand
- predicting what might occur next in the text." (Ibid.)

What materials are suggested?

- *Comprehension Strategies for Middle Grade Learners,* by Charlotte Rose Sadler. Newark, DE: International Reading Association, 2001

- *Help for Struggling Readers: Strategies for Grades 3–8,* by Michael C. McKenna. New York: The Guilford Press, 2002

- *New Directions in Reading Instruction, Revised,* by Bess Hinson, Editor. Newark, DE: International Reading Association, 2003

- *Writing Road to Reading: The Spalding Method® for Teaching Speech, Spelling, Writing, and Reading,* Fifth Edition. by Romalda Spalding. Phoenix, AZ: Spalding Education International, 2003

Reference:

Armbruster, Bonnie B., Fran Lehr, and Jean Osborn. September 2001. *Put Reading First: The Research Building Blocks for Teaching Children to Read.* Copies available from National Institute for Literacy at ED Pubs, PO Box 1398, Jessup, MD 20794-1398. Phone 1-800-228-8813; Fax 301-430-1244. To download go to the National Institute for Literacy Web site at www.nifl.gov.

READING AND WRITING CONNECTION

BIBLICAL PRINCIPLE AND LEADING IDEAS
Conscience Is the Most Sacred of All Property:
- *God gave me a property in my ability to speak, read, and write*
- *Exercising my gifts makes me a good steward, accountable to God*
- *I use my gift of language to serve God's glory and to keep a good conscience*

What is the research?

Research says that reading and writing are connected. Better readers are generally better writers. Writing improves more when connected to reading than to grammar study or extra writing practice. As children write, they connect to the text and the author's views, assumptions, and struggles. "Through writing, children learn that the purpose of text is not to be read but to be understood . . . reading is about thinking . . . learning to read depends integrally on thinking and understanding." (Adams 1990, 405)

Students should write frequently with their attention directed towards a particular purpose. Nancy Whisler tells us that, contrary to popular belief, mere writing, with no purpose or instructional guidance, does not bring about better writings skills. Writing ability improves as a result of prewriting experiences. Some experiences that influence active thinking are discussion, questioning, mapping, and organizing ideas. Writing experiences that follow the reading act increase comprehension. Whisler concludes that writing should be a part of the regular reading program, not a separate subject. Writing can be used as an aid to reading as well as to written language skills. Writing after reading causes students to rethink, reprocess, and reconstruct ideas, and reuse the vocabulary. Comprehension is thereby improved. (Whisler 1982, 5)

What are the ways to connect reading and writing?

Steps based on the Spalding® Model (Spalding 2003, 164–166)

Modeling: teacher demonstrates and explains	Begin with oral sentence and then written sentences. The teacher explains the concept of related thoughts and models composing three or four related sentences.
Coaching: teacher guides and prompts as student produces	Student practices writing related sentences. The teacher models writing a 3 or 4 sentence paragraph about the particular topic.
Scaffolding and Fading: teacher supports then withdraws as student gains mastery	Teacher guides as students jointly compose three or four sentence paragraphs. Students then independently compose short paragraphs. These are revised, as needed, rewritten and shared with peers.

Using the Bible in Composition: Paraphrasing—Students listen to the Bible and read passages as models for writing. Using Scripture for writing was the pattern in Old Testament times. The kings of Israel were commanded to write a copy of the law on a scroll, read it and follow it (Deuteronomy 17:18–19). Matthew Henry reminds us that by writing it, the law would imprint on the king's mind. He continues, "it is of great use for each of us to write down what we observe as most affecting and edifying to us, out of the Scriptures and good books, and out of the sermons we hear. A prudent pen may go far towards making up the deficiencies of the memory, and the furnishing of the treasures of the good householder with things new and old. . . . And we must persevere in the use of the written word of God as long as we live. Christ's scholars never learn above their Bibles." (Henry 1706, 797)

References:

Adams, Marilyn Jager. 1990. *Beginning To Read: Thinking and Learning about Print.* Cambridge, MA: The MIT Press.

Henry, Matthew. 1706. *Matthew Henry's Commentary on the Whole Bible,* Volume 1. Iowa Falls, IA: World Bible Publishers.

Spalding, Romalda. 2003. *The Writing Road to Reading: The Spalding Method® for Teaching Speech, Spelling, Writing, and Reading,* Fifth Edition. Phoenix, AZ: Spalding Education International.

Whisler, Nancy G. 1982. *3 Steps to Language Success: Prior Knowledge, Oral Language & the Reading/Writing Connection,* U.S. Dept. of Education, Educational Resources Information Center, edrs@inet.gov, Document: ERIC: ED 241 9181.

The Whole Principle Approach® Curriculum

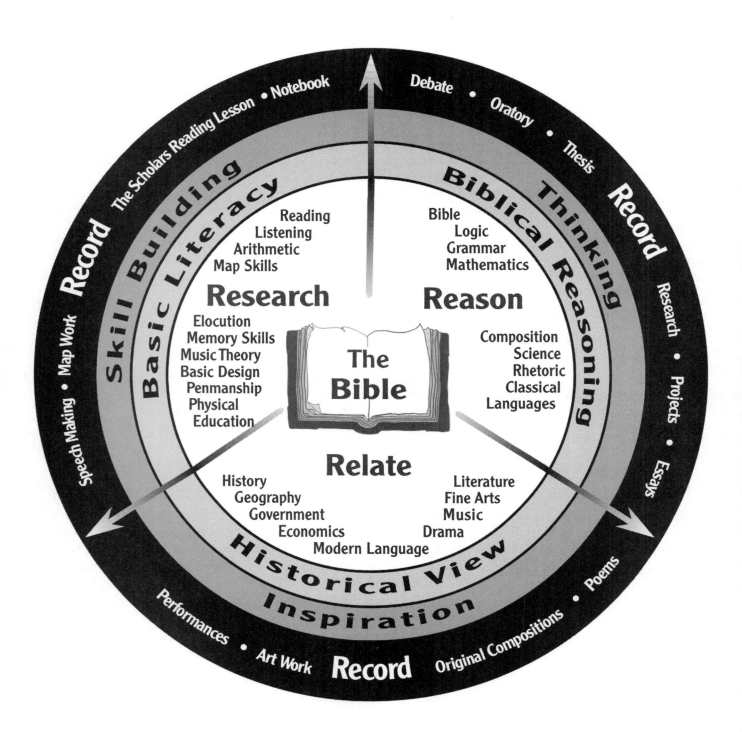

Record · The Scholars Reading Lesson · Notebook · Debate · Oratory · Thesis · **Record**

Skill Building · **Basic Literacy**

Biblical Reasoning · **Thinking**

Research
- Reading
- Listening
- Arithmetic
- Map Skills
- Elocution
- Memory Skills
- Music Theory
- Basic Design
- Penmanship
- Physical Education

Reason
- Bible
- Logic
- Grammar
- Mathematics
- Composition
- Science
- Rhetoric
- Classical Languages

The Bible

Relate
- History
- Geography
- Government
- Economics
- Modern Language
- Literature
- Fine Arts
- Music
- Drama

Historical View · **Inspiration**

Speech Making · Map Work · Research · Projects · Essays

Performances · Art Work · **Record** · Original Compositions · Poems

THE NOAH PLAN® © 2005 · FOUNDATION FOR AMERICAN CHRISTIAN EDUCATION

Cultivating Reasoning through the Grades

Grade Level	Metaphor	Research	Reason	Relate	Record
Kindergarten	Planting the seeds of all knowledge	Identifying the subjects by their principles being demonstrated	Understanding symbols (Examples: flag; snowflakes; fingerprints)	Oral language; mimicry; narrative; showing	Recognizing the notebook as a tool of learning
Primary School	Tending the seedlings (sunning; weeding; watering; regulating; fertilizing; guarding; cultivating)	Mastering the art of computation and the vocabulary of each subject	Understanding internal to external; concrete thinking; using manipulatives; skill building	Recitation; rote; expository (writing); drama; guided projects	The notebook as a tool of scholarship— notebook skills practiced and guided by teacher
Middle School	Growing the plant (pruning; guiding; correcting; transplanting; maturing; seasoning; making hardy)	Defining the principles of the subjects	Understanding cause to effect; questioning; logic; critical thinking; scientific method	Independent projects; essays; original speech (8th); high school thesis (12th)	Notebook mastery — a tool for lifelong independent learning
High School	Reaping the fruit! (cycling growth and harvesting the fruit)	Expressing and applying the principles in life and learning	Original thinking and actual reasoning from a Biblical worldview	Apprenticeship; service; debate; rhetoric; creative writing & speech; independent primary source research; original science project; thesis defense; portfolio projects	Habit and spirit of organized learning and Biblical scholarship inculcated

I walke manie times . . .
into the pleasant fieldes
of the Holye Scriptures,
where I pluck up the
goodlie greene herbes of sentences,
eate them by reading,
chew them up musing,
and laie them up at length
in the seate of memories . . .
so I may the lesse perceive
the bitterness of this miserable life.

Queen Elizabeth I

(Quoted in Otto L. Bettman. 1987. *The Delights of Reading.*
Boston: David R. Godine, Publisher.)

Chapter One

The Curriculum,
Curriculum Charts, and Model Lessons

Song VIII

Praise to God for Learning to Read

by Isaac Watts

The praises of my tongue
I offer to the Lord,
That I was taught, and learned so young,
To read his holy word;

That I am brought to know
The danger I was in;
By nature and by practice too,
A wretched slave to sin.

That I am led to see
I can do nothing well;
And whither shall a sinner flee,
To save himself from hell?

Dear Lord, this book of thine,
Informs me where to go,
For grace to pardon all my sin,
And make me holy too.

Here I can read and learn,
How Christ, the Son of God,
Did undertake our great concern;
Our ransom cost his blood.

And now he reigns above,
He sends his Spirit down,
To show the wonders of his love,
And make his gospel known.

Oh may that Spirit teach,
And may my heart receive,
Those truths which all thy servants preach,
And all thy saints believe!

Then shall I praise the Lord
In a more cheerful strain,
That I was taught to read his word,
And have not learned in vain.

From *Divine & Moral Songs for Children* by Isaac Watts.
Compiled, arranged, and edited by Carris J. Kocher. 1991.
Evensville, TN: Cumberland Missionary Society.

Enlightened Learning through Reading the Word of God

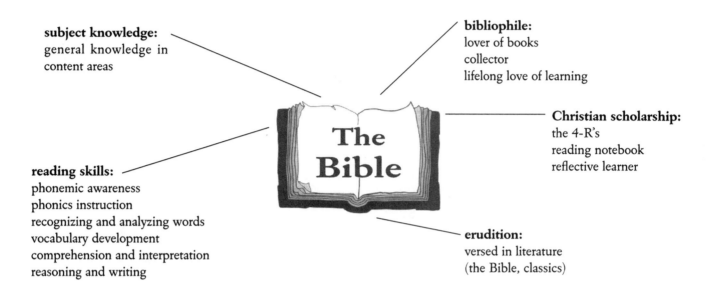

subject knowledge:
general knowledge in
content areas

bibliophile:
lover of books
collector
lifelong love of learning

The Bible

Christian scholarship:
the 4-R's
reading notebook
reflective learner

reading skills:
phonemic awareness
phonics instruction
recognizing and analyzing words
vocabulary development
comprehension and interpretation
reasoning and writing

erudition:
versed in literature
(the Bible, classics)

Components of Principle Approach® Reading

The Principle Approach philosophy of teaching reading cultivates an enlightened learner through reading the Word of God—the Bible. To be *enlightened* is to be illuminated with divine knowledge, or a knowledge of the truth. God's Word is truth and the study thereof makes one to know wisdom. The Bible contains the revelation of God, the principles of Christian faith, and the rules of practice. (Webster's 1828 *Dictionary*) The psalmist declares:

> O send out thy light and thy truth.
> (Psalm 43:3)

> For thou wilt light my candle: the LORD my God will enlighten my darkness.
> (Psalm 18:28)

> And thy law is the truth.
> (Psalm 119:142)

To learn by reading, one must master the skills of reading which include phonemic awareness, phonics, recognizing and analyzing words, developing vocabulary, comprehending and interpreting text. One reasons through leading ideas to the Biblical principles, and then records them.

Webster's definition of *reading* requires that a reader not only acquire basic skills but also obtain a general knowledge in content areas; be studious and demonstrate scholarship; be versed in books of literature (erudition); and be a lover of learning, a bibliophile. To be knowledgeable in content areas one applies facts or ideas acquired by study, investigation, observation, or experience. Scholarship is developed through the notebook method and the 4-R's (research, reason, relate, and record) to train children early to think, reason, and write with the revelation of God's Word. To be a scholar, one must be given to books or to learning, devoted to the acquisition of knowledge from books. A lover of books is a *biobliophile*. He is also a collector of books. He establishes a personal library, fostering a lifelong love of learning. The learned man is a man of erudition. *Erudition* is particularly learning in literature as distinct from the sciences, as in history, antiquity, and languages. The learned person is well-versed in literature including the classics and the Bible.

Teaching using Biblical principles and leading ideas with the Bible as a primary reader develops students with Christian character and scholarship and forms a Biblical worldview.

Kindergarten Reading Curriculum

Purpose

1. Cultivate enlightened learners through reading the Word of God—the Holy Bible
2. Inspire and equip students with a lifelong love of reading, especially reading the Bible, literary classics, and poetry
3. Unify all elements of language learning including phonics, literature, composition, grammar, spelling, penmanship, listening, and speaking
4. Lay the foundation of reading skills in an order and sequence that produces mastery of language and literacy
5. Establish the habits of study and scholarship
6. Build into the lives of students the foundation stones of Christian character and the truths of the Bible for the practice of Christian liberty

Teacher Objectives

1. Use the *Early Reader's Bible* as a primary reader
2. Provide a rich variety of inspirational activities that encourage children to look and listen attentively and to express their thoughts and feelings
3. Teach the sounds of the language using the intensive phonics procedures and multi-sensory methods of *The Writing Road to Reading®* phonics program
4. Prepare students for the thought, content, and theme of a lesson using the Guide to Writing Reading Lesson Plans, *NPRG*, 24–25
5. Form questions and leading ideas that guide students to think and reflect
6. Lead students to relate and apply Biblical principles to their lives
7. Define vocabulary from Webster's 1828 *Dictionary*
8. Have students illustrate and write to reinforce reading skills
9. Develop comprehension by providing guidance before, during, and after reading
    a) Set purposes for reading
    b) Guide involvement during reading by self-monitoring and questioning
    c) Plan for follow-up organization and retention of information
10. Model reading aloud using classic literature
11. Provide for the learning needs of each student whether enrichment or remedial
12. Evaluate the success of the lesson

Student Performance

1. Listens to *The Early Reader's Bible* as teacher reads aloud; reads along as decoding ability increases
2. Makes auditory and visual discrimination of letter-sound associations
3. Demonstrates a sense of directionality in writing and reading
4. Develops oral language and listening skills
    a) Listens to a variety of literary forms, including the Bible, stories, and poems
    b) Recognizes rhythm and rhyme
    c) Follows one-step and two-step directions
5. Demonstrates a speaking vocabulary that enables ideas to be expressed clearly
6. Develops basic phonic principles as introduced in *The Writing Road to Reading* phonics program
7. Practices early reading strategies
    a) Uses a variety of clues (picture, context, letter-sound correspondence)
    b) Focuses on meaning
    c) Self-corrects when reading makes no sense
    d) Memorizes Scripture verses and poems
8. Comprehends and retells stories; sequences events; identifies main idea
9. Writes complete sentences in shared-writing activity

Teacher Resources

1. *An American Dictionary of the English Language*, Webster, 1828
2. Dickson Bible, KJV, World
3. Matthew Henry's Commentary
4. *Phonemic Awareness in Young Children*, Adams
5. *Sounds Sensible Kit*, Clark-Edmonds
6. *Spalding's Spelling Assessment Manual*, Spalding
7. *Strong's Concordance of the Bible*
8. *The Children's Illustrated Bible*, Hastings
9. *The Comprehension Connection*, Book A, Spalding
10. *The Early Reader's Bible*, Beers
11. *The Noah Plan® English Language Curriculum Guide*, Adams
12. *The Noah Plan Literature Curriculum Guide*, Slater
13. *The Noah Plan Reading Curriculum Guide*, Shirley
14. *The Writing Road to Reading Phonogram Cards*, Spalding
15. *The Writing Road to Reading*, Spalding

Student Instructional Readers

1. *Test Lessons in Primary Reading*, McCall-Harby
2. *The Early Reader's Bible*, Beers
3. *Primary Phonics* (storybooks, sets 1–5), Makar

Definitions

1. **read:** "to pronounce written or printed words, in the proper order; to inspect and understand words; to peruse or read with attention; to understand and interpret, to reason and make inferences." (1828)
2. **skill:** "the familiar knowledge of any art or science, united with readiness and dexterity in execution or performance, or in the application to practical purposes." (1828)
3. **erudition:** "knowledge gained by study, or from books and instruction; particularly from the Bible and classic literature, themes, and characterization." (1828)
4. **knowledge:** "general knowledge in content areas; applies to facts or ideas acquired by study, investigation, observation or experience." (1828)
5. **scholarship:** The 4-R's. "Studious; given to books or to learning, contemplative; given to thought or examination of subjects by contemplation." (1828)
6. **bibliophile:** "lifelong learning. A person who loves or admires books, a collector of books." (1828)

THE NOAH PLAN® ©2005 • FOUNDATION FOR AMERICAN CHRISTIAN EDUCATION

Components of Reading for Kindergarten

1. Reading Skills

Perceptual Skills

Discriminates the sounds of the language and associates them with each letter (phonemic awareness)

Organizes letters and words visually and demonstrates a sense of directionality in writing and reading

Visual discrimination:
1. Likenesses and differences of letters
2. Recognition of correct orientation of letters in space
3. Organization of letters into groups as syllables or words

Auditory Discrimination:
1. Discrimination and matching of sounds, sequencing of sounds initial and final positions
2. Rhyming from pairs to a series of words
3. Blending of isolated sounds so that a recognizable word results

Laterality:
1. Directions of before and after
2. Orientation: right, left, up, down
3. Left-to-right progression

Vocabulary Development

Development of a rich oral vocabulary
1. Daily reading aloud after mastery of single-letter phonograms
   a) Teacher
   b) Parents
   c) Peers
2. Read aloud simultaneously in a group—choral reading
3. Partner reading—take turns listening and reading
4. Readers Theatre—read from scripts rich in dialogue
5. Time structure questions, e.g., What day is today? tomorrow? yesterday?
6. What are the days of the week?
7. Before and after questions, e.g., What day is before Monday? after Tuesday? Name the year, the month. What will next month be?
8. Follow precise oral directions
9. Recognize and use complete sentences
10. Remember and retell a story sequence
11. Questioning: Who? What? When? Where? Why? How?

Recognizing and Analyzing Words

The Writing Road to Reading®
1. A–Z single letter phonograms:
   a) Hear the sound
   b) Say the sound
   c) See the visual symbol (letter)
   d) Write the letter
2. Mastery of phonograms #1–54
3. Introduction of phonograms #55–70
4. Blend a vowel with a beginning sound
5. Single short vowel words
6. WRTR rules 1–8
7. Introduce Ayres List A–G (90 words)
8. Sight words
9. Phonic clues (letter-sound relationship, rules)
10. Context clues (pictures, sentence pattern, ideas of content)
11. Word structure clues

Reasoning and Writing

1. Write complete sentences observing punctuation and capitals
2. Group composition writing
3. Answer literal and inferential comprehension questions as teacher reads stories from *The Early Reader's Bible* to correspond to Bible lesson
4. Identify narrative elements—setting, characters, events, and theme—as teacher reads aloud passages
5. Apply the five mental actions as student listens to passages so the focus is on comprehension rather than on decoding words
6. Reinforce comprehension in writing lessons; student gives oral then written sentences. Teacher models then guides joint composition of related sentences, then paragraphs

2. Erudition

The Bible and Classic Literature

The Literature of the Bible: Psalms—Read and memorize Psalm 100 (KJV)

1. Appreciate the Bible as the greatest literary masterpiece
2. Listen to Scripture, stories, and poems read aloud by the teacher
3. *Little House in the Big Woods*, Wilder
4. Poetry of Isaac Watts
5. Lamb's *Tales from Shakespeare*
6. Learn lullabies, nursery rhymes, fables, myths, and fairy tales
7. Listen to a biography (*Abraham Lincoln*, d'Aulaire) and classic literature (*Winnie the Pooh* and *Bambi*)
8. Memorize Scripture verses
9. Recite verses or songs from memory
10. Enjoy identifying the elements of literature and selections read

3. Subject Knowledge

Content Areas

(Kindergarten students increase in knowledge through participation in special days, field trip and special visitors)

1. Field trip to pumpkin patch
2. Jamestown/Plymouth historical study and performance at the school celebration
3. Christmas celebration activities
4. Public speaking—speech meet competition
5. Art museum visit
6. Winnie the Pooh Tea Party
7. Pioneer Day (Special Day)
8. Community helper—e.g., firemen, policemen, nurse
9. Special guests—e.g., missionaries, authors, etc.

4. Christian Scholarship

The 4-R's

1. Students learn to recognize the notebook as a tool of learning
2. Students learn about study and research
3. Teacher leads identification of subject by principles and leading ideas
4. Students learn to classify by comparing likenesses and difference between members of various classes of pictured objects
5. Students use alphabetical order

5. Bibliophile

Lifelong Learning

1. Bookworms Club for selected students
2. Class speech meet, presents a poem or Scripture from memory
3. Library visits, *storytelling*
4. Supplementary reading aloud with parent
5. Personal library
6. Summer reading program
7. Choral reading
8. Special day (e.g., Pioneer Day)

First Grade Reading Curriculum

Purpose

1. Cultivate enlightened learners through reading the Word of God—the Holy Bible
2. Inspire and equip students with a lifelong love of reading, especially reading the Bible, literary classics, and poetry
3. Unify all elements of language learning including phonics, literature, composition, grammar, spelling, penmanship, listening, and speaking
4. Lay the foundation of reading skills in an order and sequence that produces mastery of language and literacy
5. Establish the habits of study and scholarship
6. Build into the lives of students the foundation stones of Christian character and the truths of the Bible for the practice of Christian liberty

Teacher Objectives

1. Use *The Young Reader's Bible* as a primary reader
2. Prepare the students for the theme, content, and purpose of each lesson using the Guide to Writing Reading Lesson Plans, *NPRG,* 24–25
3. Form questions and develop leading ideas that guide the student's reasoning and reflective thinking
4. Lead students to relate and apply Biblical principles to their lives
5. Use Webster's *1828 Dictionary* to define vocabulary
6. Use multi-sensory methods to teach intensive phonics
7. Reinforce reading through writing
8. Develop comprehension by providing guidance before, during, and after reading
   a) Set purposes for reading
   b) Guide involvement during reading by self-monitoring and questioning
   c) Plan for follow-up organization and retention of information
9. Model reading aloud using classic literature and Bible
10. Provide for the learning needs of each student whether enrichment or remedial
11. Evaluate the success of the lesson

Student Performance

1. Reads with instruction *The Young Reader's Bible*
2. Listens and responds to literature
3. Increases oral language and listening vocabulary
4. Reads familiar selections aloud with fluency and expression
5. Uses a variety of reading skills and strategies
   a) Focuses on decoding and meaning
   b) Applies phonic principles to reading and writing
6. Begins to read silently
7. Identifies characters, plot, and setting
8. Understands main ideas and sequence
9. Applies comprehension in other content areas
10. Learns that writing is the communication of ideas
11. Becomes familiar with beginning library and research skills
12. Produces a student notebook

Definitions

1. **read:** "to pronounce written or printed words, in the proper order; to inspect and understand words; to peruse or read with attention; to understand and interpret, to reason and make inferences." (1828)
2. **skill:** "the familiar knowledge of any art or science, united with readiness and dexterity in execution or performance, or in the application to practical purposes." (1828)
3. **erudition:** "knowledge gained by study, or from books and instruction; particularly from the Bible and classic literature, themes, and characterization." (1828)
4. **knowledge:** general knowledge in content areas; applies to facts or ideas acquired by study, investigation, observation or experience." (1828)
5. **scholarship:** The 4-R's . . . "Studious: given to books or to learning, contemplative; given to thought or examination of subjects by contemplation." (1828)
6. **bibliophile:** "lifelong learning. A person who loves or admires books, a collector of books." (1828)

Teacher Resources

1. *An American Dictionary of the English Language,* Webster, 1828
2. Dickson Bible, KJV, World
3. Matthew Henry's *Commentary on the Bible*
4. Life Application Bible, NIV, Tyndale
5. *Nelson's Complete Book of Bible Maps and Charts,* Thomas Nelson
6. *Phonemic Awareness in Young Children,* Adams
7. *Spelling Assessment Manual,* Spalding
8. *SRA Reading Laboratory Ia,* SRA
9. *Strong's Concordance of the Bible*
10. *The Children's Illustrated Bible,* Hastings
11. *The Comprehension Connection,* Book A, Spalding
12. *The Noah Plan® English Language Curriculum Guide,* Adams
13. *The Noah Plan Literature Curriculum Guide,* Slater
14. *The Noah Plan Reading Curriculum Guide,* Shirley
15. *The Reading Teacher's Book of Lists,* Fry
16. *The Writing Road to Reading® Phonogram Cards,* Spalding
17. *The Writing Road to Reading,* Spalding
18. *The Young Reader's Bible,* Bruno and Reinsma

Student Instructional Readers

1. *Getting the Main Idea,* Books A–C of Specific Skills Series, Boning
2. *Standard Test Lessons in Reading,* Books A–B, McCall-Crabbs
3. *Test Lessons in Primary Reading,* McCall and Harby
4. *Primary Phonics* (storybooks), Makar
5. *SRA Reading Laboratory Ia,* SRA
6. *The Young Reader's Bible,* Bruno and Reinsma

Components of Reading for First Grade

1. Reading Skills

Recognizing and Analyzing Words

Phonemic awareness: discriminates the sounds of the language and associates them with each letter

1. *The Writing Road to Reading*®:
   a) Single-letter phonograms, consonants
   b) Multi-letter phonograms
   c) Spelling rules 1–29, taught as introduced in Ayres List
   d) Spelling notebook
   e) Mastery of Ayres List A–G
   f) Introduce Ayres List H–O
2. Rules for syllabication
3. Structural analysis:
   a) Word roots, base words
   b) Prefixes, suffixes
   c) Compound words
   d) Contractions
   e) Syllabication
4. Configuration clues (capitals, word length, double letters, lowercase letters)
5. Context clues (pictures and words)
6. Blending sounds into words
7. Rhyming words

Vocabulary Development Skills

1. Definitions
2. Compound words
3. Synonyms, antonyms, homonyms
4. Classifying words (comparative degrees, comparisons)
5. Possessives
6. Multiple meanings
7. Sight words
8. Read aloud simultaneously in a group—choral reading
9. Partner reading—take turns listening and reading
10. Readers Theatre—read from scripts rich in dialogue

Comprehension and Interpretation Skills

Oral expression: keep eye ahead of voice, enunciate and pronounce clearly, read in thought units, vary pitch and volume

1. Main idea/details
2. Factual questions
3. Retelling
4. Summarizing
5. Sequencing
6. Classification
7. Predictions
8. Compare/contrast
9. Internal/external
10. Drawing conclusions
11. Relating information
12. Dramatizing
13. Following directions
14. Reasoning questions
15. Identify individual characters and relationships between characters
16. Preview, have a purpose for reading text, read with accuracy, and self-correct when necessary
17. Answer literal and inferential comprehension questions as teacher reads stories from *The Young Reader's Bible* to correspond to Bible lesson. Teach comprehension by applying the five mental actions as student listens to passages so the focus is on comprehension rather than on decoding words. Use elements in literature to identify types of writing and to vary the reading rate

Reasoning and Writing

1. Sentence writing
2. Reasoning questions
3. Paraphrasing
4. Relating information
5. Summarizing
6. Identify individual characters
7. Introduce/practice author's purpose in narratives, informative, and informative-narratives
8. Identify elements: setting, characters, events, point of view, theme, and style as teacher reads aloud passages
9. Reinforce comprehension in writing lessons; student gives oral then written sentences. Teacher models then guides joint composition of related sentences then paragraphs

2. Erudition

The Bible and Classic Literature

The Literature of the Bible: Genesis—Noah, Isaac, Joseph

1. Listen to classics read aloud by the teacher (see *The Noah Plan® Literature Curriculum Guide*)
   a) *Pinocchio*
   b) *Cinnabar, the One O'clock Fox*
   c) *Lamb's Tales from Shakespeare*
   d) *Abigail Adams, Writer*
   e) *Bay Psalm Book*
2. Poetry
   a) Henry W. Longfellow
   b) Isaac Watts
   c) William Blake
   d) Robert Louis Stevenson
3. Shakespeare's *Romeo and Juliet*
4. Memorization of short poems and Scripture passages
5. Choral reading

3. Subject Knowledge

Content Areas

1. Listening to readings on various subject areas to build vocabulary and comprehension
2. Dictionary skills:
   a) Master alphabetical order to first letter
   b) Alphabetical order to second and third letter
   c) Guide words
   d) Sections of dictionary; table of contents, etc.
   e) Special pages
3. Etymology: roots
4. Map reading skills, especially Bible atlas
5. Locate books, chapters, verses in the Bible
6. Dictation of words, phrases, sentences

4. Christian Scholarship

The 4-R's

1. Bible/Reading notebook: (Research, Reason, Relate, Record); beginning the notebook method
   a) Identify principles
   b) Classifications
   c) Discussions
2. Timelines

5. Bibliophile

Lifelong Learning

1. Supplementary reading aloud with parent
2. Participate in school speech meet to present a poem or Scripture passage from memory
3. Bookworms Club
4. Summer reading program
5. Personal library
6. Quiet reading time
7. Special days (e.g., Italy Day, etc.)

Second Grade Reading Curriculum

Purpose

1. Cultivate enlightened learners through reading the Word of God—the Holy Bible
2. Inspire and equip students with a lifelong love of reading, especially reading the Bible, literary classics, and poetry
3. Unify all elements of language learning including phonics, literature, composition, grammar, spelling, penmanship, listening, and speaking
4. Lay the foundation of reading skills in an order and sequence that produces mastery of language and literacy
5. Establish the habits of study and scholarship
6. Build into the lives of students the foundation stones of Christian character and the truths of the Bible for the practice of Christian liberty

Teacher Objectives

1. Use the Kid's Study Bible (NIrV) as a primary reader
2. Prepare the students for the theme, content, and purpose of each lesson using the Guide to Writing Reading Lesson Plans, *NPRG*, 24–25
3. Form questions and develop leading ideas that guide the student's reasoning and reflective thinking
4. Lead students to relate and apply Biblical principles to their lives
5. Use Webster's *1828 Dictionary* to define vocabulary
6. Use multi sensory methods to review phonics
7. Reinforce reading through writing
8. Develop comprehension by providing guidance before, during, and after reading
   a) Set purposes for reading
   b) Guide involvement during reading by self-monitoring and questioning
   c) Plan for follow-up organization and retention of information
9. Model reading aloud using classic literature and Bible
10. Provide for the learning needs of each student whether enrichment or remedial
11. Evaluate the success of the lesson

Student Performance

1. Reads with instruction the Kid's Study Bible, NIrV
2. Listens and responds to literature
3. Increases oral language and listening vocabulary
4. Reads familiar selections aloud with fluency and expression
5. Uses a variety of reading skills and strategies
   a) Focuses on decoding and meaning
   b) Applies phonic principles to reading and writing
6. Begins to read silently
7. Identifies point of view, theme, and style
8. Understands main ideas and sequence
9. Applies comprehension strategies in other content areas
10. Learns that writing is the communication of ideas
11. Becomes familiar with beginning library and research skills
12. Produces a student notebook

Definitions

1. **read:** "to pronounce written or printed words, in the proper order; to inspect and understand words; to peruse or read with attention; to understand and interpret, to reason and make inferences." (1828)
2. **skill:** "the familiar knowledge of any art or science, united with readiness and dexterity in execution or performance, or in the application to practical purposes." (1828)
3. **erudition:** "knowledge gained by study, or from books and instruction; particularly from the Bible and classic literature, themes, and characterization." (1828)
4. **knowledge:** "general knowledge in content areas; applies to facts or ideas acquired by study, investigation, observation or experience." (1828)
5. **scholarship:** The 4-Rs. "Studious: given to books or to learning, contemplative; given to thought or examination of subjects by contemplation." (1828)
6. **bibliophile:** "lifelong learning. A person who loves or admires books, a collector of books." (1828)

Teacher Resources

1. *An American Dictionary of the English Language*, Webster, 1828
2. Dickson Bible, KJV, World
3. *How to Spell*, Workbook 1, Rudginsky and Haskell
4. *How to Teach Spelling*, Rudginsky and Haskell
5. Kids' Study Bible, NIrV, Zondervan
6. Life Application Bible, NIV, Tyndale
7. Matthew Henry's *Commentary*
8. *Standard Test Lessons in Reading*, Books A–C, McCall-Crabbs
9. *Nelson's Complete Book of Bible Maps and Charts*, Thomas Nelson
10. SRA *Reading Laboratory* 1b, SRA
11. Strong's *Concordance of the Bible*
12. *The Children's Illustrated Bible*, Hastings
13. *The Comprehension Connection*, Books A–E, Spalding
14. *The Noah Plan® English Language Curriculum Guide*, Adams
15. *The Noah Plan Literature Curriculum Guide*, Slater
16. *The Noah Plan Reading Curriculum Guide*, Shirley
17. *The Reading Teacher's Book of Lists*, Fry

Student Instructional Readers

1. *Getting the Main Idea*, Books B–D of Specific Skills Series, Boning
2. Kids' Study Bible, NIrV, Zondervan
3. *Standard Test Lessons in Reading*, Books A–C, McCall-Crabbs
4. *SRA Reading Laboratory*, Book 1b, SRA

Components of Reading for Second Grade

1. Reading Skills

Recognizing and Analyzing Words

1. *The Writing Road to Reading®*: review phonograms and spelling rules
2. Rules for syllabication
3. Structural analysis:
   a) Word roots, base words
   b) Prefixes, suffixes
   c) Compound words
   d) Contractions
   e) Syllabication
4. Configuration clues (capitals, lowercase letters)
5. Context clues (pictures and words)
6. Blending sounds into words
7. Rhyming words

Vocabulary Development Skills

1. Definitions
2. Compound words
3. Synonyms, antonyms, homonyms
4. Classifying words (comparative degrees, comparisons)
5. Plurals
6. Possessives
7. Multiple-meanings
8. Sight words
9. Figurative language
10. Read aloud simultaneously in a group—choral reading
11. Partner reading—take turns listening and reading
12. Readers Theatre—read from scripts rich in dialogue

Comprehension and Interpretation Skills

Oral expression: keep eye ahead of voice, enunciate and pronounce clearly, read in thought units, vary pitch and volume

1. Main idea/details
2. Factual questions
3. Retelling
4. Summarizing
5. Sequencing
6. Classification
7. Predictions
8. Compare/contrast
9. Internal/external
10. Drawing conclusions

Comprehension instruction: apply the five mental actions as student reads passages

Use elements in literature to identify types of writing and to vary reading rate

Reasoning and Writing

1. Sentence and paragraph writing
2. Reasoning questions
3. Paraphrasing
4. Relating information
5. Compare/contrast
6. Cause/effect
7. Inference
8. Master identifying author's purpose in narratives, informative, and informative-narratives
9. Master identifying elements: setting, characters, events, point of view, and theme
10. Reinforce comprehension in writing lessons; student gives oral then written sentences. Teacher models then guides joint composition of related sentences then paragraphs. Student writes three basic types of paragraphs

2. Erudition

The Bible and Classic Literature

The Literature of the Bible: The Psalms—David, memorize Psalm 23

1. Memorization of short poems or Scripture passage
2. *Benjamin Franklin*, d'Aulaire
3. Listen to classics and poetry read aloud by the teacher (see *The Noah Plan® Literature Curriculum Guide*)
4. Classics:
   a) *Heidi*
   b) *Song of Hiawatha*
   c) *Pocahontas*, d'Aulaire
   d) *Benjamin West and His Cat Grimalkin*, Henry
   e) *Lamb's Tales from Shakespeare*
5. Poets:
   a) Lewis Carroll
   b) Emily Dickinson
   c) Eugene Field
   d) Henry W. Longfellow
   e) William Wordsworth
6. Shakespeare's *Comedy of Errors*

3. Subject Knowledge

Content Areas

1. Listen to readings from various subject areas to build vocabulary and comprehension
2. Dictionary skills:
   a) Extend and refine skills introduced in first grade
   b) Main entry and its elements
   c) Identify the part of speech
   d) Locate or define words
   e) Locate and use a glossary
3. Use table of contents to locate stories and chapters in books
4. Use maps, charts, tables, and graphs to answer questions
5. Find and use factual information in a reading selection (locate information to answer who, what when, why, where, and how questions)
6. Etymology: roots
7. Bible:
   a) Map reading skills
   b) Bible atlas
   c) Locate books, chapters, verses

4. Christian Scholarship

The 4-R's

1. Bible/Reading notebook: (Research, Reason, Relate, Record); student makes a written record of his learning and reflecting
2. Timeline
3. Mammal science project
4. Jamestown guided history project

5. Bibliophile

Lifelong Learning

1. Book reviews
2. Participate in school speech meet to present a poem or Scripture passage from memory
3. Supplementary reading aloud with parents
4. Bookworms Club
5. Personal library
6. Library visits
7. Record personal reading
8. Summer reading program
9. Choral reading
10. Special days (e.g., Heidi Day)

Third Grade Reading Curriculum

Purpose

1. Cultivate enlightened learners through reading the Word of God—the Holy Bible
2. Inspire and equip students with a lifelong love of reading, especially reading the Bible, literary classics, and poetry
3. Unify all elements of language learning including phonics, literature, composition, grammar, spelling, penmanship, listening, and speaking
4. Lay the foundation of reading skills in an order and sequence that produces mastery of language and literacy
5. Establish the habits of study and scholarship
6. Build into the lives of students the foundation stones of Christian character and the truths of the Bible for the practice of Christian liberty

Teacher Objectives

1. Use the Kid's Study Bible, NIrV, as a primary reader
2. Prepare the students for the theme, content, and purpose of each lesson using the Guide to Writing Reading Lesson Plans, *NPRG*, 24–25
3. Form questions and develop leading ideas that guide the student's reasoning and reflective thinking
4. Lead students to relate and apply Biblical principles to their lives
5. Use Webster's 1828 *Dictionary* to define vocabulary
6. Use multi-sensory methods to review phonics
7. Reinforce reading through writing
8. Develop comprehension by providing guidance before, during, and after reading
   a) Set purposes for reading
   b) Guide involvement during reading by self-monitoring and questioning
   c) Plan for follow-up organization and retention of information
9. Model reading aloud using classic literature and Bible
10. Provide for the learning needs of each student whether enrichment or remedial
11. Evaluate the success of the lesson

Student Performance

1. Reads with instruction the Kid's Study Bible, NIrV
2. Listens and responds to fiction, nonfiction, and poetry
3. Expands oral language and listening vocabulary, paraphrasing
4. Presents brief oral reports
5. Reads wide range of books and stories with fluency and expression
6. Uses a variety of reading skills and strategies
   a) Focuses on decoding and meaning
   b) Applies phonic and structural analysis to vocabulary
7. Increases silent reading rate beyond oral reading rate
8. Identifies characters, plot, and setting
9. Applies comprehension strategies in other content areas
10. Writes short reports about what is read
11. Writes stories, letters, explanations, etc.
12. Uses the dictionary, encyclopedia, and other reference books
13. Produces a student notebook

Definitions

1. **read:** "to pronounce written or printed words, in the proper order; to inspect and understand words; to peruse or read with attention; to understand and interpret; to reason and make inferences." (1828)
2. **skill:** "the familiar knowledge of any art or science, united with readiness and dexterity in execution or performance, or in the application to practical purposes." (1828)
3. **erudition:** "knowledge gained by study, or from books and instruction; particularly from the Bible and classic literature, themes, and characterization." (1828)
4. **knowledge:** "general knowledge in content areas; applies to facts or ideas acquired by study, investigation, observation or experience." (1828)
5. **scholarship:** The 4-R's. "Studious: given to books or to learning, contemplative; given to thought or examination of subjects by contemplation." (1828)
6. **bibliophile:** "lifelong learning. A person who loves or admires books, a collector of books." (1828)

Teacher Resources

1. *An American Dictionary of the English Language*, Webster, 1828
2. Dickson Bible, KJV, World
3. *How to Spell*, Workbook 2, Rudginsky and Haskell
4. *How to Teach Spelling*, Rudginsky and Haskell
5. Kids' Study Bible, NIrV, Zondervan
6. Life Application Bible, NIV, Tyndale
7. Matthew Henry's Commentary
8. *Nelson's Complete Book of Bible Maps and Charts*, Thomas Nelson
9. *SRA Reading Laboratory* 1c, SRA
10. Strong's Concordance of the Bible
11. Student's Life Application Bible, New Living Translation, Tyndale
12. *The Children's Illustrated Bible*, Hastings
13. *The Comprehension Connection*, Book B–E, Spalding
14. *The Noah Plan® English Language Curriculum Guide*, Adams
15. *The Noah Plan Literature Curriculum Guide*, Slater
16. *The Noah Plan Reading Curriculum Guide*, Shirley
17. *The Reading Teacher's Book of Lists*, Fry

Student Instructional Readers

1. Kids' Study Bible, NIrV, Zondervan
2. *Standard Test Lessons in Reading*, Book B, McCall-Crabbs
3. *Reading Comprehension in Varied Subject Matter*, Book 1, Ervin
4. *Getting the Main Idea*, Book C of Specific Skills Series, Boning
5. *SRA Reading Laboratory*, Book 1c, SRA

Components of Reading for Third Grade

1. Reading Skills

Recognizing and Analyzing Words

1. Review phonograms and spelling rules
2. Rules for syllabication
3. Structural analysis:
   a) Word roots, base words
   b) Prefixes, suffixes
   c) Compound words
   d) Contractions
   e) Syllabication
   f) Inflectional endings
4. Configuration clues (capitals, lowercase letters)
5. Context clues (pictures and words)
6. Blending sounds into words
7. Rhyming words

Vocabulary Development Skills

1. Definitions
2. Synonyms, antonyms, homonyms
3. Classifying words (comparative degrees, superlative)
4. Plurals
5. Possessives
6. Multiple meanings
7. Sight words
8. Figurative language
9. Idioms
10. Read aloud simultaneously in a group—choral reading
11. Partner reading—take turns listening and reading
12. Readers Theatre—read from scripts rich in dialogue

Comprehension and Interpretation Skills

Oral expression: keep eye ahead of voice, enunciate and pronounce clearly, read in thought units, vary pitch and volume

1. Main idea/details
2. Factual questions
3. Interpretative questions
4. Evaluative questions
5. Retelling
6. Summarizing
7. Sequencing
8. Classification
9. Predictions
10. Compare/contrast
11. Internal/external
12. Drawing conclusions

Comprehension instruction: review/reinforce the five mental actions as student reads passages

Use elements in literature to identify types of writing and to vary reading rate

Reasoning and Writing

1. Sentence writing
2. Reasoning questions
3. Paraphrasing
4. Relating information
5. Compare/contrast
6. Cause/effect
7. Review/reinforce identifying author's purpose in narratives, informative, and informative-narratives
8. Review identifying elements: setting, characters, events, point of view, and theme
9. Reinforce comprehension in writing lessons; student gives oral then written sentences. Teacher models then guides joint composition of related sentences then paragraphs. Student writes three basic types of paragraphs

2. Erudition

The Bible and Classic Literature

The Literature of the Bible: Jonah
1. Memorization of short poems or Scripture passage
2. Listen to classics and poetry read aloud by the teacher (see *The Noah Plan® Literature Curriculum Guide*)
4. Classics:
   a) *Hans Brinker, or the Silver Skates*
   b) *Johann Sebastian Bach: The Boy from Thuringia*
   c) *The Lion, the Witch, and the Wardrobe*
   d) *Lamb's Tales from Shakespeare*
5. Poets:
   a) Emily Dickinson
   b) Robert Louis Stevenson
   c) Henry Wadsworth Longfellow
6. Shakespeare's *Merchant of Venice*

3. Subject Knowledge

Content Areas

1. Listen to readings from various subject areas to build vocabulary and comprehension
2. Dictionary skills:
   a) Extend and refine skills introduced in second grade
   b) Main entry and its elements
   c) Identify the part of speech
   d) Locate or define words
   e) Locate and use a glossary
3. Use table of contents to locate stories and chapters in books
4. Use maps, charts, tables, and graphs to answer questions
5. Find and use factual information in a reading selection (locate information to answer who, what when, why, where, and how questions)
6. Etymology: roots
7. Bible:
   a) Map reading skills
   b) Bible atlas
   c) Locate books, chapters, verses

4. Christian Scholarship

The 4-R's

1. Bible/Reading notebook: (Research, Reason, Relate, Record); student makes a written record of his learning and reflecting
2. Timeline
3. Solar system project (optional)
4. Bird reports
5. Plymouth Plantation Day
6. Book reviews—written and oral

5. Bibliophile

Lifelong Learning

1. Quarterly book review—written and oral
2. Participates in school speech meet to present a poem or Scripture passage from memory
3. Presents informal oral reports
4. Scholars Reading Lesson
5. Choral reading
6. Supplementary reading aloud with parent
7. Bookworms Club
8. Personal library
9. Read-along tapes
10. Library visits
11. Summer reading program
12. Special days (e.g., Dutch Day)

Fourth Grade Reading Curriculum

Purpose

1. Cultivate enlightened learners through reading the Word of God—the Holy Bible
2. Inspire and equip students with a lifelong love of reading, especially reading the Bible, literary classics, and poetry
3. Unify all elements of language learning including phonics, literature, composition, grammar, spelling, penmanship, listening, and speaking
4. Lay the foundation of reading skills in an order and sequence that produces mastery of language and literacy
5. Establish the habits of study and scholarship
6. Build into the lives of students the foundation stones of Christian character and the truths of the Bible for the practice of Christian liberty

Teacher Objectives

1. Use the Adventure Bible, NIV, as a primary reader
2. Prepare the students for the theme, content, and purpose of each lesson using the Guide to Writing Reading Lesson Plans, *NPRG, 24–25*
3. Form questions and develop leading ideas that guide the student's reasoning and reflective thinking
4. Lead students to relate and apply Biblical principles to their lives
5. Use Webster's 1828 *Dictionary* to define vocabulary
6. Reinforce reading through writing; the teacher is the model
7. Develop comprehension by providing guidance before, during, and after reading
   a) Set purposes for reading
   b) Guide involvement during reading by self-monitoring and questioning
   c) Plan for follow-up organization and retention of information
8. Model reading aloud using classic literature and Bible
9. Provide for the learning needs of each student whether enrichment or remedial
10. Evaluate the success of the lesson

Student Performance

1. Reads with instruction the Adventure Bible
2. Reads a variety of longer more demanding texts, poetry, biographies, and historical fiction
3. Paraphrases, makes inferences, draws conclusions, formulates questions
4. Makes and listens to oral presentations and reports
5. Reads for a variety of purposes
6. Focuses on refinement and improvement:
   a) Uses a variety of study skills and strategies
   b) Expands writing vocabulary
7. Reads silently in larger units
8. Increases rate through timed readings
9. Identifies characters, plot, setting, and author's point of view
10. Summarizes and organizes information for written reports
11. Uses the glossary, dictionary, thesaurus
12. Chooses books for personal library collection
13. Produces a student notebook

Definitions

1. **read:** "to pronounce written or printed words, in the proper order; to inspect and understand words; to peruse or read with attention; to understand and interpret, to reason and make inferences." (1828)
2. **skill:** "the familiar knowledge of any art or science, united with readiness and dexterity in execution or performance, or in the application to practical purposes." (1828)
3. **erudition:** "knowledge gained by study, or from books and instruction; particularly from the Bible and classic literature, themes, and characterization." (1828)
4. **knowledge:** "general knowledge in content areas; applies to facts or ideas acquired by study, investigation, observation or experience." (1828)
5. **scholarship:** The 4-R's. "Studious: given to books or to learning, contemplative; given to thought or examination of subjects by contemplation." (1828)
6. **bibliophile:** "lifelong learning. A person who loves or admires books, a collector of books." (1828)

Teacher Resources

1. *An American Dictionary of the English Language*, Webster, 1828
2. Dickson Bible, KJV, World
3. *How to Spell*, Workbook 3, Rudginsky and Haskell
4. *How to Teach Spelling*, Rudginsky and Haskell
5. Life Application Bible, NIV, Tyndale
6. Matthew Henry's *Commentary*
7. *Nelson's Complete Book of Bible Maps and Charts*, Thomas Nelson
8. *SRA Reading Laboratory 2a*, SRA
9. *Strong's Concordance of the Bible*
10. Student's Life Application Bible, New Living Translation, Tyndale
11. The Adventure Bible, NIV, Zondervan
12. *The Children's Illustrated Bible*, Hastings
13. *The Comprehension Connection*, Books B–E, Spalding
14. *The Noah Plan® English Language Curriculum Guide*, Adams
15. *The Noah Plan Literature Curriculum Guide*, Slater
16. *The Noah Plan Reading Curriculum Guide*, Shirley
17. *The Reading Teacher's Book of Lists*, Fry

Student Instructional Readers

1. The Adventure Bible, NIV, Zondervan
2. *SRA Reading Laboratory 2a*, SRA
3. *Standard Test Lessons in Reading*, Books B–E, McCall-Crabbs
4. *Reading Comprehension in Varied Subject Matter*, Book 2, Ervin

Components of Reading for Fourth Grade

1. Reading Skills

Recognizing and Analyzing Words

1. Skills firmly established:
   a) Basic sight words
   b) Configuration clues
   c) Phonic analysis
   d) Syllable principles
   f) Contextual clues
2. Introduce:
   a) Decoding multisyllabic words
   b) Discriminating among similar words
   c) Develop word maps using components:
      (1) Target words
      (2) Topic classification
      (3) Properties or characteristics
      (4) Familiar examples

Vocabulary Development Skills

1. Structural analysis skills firmly established:
   a) Word endings
   b) Roots
   c) Contractions
2. Introduce:
   a) Accent rules
   b) Suffixes: *ment, ness, full, less, er, or, ion, ation, ey, ed, ing*
   c) Prefixes: *re, un, in, il im, ir*
   d) Antonyms
   e) Synonyms
   f) Figures of speech: similes, personification, alliteration, onomatopoeia
   g) Homophones
   h) Homographs
   i) Classifying words
   j) Singular/plural
   k) Parts of speech

Comprehension and Interpretation Skills

1. Teach self-questioning before, during, and after reading
2. Internalize and apply what has been read
3. Predict outcomes
4. Compare and contrast
5. Perceive relationships
6. Draw inferences
7. Appreciate figurative language
8. Memorize Scripture
9. Dramatize Scripture (Readers Theatre)
10. Determine word meaning from context
11. Examine multiple meanings of vocabulary from context
12. Find main ideas in paragraphs
13. Detect the writer's purpose
14. Follow directions
15. Sequence events
16. Summarize verbally

Reasoning and Writing

1. Summarizing
2. Outlining
3. Note-taking
4. K-W-L (Know/Want to learn/Learned)
5. Graphic organizers to organize thinking for writing
6. Recalling main idea and details
7. Determining cause/effect
8. Predicting outcomes
9. Paraphrasing
10. Composition: narrative, description, exposition, proofreading, letters, short essays, biography
11. Editing

2. Erudition

The Bible and Classic Literature

The Literature of the Bible: Proverbs
Memorize Proverbs 8:5–23

1. Literature:
   a) Latham, *Carry On, Mr. Bowditch*
   b) Stevenson, *Treasure Island*
   c) Burnett, *Secret Garden*
   d) Shakespeare, *Julius Cæsar*
   e) Lamb's *Tales from Shakespeare*
2. Poetry:
   a) Alfred Noyes
   b) Robert Louis Stevenson
   c) Henry W. Longfellow
   d) Phyllis Wheatley
   e) Proverbs
3. Shakespeare, *Julius Cæsar*

3. Subject Knowledge

Content Areas

1. Dictionary skills (use Webster's 1828 *Dictionary* when possible)
   a) Use guide words
   b) Interpret syllables
   c) Interpret accent and stress
   d) Select word meaning from context
   e) Interpret pronunciation key
   f) Use cross reference
   g) Note preferred spellings
   h) Investigate word origins
2. Extend research skills introduced in earlier grades
3. Encyclopedia:
   a) Find topic
   b) Use index
   c) Use cross reference
4. Almanac
5. Telephone directory
6. Interpret tables
7. Select an appropriate reading technique (scanning, skimming, directions, context, etc.)

4. Christian Scholarship

The 4-R's

1. Bible/Reading notebook: (Research, Reason, Relate, Record); student makes a written record of his learning and reflecting in each subject area
2. Reading comprehension skills and strategies in various content areas
3. Timed readings to improve rate
4. Latin roots and multiple-meaning words
5. Colonial research paper—teacher guided
6. History journal

5. Bibliophile

Lifelong Learning

1. Quarterly book reviews—written and oral
2. Participates in school speech meet to present a poem or Scripture passage from memory
3. Presents informal oral reports
4. Scholars Reading Lesson
5. Choral reading
6. Summer reading program
7. Supplementary reading program
8. Personal library
9. Special days (e.g., Treasure Island Day)

Fifth Grade Reading Curriculum

Purpose

1. Cultivate enlightened learners through reading the Word of God—the Holy Bible
2. Inspire and equip students with a lifelong love of reading, especially reading the Bible, literary classics, and poetry
3. Unify all elements of language learning including phonics, literature, composition, grammar, spelling, penmanship, listening, and speaking
4. Lay the foundation of reading skills in an order and sequence that produces mastery of language and literacy
5. Establish the habits of study and scholarship
6. Build into the lives of students the foundation stones of Christian character and the truths of the Bible for the practice of Christian liberty

Teacher Objectives

1. Use The Student Bible, NIV, as a primary reader
2. Prepare the students for the theme, content, and purpose of each lesson using the Guide to Writing Reading Lesson Plans, *NPRG*, 24–25
3. Form questions and develop leading ideas that guide the student's reasoning and reflective thinking
4. Lead students to relate and apply Biblical principles to their lives
5. Use Webster's 1828 *Dictionary* to define vocabulary
6. Reinforce reading through writing; the teacher is the model
7. Develop comprehension by providing guidance before, during, and after reading
   a) Set purposes for reading
   b) Guide involvement during reading by self-monitoring and questioning
   c) Plan for follow-up organization and retention of information
8. Model reading aloud using classic literature and Bible
9. Provide for the learning needs of each student whether enrichment or remedial
10. Evaluate the success of the lesson

Student Performance

1. Reads with instruction The Student Bible, NIV
2. Reads a variety of longer, more demanding texts (poetry, biographies, and historical fiction)
3. Paraphrases, summarizes
4. Makes inferences, draws conclusions, formulates questions
5. Makes and listens to oral presentations and reports
6. Reads for a variety of purposes
7. Focuses on refinement and improvement:
   a) Uses a variety of study skills and strategies
   b) Expands writing vocabulary
   c) Writes for a variety of purposes
8. Reads silently in larger units
9. Increases rate through timed readings
10. Analyzes literary elements and story structure
11. Summarizes and organizes information for written reports
12. Uses a variety of references and resource material, e.g., charts, maps, and graphs
13. Chooses books for personal library
14. Produces a student notebook

Definitions

1. **read:** "to pronounce written or printed words, in the proper order; to inspect and understand words; to peruse or read with attention; to understand and interpret, to reason and make inferences." (1828)
2. **skill:** "the familiar knowledge of any art or science, united with readiness and dexterity in execution or performance, or in the application to practical purposes." (1828)
3. **erudition:** "knowledge gained by study, or from books and instruction; particularly from the Bible and classic literature, themes, and characterization." (1828)
4. **knowledge:** "general knowledge in content areas; applies to facts or ideas acquired by study, investigation, observation or experience." (1828)
5. **scholarship:** The 4-R's. "Studious: given to books or to learning, contemplative; given to thought or examination of subjects by contemplation." (1828)
6. **bibliophile:** "lifelong learning. A person who loves or admires books, a collector of books." (1828)

Teacher Resources

1. *An American Dictionary of the English Language*, Webster, 1828
2. Dickson Bible, KJV, World
3. *How to Teach Spelling*, Rudginsky and Haskell
4. Life Application Bible, NIV, Tyndale
5. Matthew Henry's *Commentary*
6. *Nelson's Complete Book of Bible Maps and Charts*, Thomas Nelson
7. *Reasoning & Reading*, Level 1, Teacher's Guide, Carlisle
8. Strong's *Concordance of the Bible*
9. Student's Life Application Bible, New Living Translation, Tyndale
10. *The Children's Illustrated Bible*, Hastings
11. *The Comprehension Connection*, Book B–E, Spalding
12. *The Noah Plan® English Language Curriculum Guide*, Adams
13. *The Noah Plan Literature Curriculum Guide*, Slater
14. *The Noah Plan Reading Curriculum Guide*, Shirley
15. The Student Bible, NIV, Zondervan

Student Instructional Readers

1. *Reasoning & Reading*, Level 1, Carlisle
2. The Student Bible, NIV, Zondervan

Components of Reading for Fifth Grade

1. Reading Skills

Recognizing and Analyzing Words

1. Skills firmly established:
   a) Basic sight words
   b) Configuration clues
   c) Phonic analysis
   d) Syllable principles
   f) Contextual clues
2. Practice:
   a) Decoding multisyllabic words
   b) Discriminating among similar words
   c) Develop word maps using components:
      (1) Target words
      (2) Topic classification
      (3) Properties or characteristics
      (4) Familiar examples
3. Etymology studies for classical and Anglo-Saxon language roots

Vocabulary Development Skills

1. Structural analysis skills firmly established:
   a) Word endings
   b) Roots
   c) Contractions
2. Introduce:
   a) Accent rules
   b) Suffixes: *ment, ness, full, less, er, or, ion, ation, ey, ed, ing*
   c) Prefixes: *re, un, in, il im, ir*
   d) Antonyms
   e) Synonyms
   f) Figures of speech: similes
   g) Homophones
   h) Homographs
   i) Classifying words
   j) Singular/plural
3. Parts of speech and modifiers, affixes, connectives, phrases, clauses

Comprehension and Interpretation Skills

1. Self-question before, during, and after reading
2. Predict outcomes
3. Compare and contrast
4. Perceive relationships
5. Draw inferences
6. Appreciate figurative language
7. Detect author's mood and purpose
8. Filter facts from opinions
9. Memorize Scripture
10. Dramatize Scripture (Readers Theatre)
11. Determine word meaning from context
12. Examine multiple meanings of vocabulary from context
13. Find main ideas in paragraphs
14. Summarize verbally
15. Follow directions
16. Sequence events
17. Detect the writer's purpose

Reasoning and Writing

1. Summarizing
2. Outlining
3. Note-taking
4. K-W-L (Know/Want to learn/Learned)
5. Paraphrasing
6. Graphic organizers to organize thinking for writing
7. Recalling main idea and details
8. Determining cause/effect
9. Predicting outcomes
10. Composition:
    a) Narrative
    b) Instruction
    c) Explanation
    d) Description
    e) Exposition
    f) Proofreading
    g) Letters
    h) Short essays
    i) Biography
    j) Dialogue

2. Erudition

The Bible and Classic Literature

The Literature of the Bible: Ruth
1. Literature:
   a) Alcott, *Little Women*
   b) Burnett, *The Secret Garden*
   c) Latham, *Trailblazer of the Seas*
   d) Shakespeare, *Macbeth*
   e) Edgar Allen Poe
2. Poetry:
   a) Robert Frost
   b) Henry W. Longfellow

3. Subject Knowledge

Content Areas

1. Dictionary skills (review from previous year and work toward mastery):
   a) Use guide words
   b) Interpret syllables
   c) Interpret accent and stress
   d) Select word meaning from context
   e) Interpret pronunciation key
   f) Use cross reference
   g) Note preferred spellings
2. Investigate word origins
3. Vocabulary studies using Webster's 1828 *Dictionary*
4. Use reference resources:
   a) Thesaurus
   b) Textbooks
   c) Newspapers
   d) Magazines

4. Christian Scholarship

The 4-R's

1. Bible/Reading notebook: (Research, Reason, Relate, Record); student makes a written record of his learning and reflecting
2. Mini-book reports (bi-weekly)
3. Science fair project
4. Biography book report
5. History project (presidents)
6. Classic literature book report
7. History project (pioneering)
8. Invention and enterprise research project

5. Bibliophile

Lifelong Learning

1. Quarterly book reports
2. Participates in school speech meet to present a poem or Scripture passage from memory.
3. Scholars Reading Lesson
4. Library visits (bi-weekly)
5. Poetry reading
6. Personal library
7. Summer reading program
8. Special days (e.g., Presidents Wax Museum)

Sixth Grade Reading Curriculum

Purpose

1. Cultivate enlightened learners through reading the Word of God—the Holy Bible
2. Inspire and equip students with a lifelong love of reading, especially reading the Bible, literary classics, and poetry
3. Unify all elements of language learning including phonics, literature, composition, grammar, spelling, penmanship, listening, and speaking
4. Lay the foundation of reading skills in an order and sequence that produces mastery of language and literacy
5. Establish the habits of study and scholarship
6. Build into the lives of students the foundation stones of Christian character and the truths of the Bible for the practice of Christian liberty

Teacher Objectives

1. Use The Student Bible, NIV, as a primary reader
2. Prepare the students for the theme, content, and purpose of each lesson using the Guide to Writing Reading Lesson Plans, *NPRG*, 24–25
3. Form questions and develop leading ideas that guide the student's reasoning and reflective thinking
4. Lead students to relate and apply Biblical principles to their lives
5. Use Webster's 1828 *Dictionary* to define vocabulary
6. Reinforce reading through writing; the teacher is the model
7. Develop comprehension by providing guidance before, during, and after reading
   a) Set purposes for reading
   b) Guide involvement during reading by self-monitoring and questioning
   c) Plan for follow-up organization and retention of information
8. Model reading aloud using classic literature and Bible
9. Provide for the learning needs of each student whether enrichment or remedial
10. Evaluate the success of the lesson

Student Performance

1. Reads with instruction The Student Bible, NIV
2. Reads a variety of longer and more demanding texts, poetry, biographies, and historical fiction
3. Paraphrases, summarizes, makes inferences, draws conclusions, formulates questions
4. Makes, listens to, and evaluates oral presentations and reports
5. Demonstrates comprehension of a variety of selections
6. Focuses on refinement and mastery:
   a) Uses a variety of study skills and strategies
   b) Expands writing vocabulary
   c) Uses writing as a tool for learning in all subjects
7. Reads and writes a diversity of poetry
8. Analyzes literary elements and story structure
9. Summarizes and organizes information for written reports
10. Uses a variety of references and resource material, e.g., charts, maps, and graphs
11. Chooses books for personal library
12. Produces a student notebook

Definitions

1. **read:** "to pronounce written or printed words, in the proper order; to inspect and understand words; to peruse or read with attention; to understand and interpret, to reason and make inferences." (1828)
2. **skill:** "the familiar knowledge of any art or science, united with readiness and dexterity in execution or performance, or in the application to practical purposes." (1828)
3. **erudition:** "knowledge gained by study, or from books and instruction; particularly from the Bible and classic literature, themes, and characterization." (1828)
4. **knowledge:** general knowledge in content areas; applies to facts or ideas acquired by study, investigation, observation or experience." (1828)
5. **scholarship:** The 4-R's. "Studious; given to books or to learning, contemplative; given to thought or examination of subjects by contemplation." (1828)
6. **bibliophile:** "lifelong learning. A person who loves or admires books, a collector of books." (1828)

Teacher Resources

1. *An American Dictionary of the English Language*, Webster, 1828
2. Dickson Bible, KJV, World
3. *How to Teach Spelling*, Rudginsky and Haskell
4. Life Application Bible, NIV, Tyndale
5. Matthew Henry's Commentary
6. *Nelson's Complete Book of Bible Maps and Charts*, Thomas Nelson
7. *Reasoning and Reading*, Level 1, Teacher's Guide, Carlisle
8. Strong's Concordance of the Bible
9. Student's Life Application Bible, New Living Translation, Tyndale
10. *The Children's Illustrated Bible*, Hastings
11. *The Noah Plan® English Language Curriculum Guide*, Adams
12. *The Noah Plan Literature Curriculum Guide*, Slater
13. *The Noah Plan Reading Curriculum Guide*, Shirley
14. *The Reading Teacher's Book of Lists*, Fry
15. The Student Bible, NIV, Zondervan

Student Instructional Readers

1. *Reasoning and Reading*, Level 1, Carlisle
2. The Student Bible, NIV, Zondervan

Components of Reading for Sixth Grade

1. Reading Skills

Recognizing and Analyzing Words

1. Skills firmly established:
   a) Configuration clues
   b) Phonic analysis
   c) Syllable principles
   d) Contextual clues
2. Mastery of:
   a) Decoding multisyllabic words
   b) Discriminating among similar words
   c) Word maps: develop using components:
      (1) Target words
      (2) Topic classification
      (3) Properties or characteristics
      (4) Familiar examples

Vocabulary Development Skills

1. Structural analysis skills firmly established: word endings, roots, contractions
2. Introduce:
   a) Accent rules
   b) Suffixes: *ment, ness, full, less, er, or, ion, ation, ey, ed, ing*
   c) Prefixes: *re, un, in, il im, ir*
   d) Antonyms
   e) Synonyms
   f) Figures of speech: similes
   g) Homophones
   h) Homographs
   i) Classifying words
   j) Singular/plural
3. Parts of speech and modifiers, affixes, connectives, phrases, clauses

Comprehension and Interpretation Skills

1. Self-question before, during, and after reading
2. Predict outcomes
3. Compare and contrast acts, events, and authors
4. Perceive relationships
5. Draw inferences
6. Appreciate figurative language
7. Detect author's mood
8. Filter facts from opinions
9. Memorize Scripture
10. Dramatize Scripture (Readers Theatre)
11. Determine word meaning from context
12. Examine multiple meanings of vocabulary from content
13. Find main ideas in paragraphs
14. Summarize verbally
15. Follow directions
16. Sequence events
17. Detect the writer's purpose

Reasoning and Writing

1. Summarizing
2. Outlining
3. Note-taking
4. K-W-L (Know/Want to learn/Learned)
5. Paraphrasing
6. Mapping
7. Recalling main idea and details
8. Determining cause/effect
9. Predicting outcomes
10. Composition:
    a) Narrative
    b) Instruction
    c) Explanation
    d) Description
    e) Exposition
    f) Proofreading
    g) Letters
    h) Short essays
    i) Biography
    j) Dialogue

2. Erudition

The Bible and Classic Literature

The Literature of the Bible: Epistles
Read Philippians
1. Literature:
   a) Hawthorne, *A Wonder Book*
   b) Schultz, *Wizard of the North*
   c) Scott, *Ivanhoe*
   d) Shakespeare, *Twelfth Night*
2. Poetry:
   a) Henry W. Longfellow
      (1) "Village Blacksmith"
      (2) "Psalm of Life"
      (3) "Christmas Bells"
      (4) "Ship of State"
   b) Robert Frost
      (1) "Stopping by the Woods"
      (2) "Road Not Taken"
      (3) "Mending Wall"
   c) James Russell Lowell
   d) John Greenleaf Whittier
   e) Julia Ward Howe
3. Epistles of the Bible

3. Subject Knowledge

Content Areas

1. Dictionary skills (extend and refine skills introduced in earlier grades):
   a) Use guide words
   b) Interpret syllables
   c) Interpret accent and stress
   d) Select word meaning from context
   e) Interpret pronunciation key
   f) Use cross reference
   g) Note preferred spellings
   h) Investigate word origins
2. Encyclopedia
   a) Find topic
   b) Use index volume
   c) Use cross reference
3. Almanac
4. Telephone directory
5. Interpret tables
6. Use footnotes
7. Select an appropriate reading technique (scanning, skimming, directions, context, etc.)

4. Christian Scholarship

The 4-R's

1. Bible/Reading notebook: (Research, Reason, Relate, Record); student makes a written record of his learning and reflecting
2. History research paper—ancient civilization

5. Bibliophile

Lifelong Learning

1. Quarterly book reports
2. Participates in school speech meet to present a poem or Scripture passage from memory
3. Scholars Reading Lesson
4. Library visits (bi-weekly)
5. Choral reading
6. Summer reading program
7. Book fairs
8. Library visits
9. Personal library
10. Special days (e.g., Ivanhoe Day)

Seventh Grade Reading Curriculum

Purpose

1. Cultivate enlightened learners through reading the Word of God—the Holy Bible
2. Inspire and equip students with a lifelong love of reading, especially reading the Bible, literary classics, and poetry
3. Unify all elements of language learning including phonics, literature, composition, grammar, spelling, penmanship, listening, and speaking
4. Lay the foundation of reading skills in an order and sequence that produces mastery of language and literacy
5. Establish the habits of study and scholarship
6. Build into the lives of students the foundation stones of Christian character and the truths of the Bible for the practice of Christian liberty

Teacher Objectives

1. Use the Life Application Bible, KJV
2. Prepare the students for the theme, content, and purpose of each lesson using the Guide to Writing Reading Lesson Plans, *NPRG*, 24–25
3. Form questions and develop leading ideas that guide the student's reasoning and reflective thinking
4. Lead students to relate and apply Biblical principles to their lives
5. Use Webster's 1828 *Dictionary* to define vocabulary
6. Model writing; give guidance, correction, and encouragement
7. Present content and skills concurrently to allow direct application
8. Teach students how to be independent strategic readers who are concerned with the process of learning, not just the product:
   a) Plan appropriate strategy
   b) Read—analyze their thinking
   c) Evaluate whether something is making sense and why
9. Model reading aloud using classic literature and Bible
10. Provide for the learning needs of each student whether enrichment or remedial
11. Evaluate the success of the lesson

Student Performance

1. Reads with instruction the Life Application Bible, KJV
2. Makes the transition from mainly story reading to reading for content—narrative vs. expository
3. Adjusts to departmentalized and content-focused system
4. Discusses, evaluates, and organizes the ideas encountered in print moving from structured to a more independent study in reading and writing
5. Focuses on the main idea of what is read and written—seeing the whole, seeing the parts in relation to the whole, seeing the interrelationships:
   a) Uses a variety of study skills and strategies
   b) Expands writing vocabulary
   c) Uses writing as a tool for learning in all subjects
6. Reads and writes a diversity of poetry
7. Analyzes literary elements and story structure
8. Summarizes and organizes information for written reports
9. Uses a variety of references and resource material, e.g., charts, maps, and graphs
10. Chooses books for personal library
11. Produces a student notebook

Definitions

1. **read:** " to pronounce written or printed words, in the proper order; to inspect and understand words; to peruse or read with attention; to understand and interpret, to reason and make inferences." (1828)
2. **skill:** "the familiar knowledge of any art or science, united with readiness and dexterity in execution or performance, or in the application to practical purposes." (1828)
3. **erudition:** "knowledge gained by study, or from books and instruction; particularly from the Bible and classic literature, themes, and characterization." (1828)
4. **knowledge:** " general knowledge in content areas; applies to facts or ideas acquired by study, investigation, observation or experience." (1828)
5. **scholarship:** The 4-R's. "Studious: given to books or to learning, contemplative; given to thought or examination of subjects by contemplation." (1828)
6. **bibliophile:** "lifelong learning. A person who loves or admires books, a collector of books." (1828)

Teacher Resources

1. *An American Dictionary of the English Language*, Webster, 1828
2. Dickson Bible, KJV, World
3. *How to Teach Spelling*, Rudginsky and Haskell
4. Life Application Bible, NIV, Tyndale
5. Matthew Henry's Commentary
6. *Nelson's Complete Book of Bible Maps and Charts*, Thomas Nelson
7. *Reasoning and Reading*, Level 2, Teacher's Guide, Carlisle
8. Strong's Concordance of the Bible
9. Student's Life Application Bible, New Living Translation, Tyndale
10. *The Children's Illustrated Bible*, Hastings
11. The Life Application Bible, KJV, Tyndale
12. *The Noah Plan® English Language Curriculum Guide*, Adams
13. *The Noah Plan Literature Curriculum Guide*, Slater
14. *The Noah Plan Reading Curriculum Guide*, Shirley
15. *The Reading Teacher's Book of Lists*, Fry

Student Instructional Readers

1. *Reasoning and Reading*, Level II, Carlisle
2. The Life Application Bible, KJV, Tyndale

Components of Reading for Seventh Grade

1. Reading Skills

Recognizing and Analyzing Words

1. Skills firmly established:
   a) Configuration clues
   b) Phonic analysis
   c) Syllable principles
   d) Contextual clues
2. Mastery of:
   a) Decoding multisyllabic words
   b) Discriminating among similar words
   c) Word maps: develop using components:
      (1) Target words
      (2) Topic classification
      (3) Properties or characteristics
      (4) Familiar examples

Vocabulary Development Skills

1. Teach the PAR method—Vocabulary development can be done in three stages:
   a) Preparation for reading
   b) Assistance given during reading
   c) Reflection on vocabulary after reading to see how terms convey meaning and relationships
2. Nuances and shades of meaning need to be taught
3. Multiple meanings
4. Graphic organizers
5. Semantic mapping—diagrams that show relationships among words
6. Cloze exercises—select a passage and omit words such as every fifth or tenth, etc.; the student uses context to fill in the missing words

Comprehension and Interpretation Skills

1. Self-question before, during, and after reading
2. Predict outcomes
3. Compare and contrast acts, events, and authors
4. Perceive relationships
5. Draw inferences
6. Appreciate figurative language
7. Detect author's mood
8. Filter facts from opinions
9. Memorize Scripture
10. Dramatize Scripture
11. Determine word meaning from context
12. Examine multiple meanings of vocabulary from content
13. Find main ideas in paragraphs
14. Summarize verbally
15. Follow directions
16. Sequence events
17. Detect the writer's purpose

Reasoning and Writing

1. Summarizing
2. Outlining
3. Note-taking
4. K-W-L (Know/Want to learn/Learned)
5. Paraphrasing
6. Mapping
7. Recalling main idea and details
8. Determining cause/effect
9. Predicting outcomes
10. Composition:
    a) Narrative
    b) Instruction
    c) Explanation
    d) Description
    e) Exposition
    f) Proofreading
    g) Letters
    h) Short essays
    i) Biography
    j) Dialogue

2. Erudition

The Bible and Classic Literature

The Literature of the Bible: Poetry of the Bible

1. Literature:
   a) Dickens, *David Copperfield*
   b) Sandburg, *Abe Lincoln Grows Up*
   c) The Bible as Literature
   d) Shakespeare, plays rotate according to drama class presentation: *Midsummer Night's Dream, Much Ado about Nothing, Romeo and Juliet, Love's Labour's Lost*
   e) Study of essay
   f) Study of short story
   g) Novels
   h) Biography
2. Poetry: (see *The Noah Plan® Literature Curriculum Guide*)

3. Subject Knowledge

Content Areas

1. Dictionary skills:
   a) Interpret accent and stress
   b) Select word meaning from context
   c) Interpret pronunciation key
   d) Use cross reference
   e) Note preferred spellings
   f) Investigate word origins
2. Geography:
   a) Mapmaking
   b) Atlas usage
3. English/history:
   a) Thesaurus
   b) Encyclopedia
   c) Dictionary
4. English/Latin:
   a) Root words
   b) Derivatives
   c) Prefixes, suffixes, affixes
   d) Composition
   e) Grammar

4. Christian Scholarship

The 4-R's

1. Bible/Reading notebook: (Research, Reason, Relate, Record); student makes a written record of his learning and reflecting
2. Various reading for research and projects:
   a) History (independent research)
   b) Science
   c) Latin
   d) Geography
   e) Arithmetic
   f) Poetry

5. Bibliophile

Lifelong Learning

1. English book reviews
2. Summer reading program
3. Personal library

Eighth Grade Reading Curriculum

Purpose

1. Cultivate enlightened learners through reading the Word of God—the Holy Bible
2. Inspire and equip students with a lifelong love of reading, especially reading the Bible, literary classics, and poetry
3. Unify all elements of language learning including phonics, literature, composition, grammar, spelling, penmanship, listening, and speaking
4. Lay the foundation of reading skills in an order and sequence that produces mastery of language and literacy
5. Establish the habits of study and scholarship
6. Build into the lives of students the foundation stones of Christian character and the truths of the Bible for the practice of Christian liberty

Teacher Objectives

1. Use the Life Application Bible, KJV
2. Prepare the students for the theme, content, and purpose of each lesson using the Guide to Writing Reading Lesson Plans, *NPRG*, 24–25
3. Form questions and develop leading ideas that guide the student's reasoning and reflective thinking
4. Lead students to relate and apply Biblical principles to their lives
5. Use Webster's 1828 *Dictionary* to define vocabulary
6. Model writing; give guidance, correction, and encouragement
7. Present content and skills concurrently to allow direct application
8. Teach students how to be independent strategic readers who are concerned with the process of learning, not just the product:
   a) Plan appropriate strategy
   b) Read—analyze their thinking
   c) Evaluate whether something is making sense and why
9. Model reading aloud using classic literature and Bible
10. Provide for the learning needs of each student whether enrichment or remedial
11. Evaluate the success of the lesson

Student Performance

1. Reads with instruction the Life Application Bible, KJV
2. Makes the transition from mainly story reading to reading for content—narrative vs. expository
3. Adjusts to departmentalized and content-focused system
4. Discusses, evaluates, and organizes the ideas encountered in print moving from structured to a more independent study in reading and writing
5. Focuses on the main idea of what is read and written—seeing the whole, seeing the parts in relation to the whole, seeing the interrelationships
6. Uses flexible reading rates and varied study strategies
7. Summarizes and organizes information for written reports
8. Uses a variety of references and resource material, e.g., charts, maps, and graphs
9. Understands his individual reading style and engages in voluntary reading
10. Establishes lifelong reading habits
11. Chooses books for personal library
12. Produces a student notebook—a tool for lifelong independent learning
13. Writes an original speech and presents it at graduation

Definitions

1. **read:** "to pronounce written or printed words, in the proper order; to inspect and understand words; to peruse or read with attention; to understand and interpret, to reason and make inferences." (1828)
2. **skill:** "the familiar knowledge of any art or science, united with readiness and dexterity in execution or performance, or in the application to practical purposes." (1828)
3. **erudition:** "knowledge gained by study, or from books and instruction; particularly from the Bible and classic literature, themes, and characterization." (1828)
4. **knowledge:** "general knowledge in content areas; applies to facts or ideas acquired by study, investigation, observation or experience." (1828)
5. **scholarship:** The 4-R's. "Studious: given to books or to learning, contemplative; given to thought or examination of subjects by contemplation." (1828)
6. **bibliophile:** "lifelong learning. A person who loves or admires books, a collector of books." (1828)

Teacher Resources

1. *An American Dictionary of the English Language*, Webster, 1828
2. Dickson Bible, KJV, World
3. *How to Teach Spelling*, Rudginsky and Haskell
4. Life Application Bible, NIV, Tyndale
5. Matthew Henry's Commentary
6. *Nelson's Complete Book of Bible Maps and Charts*, Thomas Nelson
7. *Reasoning and Reading*, Level 2, Teacher's Guide, Carlisle
8. Strong's *Concordance of the Bible*
9. Student's Life Application Bible, New Living Translation, Tyndale
10. *The Children's Illustrated Bible*, Hastings
11. The Life Application Bible, KJV, Tyndale
12. *The Noah Plan® English Language Curriculum Guide*, Adams
13. *The Noah Plan Literature Curriculum Guide*, Slater
14. *The Noah Plan Reading Curriculum Guide*, Shirley
15. *The Reading Teacher's Book of Lists*, Fry

Student Instructional Readers

1. *Reasoning and Reading*, Level 2, Carlisle
2. The Life Application Bible, KJV, Tyndale

Components of Reading for Eighth Grade

1. Reading Skills

Recognizing and Analyzing Words

1. Context clue discovery
2. Definitions
3. Signal words
4. Direct explanations
5. Synonyms
6. Antonyms
7. Inferences
8. Structural analysis
9. Word analysis paradigms:
   a) Meaning from context
   b) Examine roots
   c) Syllables
   d) Comparing with known words
   e) Check glossaries
   f) Use Webster 1828 *Dictionary*
10. Vocabulary lists
11. Quadrant cards:
    a) Use a 4" x 6" card
    b) Divide it into 4 sections
    c) Put word, synonym, antonym, and words associated with target word
12. Organizational charts—show relationships in words, e.g., compare/contrast
13. Word analogies

Vocabulary Development Skills

1. Teach the PAR method—Vocabulary development can be done in three stages:
   a) Preparation for reading
   b) Assistance given during reading
   c) Reflection on vocabulary after reading to see how terms convey meaning and relationships
2. Nuances and shades of meaning need to be taught
3. Multiple meanings
4. Graphic organizers
5. Semantic mapping—diagrams that show relationships among words
6. Cloze exercises—select a passage and omit words such as every fifth or tenth, etc.; the student uses context to fill in the missing words

Comprehension and Interpretation Skills

1. Self-question before, during, and after reading
2. Retain and apply what has been read
3. Predict outcomes
4. Compare and contrast facts, events, and authors
5. Perceive relationships
6. Draw inferences
7. Appreciate figurative language
8. Detect author's mood
9. Filter facts from opinions
10. Memorize Scripture
11. Dramatize Scripture
12. Determine word meaning from context
13. Examine multiple meanings of vocabulary from context
14. Find main ideas in paragraphs
15. Recognize literary form
16. Detect the writer's purpose
17. Follow directions
18. Sequence events
19. Summarize verbally

Reasoning and Writing

1. Summarizing
2. Outlining
3. Note-taking
4. K-W-L (Know/Want to learn/Learned)
5. Mapping
6. Paraphrasing
7. Recalling main idea and details
8. Determining cause/effect
9. Composition:
   a) Narrative
   b) Opinion
   c) Instruction
   d) Explanation
   e) Description
   f) Exposition
   g) Proofreading
   h) Letters
   i) Short essays
   j) Argument—point of view
   k) Types of persuasion
   l) Biography
   m) Dialogue

2. Erudition

The Bible and Classic Literature

The Literature of the Bible: Contrast Jews, Greeks, Romans

1. Literature:
   a) Wallace, *Ben Hur*
   b) Shakespeare, *Comedy of Errors*
   c) Pyle, *King Arthur and His Knights of the Round Table*
   d) Brayer, *The Walls of Windy Troy*
2. Poetry:
   a) Longfellow, *The Courtship of Miles Standish*
   b) Tennyson, *Idylls of the King*
   c) Homer, *The Odyssey*
3. Pyle, *Men of Iron* (read independently)

3. Subject Knowledge

Content Areas

1. Dictionary skills:
   a) Interpret accent and stress
   b) Select word meaning from context
   c) Interpret pronunciation key
   d) Use cross reference
   e) Note preferred spellings
   f) Investigate word origins
2. Geography:
   a) Mapmaking
   b) Atlas usage
3. English/history:
   a) Thesaurus
   b) Encyclopedia
   c) Dictionary
4. English/Latin:
   a) Root words
   b) Derivatives
   c) Prefixes, suffixes, affixes
   d) Composition
   e) Grammar

4. Christian Scholarship

The 4-R's

1. Bible/Reading notebook: (Research, Reason, Relate, Record); student makes a written record of his learning and reflecting in each subject area
2. *Rudiments of America's Christian History and Government*, Rosalie Slater and Verna Hall, 1994
3. *Christian History of the Constitution of the United States of America*, Vol. I: *Christian Self-Government*, Verna Hall, 1960

5. Bibliophile

Lifelong Learning

1. Summer reading program
2. Quarterly book reviews
3. Reading of selected materials in preparation for Christian history tour of Boston and Plymouth
4. Poetry selections
5. Personal library
6. Special days (select and prepare a special day)

Governing Steps for Writing Lessons Using the Bible as Reader Program

For the LORD *is our judge, the* LORD *is our lawgiver, the* LORD *is our king.*
(Isaiah 33:22)

STEP 1 I Plan

1. Use the Expanded Quarterly Topics Chart to complete the planning form for the Bible as Reader (*NPRG*, 125).

2. Select the Bible text that teaches the topic.

   a. For example the "Dominion Mandate" topic from second quarter of fourth grade is taught in Genesis 1–11.

   b. Choose age-appropriate passages and manageable portions of text for guided reading and thinking.

3. Determine the overarching theme.

   a. Identify the Biblical principle and leading idea. Use The Art and Love of Learning (*NPRG*, 80–81) and Guide to Writing Reading Lesson Plans (*NPRG*, 24–25).

   b. For example, the fourth grade topic is "Dominion Mandate." The principle is that God has given man dominion over the earth to subdue it. The leading idea is the application of the principle. Christian self-government is thinking governmentally—I plan, I do, I evaluate.

   c. What truth is the Word teaching you? What is the rule of action to be learned? What questions lead to reflective thinking?

4. Examine the Reading Curriculum Chart for your grade level (*NPRG*, 4–21).

   a. Highlight the details of each component to be taught in the week/quarter.

   b. Use the Reading Quarterly Plan Sheet for Teaching Reading (*NPRG*, 23) for recording the skills and strategies to teach.

5. Write the lesson plan using the Six-step Lesson Plan form and the Guide to Writing Lesson Plans (*NPRG*, 24–26).

STEP 2 I Do

1. Assemble Bible helps, maps, pictures, graphic organizer forms, etc.

2. Teach and apply the Strategic Reading Process (*NPRG*, 90). to develop comprehension.

   a. Set purposes for reading before reading.

   b. Guide involvement during reading by self-monitoring and questioning.

   c. After reading, plan for evaluation and reflection.

STEP 3 I Evaluate

1. Was each student actively involved in the reading lesson?

2. What follow-up teaching needs to done to ensure understanding and scholarship?

PLAN	DO (See Chapter Four for complete list.)		EVALUATE
	Methods	**Strategies & Tools**	
• Bible/BAR overview	• 4-R's	• Character chart	• Tutorial approach
• Bible Text	• Notebook method	• K-W-L chart	• Notebook grading
• Biblical Principles & Leading Ideas	• Paraphrasing	• T-chart	• Individual reading progress
• Timeline	• Key word studies, Webster's 1828 *Dictionary*	• Sequence chain	• Oral reading assessment
• Maps	• Strategic reading process	• Story mapping	• Rate and fluency
• 6-Step Reading Lesson Plan	• Fluency instruction	• Story circle	
	• Graphic organizers	• Venn diagram	
		• Word mapping	

Quarterly Plan Sheet for Teaching Reading

Quarter____ Teacher____ Grade____

Week	Bible Text & Memory Verse	Biblical Principles & Leading Ideas	Vocabulary Development	Comprehension & Interpretation	Reasoning & Writing	Enrichment/ Remediation
1						
2						
3						
4						
5						
6						
7						
8						
9						

Guide to Writing Reading Lesson Plans

BIBLE REFERENCE: book, chapter, verse

PAGE NUMBERS: pages of student text

LITERARY TYPE: 1. biography, 2. autobiography, 3. letter, epistle, 4. sermon, 5. poetry and song, epigram (type of poem), 6. historical narrative, 7. short story, 8. drama, 9. wisdom (proverbs), 10. parable, 11. allegory, 12. prophecy

AUTHOR: the writer of the Bible book or psalm

BIBLE: Grade-level Bible

MATERIALS: Study Bibles, reference books, maps, charts, diagrams, resources, pictures, visual aids, tapes, records, teaching tools, and manipulatives

OVERARCHING THEME OF BOOK OR CHAPTER:
A Bible Helps section usually gives suggested divisions or segments with themes or headings which can be used for the entire unit of lesson plans.

BIBLICAL PRINCIPLE: Biblical truth, foundational premise, seeds of truth. Principle chosen based upon the questions: What is the Word teaching us? What is the rule of action to be learned?

LEADING IDEAS: Bridges story content with the Biblical principle and guides the pathway of reasoning for the student. Teacher predetermines where he wants reasoning to go. Some passages will have several principles. The teacher decides the overarching theme. Questions that ask why, what, and how lead to thinking and reflecting. The response to the questions is the principle. Begin with the questions and guide the thinking.

SKILLS TO BE DEVELOPED OR STRENGTHENED:
Refer to the grade level Reading Curriculum Chart.

• Phonics Instruction

• Recognizing and Analyzing Words

• Vocabulary Development Skills

• Comprehension and Interpretation Skill

• Reasoning and Writing

1. SETTING THE STAGE AND UNFAMILIAR VOCABULARY
Inspiring interest in the selection

• Teach unfamiliar vocabulary, unusual words, or names of characters
• Prereading strategies:
  1. Activate prior knowledge
  2. Relate the story to the student's experience
  3. Describe the setting and/or the time
  4. Study the illustrations
  5. Anticipate what they will read or hear
  6. What are the major points?
  7. How is the passage organized?
  8. Describe the background of the author
• Provide a purpose for reading

2. VOCABULARY DEVELOPMENT
Improving vocabulary knowledge, phonics drill/word analysis and usage

• Teach new words, review difficult words, and practice word recognition skills:
  1. Relate new words to previously known words
  2. Emphasize the base words in word families
  3. Use root word meanings—Latin, Greek, etc.
  4. Define prefix and suffix meanings
  5. Present words in context
  6. Arrange words in categories
  7. Practice phonetic and structural analysis
  8. Expand multiple meanings
  9. Use synonyms, antonyms, homonyms
  10. Compile individual word bank
• Define words from memory verses that amplify leading ideas and Biblical principles
• Select words from memory verses that amplify leading ideas and Biblical principles
• Incorporate vocabulary in writing assignments

Guide to Writing Reading Lesson Plans

3. GUIDED READING

SILENT
Strengthening independence in reading (process, not product)

- Guide the thinking of students as they read
- Develop comprehension of the selection
  1. Provide before, during, and after guidance:
     - Set purposes for reading using "setting the stage" information
     - Guide student's involvement during reading by self-monitoring
     - Plan for follow-up organization and retention of information
  2. Discuss the action of the story/selection section by section
  3. What was the order of events?
  4. Who were the people? What did they do? Why? How? When? Where?
  5. What inferences can be drawn?
  6. Was there a cause and effect relationship?
  7. Is there a relationship to other stories, other characters and other events?
  8. Integrate story/selection parts
  9. Look back over story/selection to correct answers
  10. Evaluate students on what they understand, not just recall
- Read cross-reference passages

ORAL
Listening and interpreting manageable sections of text

- Teacher needs to model reading aloud
  1. Read all poetry selections aloud; clap rhythm, show meter on blackboard
  2. Provide good listening experiences
- Direct oral reading by the following:
  1. Read a favorite part
  2. Read to vary emphasis on words and phrases
  3. Read in thought units
  4. Read to check pronunciation of new vocabulary
  5. Practice keeping eye ahead of voice
  6. Read conversation parts with expression
  7. Read to support answers
  8. Re-read to develop fluency
- Supplementary reading with parent monitoring at the independent or free reading level
- In early reading instruction, teach oral reading then silent reading
- In mid- and late primary grades, students should read silently most of the time; oral reading is used for enrichment or to check decoding progress
- After the basic skills are mastered (usually at the end of third grade) emphasize reading rate and comprehension, and strategic reading

4. REASONING AND WRITING
Developing the daily habit of Biblical reasoning and scholarship

- Extend skills development and comprehension:
  1. Reason questions
  2. Provide practice of words in different contexts
  3. Activities: reading, writing, speaking, listening
  4. Research reference materials for more information
  5. Summarize the content
  6. Make a timeline
  7. Memorize Scripture passages and memory verses
- Reinforce reading through writing

5. ENRICHMENT AND REMEDIATION
Providing for the individuality of the learners

- Memorize parallel Scripture passages
- Reading appreciation:
  1. Provide time for related free reading in library books
  2. Dramatize the story (Readers Theatre)
  3. Incorporate art, music, current events
- Teach qualities of a "noble" book
- Take children to a large library and teach library skills

Remediation must be based on an understanding of the child's instructional needs:

1. Word recognition problems
2. Comprehension difficulties
3. Word meanings
4. Insufficient sight vocabulary
5. Weak visual/auditory perception
6. Fluency and rate of oral reading
7. Basic study skills
8. Limited ability to evaluate what is read

6. EVALUATION OF LESSON EFFECTIVENESS
Reflecting on the success of the lesson

1. Were the skills built or strengthened as planned?
2. Did the students show interest in the selection?
3. Was there sufficient practice to develop pronunciation and understanding of the unfamiliar vocabulary?
4. Were the new words analyzed and used in writing exercises?
5. Did the guided reading engage the students' understanding?
6. Were there opportunities for oral reading?
7. Was the Biblical Principle connected to the story content?
8. Who still needs help in mastering the skills?
9. What remedial activities will be planned for those students?
10. What enrichment activities will be developed for the above level readers?

Bible as Reader Weekly Lesson Plan

Teacher_____ Grade_____ Qtr_____ Week_____

BIBLE REFERENCE: **PAGE NUMBERS:** **LITERARY TYPE:** **AUTHOR:**	**BIBLE:** **MATERIALS:**

OVERARCHING THEME OF BOOK OR CHAPTER DIVISIONS: **BIBLICAL PRINCIPLE:** Biblical truth, foundational premise, seeds of truth **LEADING IDEAS:** Bridges story content with the Biblical principle and guides the pathway of reasoning for the student	**SKILLS TO TEACH OR REVIEW:** Refer to the grade level Reading Curriculum charts

1. SETTING THE STAGE AND UNFAMILIAR VOCABULARY Inspiring interest in the selection	**2. VOCABULARY DEVELOPMENT** Improving vocabulary knowledge, phonics drill/word analysis and usage

3. GUIDED READING

SILENT Strengthening independence in reading (process, not product)	**ORAL** Listening and interpreting manageable sections of text

4. REASONING AND WRITING Developing the daily habit of Biblical reasoning and scholarship	**5. ENRICHMENT AND REMEDIATION** Providing for the individuality of the learners

6. EVALUATION OF LESSON EFFECTIVENESS
Reflecting on the success of the lesson (Use the evaluation checklist, *NPRG*, 25)

Model Bible as Reader Weekly Lesson Plan

Teacher _Mrs. Ferrell_ Grade _1_ Qtr _1_ Week _2_

BIBLE REFERENCE: _Matthew 2_ **PAGE NUMBERS:** _250-255_
LITERARY TYPE: _Biography_
AUTHOR: _Matthew, a tax-collector_

BIBLE: _The Young Reader's Bible_
MATERIALS: _Timeline (NPRG, 48-53); K-W-L chart (NPRG, 127), sequence chain form (NPRG, 132) [Appendix]_

OVERARCHING THEME OF BOOK OR CHAPTER DIVISIONS:
Birth of Jesus
BIBLICAL PRINCIPLE: Biblical truth, foundational premise, seeds of truth
Those who are wise seek and worship Jesus.
LEADING IDEAS: Bridges story content with the Biblical principle and guides the pathway of reasoning for the student.
God directed the wise men to Jesus.

SKILLS TO TEACH OR REVIEW:
Refer to the grade level Reading Curriculum charts
Structural analysis of two-syllable words
Multiple meanings: wise, gifts
Sequencing events
Reasoning

1. SETTING THE STAGE AND UNFAMILIAR VOCABULARY
Inspiring interest in the selection

1. _Locate Bethlehem, Judea, and Jerusalem_
2. _Use the K-W-L chart to review story of Christ's birth_
3. _Describe Wise Men_
4. _Discuss teachers of the Law and priests_
5. _Unfamiliar vocabulary:_
   - _Herod_
   - _Israel_
   - _incense_
   - _myrrh_
   - _precious gifts_
   - _Wise Men (Magi)_
   - _Herod_

2. VOCABULARY DEVELOPMENT
Improving vocabulary knowledge, phonics drill/word analysis and usage

1. _wise_
2. _wor'ship_
3. _proph'et (prophecy, prophesy, prophetess, prophetic)_
4. _shep'herd (shepherdess)_
5. _gifts_

3. GUIDED READING

SILENT
Strengthening independence in reading (process, not product)

1. _How did the Wise Men follow God's direction?_

2. _How did King Herod try to change the Wise Men's plan to follow God?_

ORAL
Listening and interpreting manageable sections of text

1. _Students follow along as teacher reads aloud, modeling fluent reading._
2. _Students practice reading the same text to develop fluency. Use partner reading._
3. _After-reading reason questions—_
   - _What makes a person wise?_
   - _How does God guide His people?_

4. REASONING AND WRITING
Developing the daily habit of Biblical reasoning and scholarship

1. _Why do you think King Herod was upset when he heard about Jesus' birth?_
2. _How did the Wise Men find Jesus?_
3. _What did they do when they found Him?_
4. _Why did the Wise Men treat Jesus in this special way?_
5. _Sequencing chain: Students order events chronologically._

5. ENRICHMENT AND REMEDIATION
Providing for the individuality of the learners

1. _Enrichment: name some modern-day Wise Men or Women and tell why they are wise._
2. _Remediation: Use pictures or sentences to practice putting events in the correct order._

6. EVALUATION OF LESSON EFFECTIVENESS
Reflecting on the success of the lesson (Use the evaluation checklist, _NPRG, 25_)

1. _Children were able to use new vocabulary words._
2. _Students understood sequencing except Joey, Mary, Sue, and Miriam. Follow-up and reinforce._

Model Bible as Reader Weekly Lesson Plan

Teacher _Mrs. Martha Shirley_   Grade _3_   Qtr _2_   Week _3_

Bible Reference: _Genesis 6–10_   **Page Numbers:**
Literary Type: _Historical-Narrative_
Author: _Moses_

Bible: _Kid's Study Bible, NIrV_
Materials: _K-W-L chart (NPRG, 127), story map (NPRG, 130)_

OVERARCHING THEME OF BOOK OR CHAPTER DIVISIONS:
The Story of Noah
BIBLICAL PRINCIPLE:
God keeps His promises.
LEADING IDEAS:
The Lord was pleased with Noah who did everything as God commanded. God protected Noah and his family and made a covenant with him. The rainbow is the sign of God's promise.

SKILLS TO TEACH OR REVIEW:
Strategic Reading Process—K-W-L. Ask, What do I know (K) about Noah before reading the text? What do I want to know (W)? After reading, fill in what I learned (L).
Graphic Organizer—Story Map: To analyze the story of Noah and to provide a graphic representation of the key elements. The visual outline provides a framework not only for understanding and remembering a story, but also provides a starting point for composition.
Vocabulary: Grouping new words by structure and meaning.

1. SETTING THE STAGE AND UNFAMILIAR VOCABULARY

1. Read text and display pictures from the <u>Children's Illustrated Bible</u> or other appropriate pictures to give visual images. See <u>Kid's Study Bible</u>, 53, a picture of the ark.
2. Make connections to present-day floods and shipbuilding activities.
3. Use K-W-L chart. Ask:
  "What are the main events in the story of Noah? (K)
  Fill in the "K" column as answers are given.
  "What are some things you want to learn about the story of Noah?" (L)
  Write the questions in the "L" column.
4. Define and discuss new vocabulary using Webster's 1828 <u>Dictionary</u>: ark, Nephilim, cypress wood, clean animal, Ararat, covenant

2. VOCABULARY DEVELOPMENT

1. List new vocabulary as text is read and discussed. Write on note cards for grouping and regrouping into categories—structure, part-of-speech, synonyms or antonyms. For example:
  • ark—noun, type of a boat or a sacred chest, r-controlled syllable
  • flood—noun, proper noun (cap) Flood; verb, to cover with a flood, synonym—inundate
  • phonics—flood is exception, a short u sound, etc.
2. Discuss figurative language in Genesis 7:11: "God opened the windows of the skies."
3. Clarify Genesis 8:2, "The springs at the bottom of the oceans had been closed."

3. GUIDED READING

SILENT

What did God see? (Genesis 6:5) How did God feel? (Genesis 6:6) What did God say He would do? (Genesis 6:7)
Why did God think differently about Noah? What does it mean, "Noah was a Godly man?" List Noah's character qualities that found favor with God.
We live in an evil world like Noah did. Are you influencing others or are they influencing you?

ORAL

Find examples of the phrase, "Everything happened exactly as God had commanded. (Genesis 6:7)
What questions would you ask in an interview with Noah, his sons and his wife and his sons' wives as they left the ark?
What conclusions can you draw from God's covenant with Noah?

4. REASONING AND WRITING

Reason Questions:
Why did God make an exception of Noah? Use Noah's qualities described in Genesis 6:8-9 and 6:22 to answer in complete sentences.
Do you agree with the outcome of the flood? Why or why not?
Composition:
Fill in story map graphic organizer form.
Use the information from the story map to write an informative-narrative about God's covenant with Noah.
The "solution" can be the topic sentence.

5. ENRICHMENT AND REMEDIATION

1. Rewrite the story of the flood from the point-of-view of one of the animals.
2. Readers Theatre: Rehearse the story of Noah and perform for peers or others. Use the dialogue from Genesis 6-9. Assign a narrator and assemble simple props.
3. Construct or draw a model ark. Use illustration from text to compare a football field and house (NIrV, 9)

6. EVALUATION OF LESSON EFFECTIVENESS

Reflecting on the success of the lesson (Use the evaluation checklist, NPRG, 25)

Was there an understanding of the Biblical principle? Did the student connect God's faithfulness in caring for Noah with God's faithfulness to him and his family today? Were the new vocabulary words incorporated into the composition and into the dialogue of the Noah story presentation? After reading the text, was the student able to fill in the "What I Learned" (L) column using the K-W-L chart?

Model Bible as Reader Weekly Lesson Plan

Teacher: _Mrs. Shirley_   Grade: _5_   Qtr: _2_   Week: _5_

BIBLE REFERENCE: _1 Samuel 16:1-13_ **PAGE NUMBERS:** _315_
LITERARY TYPE: _Biography_
AUTHOR: _Samuel_

BIBLE: _The Student Bible, NIV_
MATERIALS: _Pictures of Samuel anointing David, horn, oil, staff; map with Bethlehem marked_

OVERARCHING THEME OF BOOK OR CHAPTER DIVISIONS:
Leadership

BIBLICAL PRINCIPLE: Biblical truth, foundational premise, seeds of truth
God's anointing rests on those whose hearts are right with Him.

LEADING IDEAS: Bridges story content with the Biblical principle and guides the pathway of reasoning for the student.
Man looks at the outward appearance but God looks at the heart.

SKILLS TO TEACH OR REVIEW:
Refer to the grade level Bible as Reader Reading Curriculum charts
Comprehension and Interpreting Skills:
1. _Sequencing events_
2. _Questioning strategies_
3. _Comparison and contrast—using a T-chart_ (NPRG, 131)
4. _Dramatizing Scripture_
5. _Memorizing Scripture_

---

1. SETTING THE STAGE AND UNFAMILIAR VOCABULARY
Inspiring interest in the selection

1. _Use a character chart to review the life of Saul. (See "People Who Impacted History" chart, NPRG, 99; form NPRG, 129.)_
2. _Discuss why God rejected Saul. 1 Samuel 15:23_
3. _Discuss why Saul failed. (Student Bible, 315)_
4. _Word mapping strategy for "anoint" (See word map graphic organizer, NPRG, 98; form NPRG, 132.)_
5. _Unfamiliar vocabulary:_
   • _Ramah_   • _Eliab_
   • _Shammah_   • _heifer_
   • _Jesse_   • _elders_

2. VOCABULARY DEVELOPMENT
Improving vocabulary knowledge, phonics drill/word analysis and usage

1. _anoint_   5. _sacrifice_
2. _consecrate_   6. _tending_
3. _mourn_   7. _ruddy_
4. _reject_

Divide words into syllables.
Put on chart paper for review and re-reading.

---

3. GUIDED READING

SILENT
Strengthening independence in reading (process, not product)

1. _Generate questions by using title—Samuel Anoints David—to ask why, when, where, and how. For example, why did Samuel anoint David?_
2. _Place the events of the story in sequence._
3. _Use a T-chart to compare and contrast Samuel anointing David as King to God anointing Jesus. Matthew 3:16-17_
4. _What is the Biblical principle in this reading?_

ORAL
Listening and interpreting manageable sections of text

Readers Theatre:
Assign parts—Lord, Samuel, Jesse, 7 sons, and David.
Re-enact anointing ceremony.
Use dialogue and actions from 1 Samuel 16

---

4. REASONING AND WRITING
Developing the daily habit of Biblical reasoning and scholarship

1. _Why do you think King Herod was upset when he heard about Jesus' birth?_
2. _How did the Wise Men find Jesus?_
3. _What did they do when they found Him?_
4. _Why did the Wise Men treat Jesus in this special way?_
5. _Sequence chain: Students order events chronologically._

5. ENRICHMENT AND REMEDIATION
Providing for the individuality of the learners

Enrichment: Read Psalm 23
1. _Who wrote this psalm?_
2. _How did the author know about shepherds and sheep?_
3. _What is the symbolism of anointing the head with oil?_
4. _Who anoints believers in the New Testament?_
   (John 1:29-34 & Matthew 3:16-17)

---

6. EVALUATION OF LESSON EFFECTIVENESS
Reflecting on the success of the lesson (Use the evaluation checklist, NPRG, 25)

Students all interacted with the leading idea and deduced the Biblical principle!
The Readers Theatre activity gave opportunities for re-reading the text and for developing oral expression.

Model Bible as Reader Weekly Lesson Plan

Teacher _Mrs. Hameloth_ Grade _6_ Qtr _3_ Week _5_

BIBLE REFERENCE: _Galatians 1-2_ PAGE NUMBERS: _2049-2056_
LITERARY TYPE: _Letter_
AUTHOR: _Paul, A.D. 50_

BIBLE: _Life Application Bible, KJV_
MATERIALS: _Cities in Galatia, map, page 2051_

OVERARCHING THEME OF BOOK OR CHAPTER DIVISIONS:
Authenticity of the Gospel

BIBLICAL PRINCIPLE: Biblical truth, foundational premise, seeds of truth
We are saved by faith in Jesus Christ, not by keeping the law.

LEADING IDEAS: Bridges story content with the Biblical principle and guides the pathway of reasoning for the student.
Old beliefs can keep us from growing spiritually.
The good news is—Christ has set us free!

SKILLS TO TEACH OR REVIEW:
Refer to the grade level Reading Curriculum charts
Summarize verbally
Compose and contrast
Draw inferences
Paraphrase

---

1. SETTING THE STAGE AND UNFAMILIAR VOCABULARY
Inspiring interest in the selection

1. _Introduce book of Galatians. Students read aloud from p. 2049 to answer questions (See Guided Reading, Oral, below.)_
2. _Introduce the mega themes of the book, p. 2050. Copy into notebook._
3. _Introduce Paul (read biographical sketch, p. 1897, "persecutor to preacher")._
4. _Unfamiliar names/places: Galatia and its cities (study map, p. 2051)_

2. VOCABULARY DEVELOPMENT
Improving vocabulary knowledge, phonics drill/word analysis and usage

1. _authenticity_   6. _persuade_
2. _gospel_   7. _grace_
3. _pervert_   8. _hypocrisy_
4. _certify_   9. _justified_
5. _revelation_   10. _transgression_

Write definitions on chalkboard and discuss;
Have students copy into Bible/Reading notebook.

---

3. GUIDED READING

SILENT
Strengthening independence in reading (process, not product)

1. _What is the "false" Gospel? (p. 2053)_
2. _Who preached it?_
3. _What is the "true" Gospel? (p. 2053)_
4. _Who preached it?_
5. _In what ways were the Galatians foolish?_
6. _What did Paul do when Peter and his friends acted hypocritically?_
7. _Whom did Paul try to please?_

ORAL
Listening and interpreting manageable sections of text

Introduction to the book
Who wrote the book?
Why was the book written?
For whom was Galatians written?
When was Galatians written?
What are some important teachings in this book?

---

4. REASONING AND WRITING
Developing the daily habit of Biblical reasoning and scholarship

1. _Why is Paul called the apostle to the Gentiles?_
2. _Complete the chart using verses from Galatians._
3. _What is the principle you have learned about salvation?_
4. _How has God showed you His grace? Be specific._

Old Covenant	New Covenant
Law	_Grace_
Works	_Faith_
Ten Commandments	_Gospel_

5. ENRICHMENT AND REMEDIATION
Providing for the individuality of the learners

Enrichment: Paraphrase Galatians 2:20.

Remediation: Have students read chapters from NIV.

---

6. EVALUATION OF LESSON EFFECTIVENESS
Reflecting on the success of the lesson (Use the evaluation checklist, NPRG, 25)

1. _The concept of freedom from the Law in light of God's salvation was clarified in this difficult passage._
2. _Most students were able to interpret the first-century thinking regarding hypocrisy._

Reading with Reason:
A Cultural Analysis Program
for High School

by Carole G. Adams

> **Read** *v.* (Sax., speech, discourse, counsel, advice, knowledge, benefit, *reason*, rule, govern, learn, know, advance) To discover or understand by characters, marks or features. To learn by observation. To know fully.
>
> **Culture** *n.* (L. from cultivate to till, to dwell) The application of labor or other means to improve good qualities in, or growth; as the culture of the mind; the culture of virtue. Any labor or means employed for improvement, correction or growth.
>
> **Analysis** *n.* (Gr. to loosen) The tracing of things to their source, and the resolving of knowledge into its original principles
>
> **Reason** *n.* (Primarily *reason* is that which is uttered.) A faculty of the mind by which it distinguishes truth from falsehood, and good from evil, and which enables the possessor to deduce Inferences from facts or from propositions.
>
> (Webster's 1828 *Dictionary*)

In the high school, the reading program (Reading with Reason) parallels the academic subjects, offering a forum to discuss and debate books selected for their value in giving breadth and depth to the curriculum. The program relates twelve leading ideas to all the subjects of the curriculum and to books, writing, theater, dance, art, and music.

The program cultivates the spirit of Daniel 1:3−4 to prepare Christian students to enter a world of diverse and often conflicting ideas: "certain of the children of Israel, and of the king's seed, and of the princes; children in whom was no blemish, but well-favored, and skillful in all wisdom and cunning in knowledge and understanding science and such as had ability in them to stand in the king's palace and whom they might teach the learning and tongue of the Chaldeans."

In terms of Reading with Reason, "A chosen progeny of strong character, cherished, disciplined, reasoning, alert, (standing in) leadership and service, to be the articulate builders (of the kingdom of God)."

Reading with Reason presents three leading ideas in each of the four years of high school for study, discussion, debate, and for recording observations and reviews. Faculty members act as mentors in cultivating an understanding of the ideas and the classical readings, pacing the reading, and reviewing and leading the forums. The teacher selects the art, drama, music, film, and other cultural expressions of the leading idea for review.

Reading with Reason expands and deepens every course in the curriculum of the high school by allowing the student time to confront, ponder, articulate, and debate twelve leading questions and ideas.

The Principle Approach® to Biblical reasoning in any field requires that we first establish the seed of Christian self-government, our philosophy of life and government, from which we research, reason, relate, and finally record our findings in any field.

Requirements and Procedures for Reading with Reason:

1. A weekly meeting is held to preview, prepare, and present the selections to complement the readings that are done independently.

2. A main book is read by the whole class.

3. Related selections are chosen by students who read and present their choices.

4. The teacher previews the leading idea with the class by defining words, discussing the meanings, and formulating questions that naturally arise from the discussion.

5. Approximately six weeks are given to each topic.

6. Students keep a reading diary for each selected book. Film, art, and music selections are recorded in the diary according to the teacher's direction.

7. When the main selection is read, a forum is held in which the questions formulated are addressed and discussed or debated.

8. Students present their readings to add to the topic. The interaction of the students in the reading, reviewing and discussion, and debating gives the desired effect of creating a forum for each student to contribute from his own reading and reasoning.

Reading with Reason:
Leading Ideas

Ninth Grade

Courses	Leading Ideas for Reading with Reason
English Literature, A.D. 450–1660; Universal History: Ancient to the Reformation; Bible/Logic; Algebra/Geometry; Astronomy; Geology; Classical or Modern Language	9A The Reach of Rome 9B The Hebrew Question 9C Origins

---

Tenth Grade

Courses	Leading Ideas for Reading with Reason
English Literature, 1660–21ˢᵗ Century; Modern History, 1660 to Present; Bible/Hermeneutics; Geometry/Algebra; Biology; Classical or Modern Language	10A The Second Creation 10B Revolutions 10C Frontiers

---

Eleventh Grade

Courses	Leading Ideas for Reading with Reason
American Literature, 1607–1820; American History Survey; Bible; Trigonometry; Chemistry; Classical or Modern Language	11A Wars 11B Statesmanship 11C The Purpose of Science

---

Twelfth Grade

Courses	Leading Ideas for Reading with Reason
American Literature, 1820–21ˢᵗ Century; Government/ Economics; Bible; Physics; Classical or Modern Language	12A Liberty and Slavery 12B Letters 12C Senior Thesis

Index of Reading with Reason Themes and
Suggested Cultural Analysis Selections

Leading Ideas	Books/Selected Readings	Film, Music, Theater, Art
9A The Reach of Rome (Law, Republic, Empire, Greece, Roman Church, Pagan gods, Architecture, Modern Italy)	*The Life and Writings of Cicero, Pillar of Iron,* Taylor Caldwell; *Quo Vadis?,* Henryk Sienkiewicz; *The Agony and the Ecstasy,* Irving Stone; Virgil; *Death Comes to the Archbishop,* Willa Cather; *The Greek Treasure,* Irving Stone; CHOC I Readings; CHOC II Readings	Film: *Ben Hur,* 1959 Art: Leonardo da Vinci, inventions Music: *The Pines of Rome,* Respighi
9B The Hebrew Question (Old Testament History, Judaism, Diaspora, the Holocaust, Modern Israel, Palestine)	*The Source,* James Michener; *Exodus,* Leon Uris; *The Diary of Anne Frank; Berlin Diary,* William Shirer; *The Merchant of Venice,* Shakespeare; *Ivanhoe,* Walter Scott; CHOC II Readings	Film: *Weapons of the Spirit,* 1988 Art: Michelangelo's *Moses, David* Music: *Messiah,* Handel
9C Origins (Creation, Evolution)	*Darwin; Genesis Flood,* Henry Morris	Film: *Inherit the Wind,* 1960 Art: Michelangelo, *Creation,* Sistine Chapel
10A The Second Creation; Life in Christ (Early Christianity, Reformation, Christian Champions)	*The Big Fisherman,* Lloyd C. Douglas; *The Robe,* Lloyd C. Douglas; *Dear and Beloved Physician,* Taylor Caldwell; *Lion of God,* Taylor Caldwell; *The Talisman,* Walter Scott	Film: *Chariots of Fire,* 1981 (How is a Christian to react to strong peer pressure that challenges his moral principles? How is a Jew to fit into a society? What value do we place on sports? What is patriotism?) Art: Fra Angelico Music: Bach
10B Revolutions (American, French, Bolshevik, and others)	*A Tale of Two Cities,* Charles Dickens; *The Scarlet Pimpernel,* Orczy; *Three Revolutions,* by Friederich Gentz, translated by John Quincy Adams; *The Spy,* James Fenimore Cooper	Film: *The Manchurian Candidate,* 1962 (How completely can the human mind be controlled?) Art: Benjamin West Music: *La Marseillaise,* Rouget de Lisle
10C Frontiers: Internal and External (Geographical exploration, science fiction, space, creative expression, experimental research)	*Christopher Columbus, Mariner,* Samuel Morison; *Apollo to the Moon,* Gregory Kennedy. Other related choices: *Alone,* Admiral Byrd; *Seven Came Through,* Edward Rickenbacker; *Last of the Mohicans,* James Fenimore Cooper; *Out of the Silent Planet,* C. S. Lewis; *John of the Mountains,* John Muir; *My Antonia,* Willa Cather	Film: *Amadeus,* 1984 (The early death of Mozart raises some important questions regarding pride, the use of gifts God bestows upon us, and the creative process.) *The Man Who Shot Liberty Valance,* 1962 (How are heroes made? How is one to deal with a complete savage? Conflict between good and evil, civilization and anarchy, fact and myth.) Art: *Columbus Departing from Palos,* Leutze Music: *The New World Symphony,* Dvorák
11A Wars (Philosophies of war: World wars, Civil War)	*Men of Iron,* Howard Pyle; *The Tree of Liberty,* Elizabeth Page; *Drums,* James Boyd; *Patton: A Genius for War,* Carlo d'Este	Film: *Bridge on the River Kwai,* 1957 (story of willpower and the futility of war) *Casablanca,* 1943 (love through sacrifice, the worth of the individual, human loyalty, freedom) Art: *Guernica,* Picasso Music: *The 1812 Overture,* Tchaikovsky
11B Statesmanship (Who has the right to rule? Statesmanship and models of statesmen)	*An American Life,* Ronald Reagan; *The Republic,* Plato; *The Prince,* Machiavelli; *The Glory and the Dream,* Michael Musmanno	Film: *Mr. Smith Goes to Washington,* 1939 (integrity in a corrupt system: one good person can make a difference.) Art: The Peale Family paintings Music: *Hail Columbia,* Hopkinson
11C The Purpose of Science	Humboldt; Agassiz; *Matthew Fontaine Maury: Scientist of the Sea,* Frances Williams; *Men under the Sea,* Edward Ellsberg; Hiroshima	Art: Photography
12A Wars (Philosophies of war: World wars, Civil War)	*Up from Slavery,* Booker T. Washington; *Narrative of the Captivity and Restoration of Mrs. Mary Rowlandson*	Film: *to Kill a Mockingbird,* 1962 (prejudice, truth, and reason) Music: Spirituals
12B Statesmanship (Who has the right to rule? Statesmanship and models of statesmen)	*The Book of John and Abigail [Adams]*	Film: *84 Charing Cross Road,* 1986

12C Senior Thesis
The Senior Thesis is the selection of an issue or problem to be researched, presented orally, and defended during the senior year.

The thesis project requires broad reading and documentation based upon the methods learned through the Reading with Reason method.

Model Lesson Plan: Reading with Reason
Sample Development of a Leading Idea
for Tenth Grade

Statement of the Leading Idea

Frontiers may be internal or external. Frontiers may be in the areas of geographic exploration, science fiction, space, creative expression, experimental research—anything that borders the known and suggests the unknown.

Main Book Selections: *Christopher Columbus, Mariner*, Samuel Eliot Morison; *Apollo to the Moon*, Gregory Kennedy

Film, music, theater, and art are for the enhancement of the discussion to give color and "story" to the themes.

Previewing the Leading Idea

Define the words: *frontier* (noun and verb), *compass* (noun and verb). Shakespeare: "There are more things in heaven and earth, Horatio, than are dreamed of in your philosophy."

Our internal liberty in Christ and our external governmental freedom in America enable us to seek to go beyond the present compass of our thoughts, our knowledge, and our experience. This impels us to seek to go beyond present limitations in all fields. Our goal is always to make life richer and freer for all mankind.

Student Requirements

- Read the main selection looking for themes and leading ideas.
- Select a second choice for independent reading (something of personal interest) and read. Make notes for the oral presentation of themes and leading ideas found in it.
- Attend the weekly meeting at which the theme is previewed, the cultural analysis of the film, art, and music selections are shared, and the final forum of discussion and debate is held.
- Keep the Reading Diary, recording notes from reading and from the cultural analysis of film, art, and music. Of most importance is the articulation of what is read, understood, and reasoned verbally. The diary is a respository of student ideas to be used in discussion and debate.

Weekly Meeting for Six Weeks

- Week One: Preview of theme
- Week Two: Analysis of the painting *Columbus Departing from Palos* by Leutze; Discussion of the main selection.
- Week Three: Viewing of the film *Amadeus*. Discussion of the creative process, the use of the gifts God gives us.
- Week Four: Analysis of *The New World Symphony* and how the frontier theme is depicted musically. Presentation of related selections read by students.
- Week Five: Viewing of another film as selected by the teacher to broaden the discussion of frontiers.
- Week Six: Forum

Forum: Student Participation

- Students should be prepared to discuss the questions raised by the leading ideas, to raise further questions, and to expound upon the conclusions.
- Students should be prepared to:
  - identify the principles related to the themes
  - identify the perspective on the theme presented in the readings
  - present the conflicting views
  - present personal conclusions
  - raise questions for debate
  - identify issues remaining unanswered

Forum: Teacher Direction

- The experience of Reading with Reason is designed to give breadth and depth to the curriculum but also to give joy to readers through the experience of sharing ideas and discussing personal perspectives and conclusions drawn from reading.
- Questions for the forum: In light of the leading idea—frontiers, and their implication for the human spirit—what does the study of Columbus mean to you? Interpret providence, barriers, character, and vision in this context. What unanswered questions do you have?

Chapter Two

Foundations for
Teaching Reading

*The moral principles and precepts contained in the Scriptures
ought to form the basis of all our civil constitutions and laws.
All the miseries and evils which men suffer from vice,
crime, ambition, injustice, oppression, slavery, and war,
proceed from their despising or neglecting
the precepts contained in the Bible.*

(Noah Webster, *An American Dictionary of the English Language*, 1828)

Defining Reading and Identifying Its Principles

Read, *v. t.* [Saxon. *ræd, rad, red,* speech, discourse, counsel, advice, knowledge, benefit, *reason*; to read, to decree, to appoint, to command, to rule or govern, to conjecture, to give or take counsel; . . . reason, . . . knowledge, instruction or learning, G. *rede,* speech; . . . Goth. *rodyan,* to speak. The primary sense of *read* is to speak, to utter, that is, to push, drive or advance. . . .]

1. To utter or pronounce written or printed words, letters or characters in the proper order; to repeat the names or utter the sounds customarily annexed to words, letters, or characters; as, to *read* a written or printed discourse; to *read* the letters of an alphabet; to *read* figures; to *read* the notes of music, or to *read* music.

2. To inspect and understand words or characters; to peruse silently; as, to *read* a paper or letter without uttering the words; to *read* to one's self.

3. To discover or understand by characters, marks or features; as, to *read* a man's thoughts in his countenance.

4. To learn by observation.

5. To know fully.

(Webster's 1828 *Dictionary*)*

Key Words

Understand, *v. t.* [*under* and *stand.* The sense is to support or hold in the mind.] To have just and adequate ideas of; to comprehend; to know; to interpret, at least mentally.

Understanding, *ppr.* Knowing; skillful.
There is a spirit in man, and the inspiration of the Almighty giveth him understanding. Job xxxii.

Peruse, *v. t.* To read, or to read with attention. To observe; to examine with careful survey.

Know, *v. t.* To perceive with certainty; to understand clearly; to have a clear and certain perception of truth, fact, or anything that actually exists.

Comprehend, *v. t.* [L. *comprehendo*; to seize or grasp; . . .]
To understand; to conceive; that is, to take, hold or contain in the mind; to possess or to have an idea;
God doeth great things, which we cannot comprehend. Job xxxvii.

Perceive, *v.t.* To have knowledge or receive . . . through the senses. To know; to understand; to observe.

Rule, *v.t.* To govern; to conduct; to manage; to control. That God rules the world he has created is a fundamental article of belief.

Govern, *v.t.* To direct and control; To regulate; to influence. *v.i.* To exercise authority.

Reason, *v.i.* To exercise the faculty of reason; to deduce inferences justly from premises. To argue; to infer conclusions from premises, or to deduce new or unknown propositions from previous propositions which are known or evident. To debate; to confer or inquire by discussion or mutual communication of thoughts, arguments or reasons. To discourse; to talk; to take or give an account.

Reason, *n.* A faculty of the mind by which it distinguishes truth from falsehood, and good from evil, and which enables the possessor to deduce inferences from facts or from propositions.
Reason is the director of man's will. *Hooker.*

Knowledge, *n.* A clear and certain perception of that which exists, or of truth and fact; Learning; illumination of mind. Skill; Information.

(Webster's 1828 *Dictionary*)

Definition of Reading

Reading is an oral exercise which requires speaking and pronouncing words, letters, or characters which must be heard and understood.

To read written language, one must look with a purpose at the text, understand the words, and comprehend the ideas presented. To *comprehend* means literally, "to take in"; it is a compound of two Latin words meaning "to seize or grasp." The reader "takes hold" of the ideas and interprets and analyzes. He must "seize" the information, insight, and inspiration from the text. Reading is governmental. One must control and regulate what he reads, having a knowledge of what is of value.

Reasoning completes the reading process. Webster says reason is a faculty of the mind by which it distinguishes truth from falsehood, and good from evil, and enables the possessor to deduce inferences from facts or from propositions.

---

* Underline the key words in your definition, then also define those key words. (See Word Study format, *NPSDS,* 23–26)

The Biblical Foundations for Reading the Bible

1. **The Bible is of divine origin.** The Bible is revelation from God. Men without revelation wander in darkness.

   a. "In the beginning was the Word, and the Word was with God, and the Word was God." (John 1:1)

   b. "All scripture is given by inspiration of God, and is profitable for doctrine, for reproof, for correction, for instruction in righteousness:" (2 Timothy 3:16)

2. **God revealed His character and will to man.** In the Scriptures we learn of creation, where we came from, why we were made, and how we should live.

   a. "In the beginning God created the heaven and the earth. . . . And God said, Let us make man in our image, after our likeness; and let them have dominion . . . And God blessed them, and God said unto them, Be fruitful, and multiply, and replenish the earth, and subdue it: and have dominion." (Genesis 1:1, 26, 28)

   b. "I will bless the LORD, who hath given me counsel . . . I have set the LORD always before me: because he is at my right hand, I shall not be moved." (Psalm 16:7–8)

3. **The first duty of man is to know God and His will for us.** The Scriptures give us the knowledge of God and what He requires. It is our duty to read the Scriptures to learn the character and will of God. His will is that we be like Him.

   a. "Thus did Moses: according to all that the LORD commanded him so did he." (Exodus 40:16)

   b. "Thy kingdom come. Thy will be done in earth, as it is in heaven." (Matthew 6:10)

   c. "[I]f we ask any thing according to his will, he heareth us." (1 John 5:14)

   d. "For it is God which worketh in you both to will and to do of his good pleasure." (Philippians 2:12)

4. **The Bible is the only inspired, inerrant, infallible Word of God.** It is trustworthy for the governing of the affairs of men socially, morally, and religiously.

   a. "[I]f ye will obey my voice indeed, and keep my covenant, then ye shall be a peculiar treasure unto me above all people: for all the earth is mine: And ye shall be unto me a kingdom of priests, and an holy nation." (Exodus 19:5–6)

   b. "And now, O LORD God, thou art that God, and thy words be true." (2 Samuel 7:28)

5. **The true religion of Christ is in the Bible only,** "the principles of which are all comprehended in two short phrases, *love to God*, and *love to men*. . . .[T]he person who loves God supremely, will reverence his character and laws, and will extend his benevolent affections and charities to all his creatures. From this source will proceed love to man, and the careful performance of all moral and social duties." (Noah Webster's *Value of the Bible*, 81)

   a. "Unto you first God, having raised up his Son Jesus, sent him to bless you, in turning away every one of you from his iniquities." (Acts 3:26)

   b. "Jesus saith unto him, I am the way, the truth, and the life: no man cometh unto the Father, but by me." (John 14:6)

The Principles for Using the Bible as a Reader

1. **Reading the Bible prepares a Biblical character in children.**

   "The LORD our God is one LORD: and thy shalt love the LORD thy God with all thine heart, and with all thy soul, and with all thy might. And these words, . . . shall be in thine heart: . . . teach them diligently unto they children, . . . talk of them when thou sittest in thy house, and when thou walkest by the way, and when thou liest down, and when thou risest up." (Deuteronomy 6:4–7)

   • Lays the foundation for character

   • Teaches self-government

   • Provides practice of true religion—love for God and love for others

2. **Reading the Bible gives the opportunity to correct the heart and purify it from all that is wrong and inconsistent with the enjoyment of God.**

   "Thy word have I hid in mine heart, that I might not sin against thee. . . . I will meditate in thy precepts, and have respect unto thy ways. (Psalm 119:11, 15)

   "Your word is a lamp to my feet and a light to my path." (Psalm 119:105)

   • Strengthens the intellect and expands its powers

   • Refines our ideas of God's purity and holiness

- Forms our conception of what is ennobling in our conduct

- Directs our path toward an elevation of character

- Prepares us to live happily with God

3. **Reading the Bible is time usefully employed.**

Reading the Bible furnishes the mind with correct notions about God, His laws, and human duty; and directs us to help others to be wiser and better.

"[H]e [the king] shall write him a copy of this law in a book. . . . it shall be with him, and he shall read therein all the days of his life: that he may learn to fear the LORD his God, to keep all the words of this law and these statutes, to do them: That his heart be not lifted up above his brethren."

(Deuteronomy 17:18–20)

4. **Reading the Bible equips man with truth for the practice of Christian liberty.**

"And ye shall know the truth, and the truth shall make you free."

(John 8:32)

The Art of Good Reading

"The technique of reading, though always subordinate and secondary to the mastery of the thought, nevertheless claims constant and careful attention. Good reading requires clear enunciation and correct pronunciation, and these can be secured only when the teacher steadily insists upon them. . . . The habit of using the dictionary freely should be firmly established in pupils. The art of good reading can be cultivated by judicious training and the school should spare no pains to realize this result. . . . The best in literature shall be the means of cultivating in pupils a taste for good reading, and at the same time shall have that refining influence on character which good literature always had." (Elson and Keck 1911, 11)

Reading Is Like the Performance of a Symphony

"Reading is the process of constructing meaning from written texts. It is a complex skill requiring the coordination of a number of interrelated sources of information.

"Reading can be compared to the performance of a symphony orchestra. This analogy illustrates three points:

"First, like the performance of a symphony, reading is a holistic act. In other words, while reading can be analyzed into subskills such as discriminating letters and identifying words, performing the subskills one at a time does not constitute reading. Reading can be said to take place only when the parts are put together in a smooth, integrated performance.

"Second, success in reading comes from practice over long periods of time, like skill in playing musical instruments. Indeed, it is a lifelong endeavor.

"Third, as with a musical score, there may be more than one interpretation of a text. The interpretation depends upon the background of the reader, the purpose for reading, and the context in which reading ocurs." (Anderson 1984, 7)

Anderson, Richard C., Elfrieda H. Hiebert, Judith A. Scott, and Ian A. G. Wilkinson. 1984. *Becoming a Nation of Readers: The Report of the Commission on Reading.* Champaign, Illinois: The Center for the Study of Reading, University of Illinois at Urbana-Champaign, National Institute of Education, U.S. Department of Education.

Elson, William H. and Christine Keck. 1911. *Elson Grammar School Reader,* Book Two. Chicago: Scott Foresman and Company.

The Bible: Rock of Our Republic

by Stephen McDowell

Editor's Note:

Stephen McDowell's extensively documented article from his newsletter *Providential Perspective*, Vol. 11, No. 3, October 1996, presents the impact the Bible has had on America and is submitted as a case for returning the Bible as a schoolbook to American classrooms. Rev. McDowell proceeds from presenting the central role of the Bible in shaping the beginnings of our nation through the Civil War and the centrality of the Bible in education. The exact words of America's founders support the value of the Bible in schools, law, government, and social transactions. The first book printed in America was the Bible. Rev. McDowell concludes, "As the Bible and its principles have been removed from our schools, missing from our leaders' ideas and actions, extirpated from the market place of ideas, and not adhered to by enough of our citizens, America has declined and will continue to decline. America must once again restore the Bible to its place of influence. We must consider the Bible, in the words of Noah Webster, 'as the great source of all the truths by which men are to be guided in government, as well as in all social transactions. . . . the Bible [is] the instrument of all reformation in morals and religion.'"

Stephen McDowell is executive director of the Providence Foundation, an educational organization whose purpose is to study the relationship between religion and public life and to train people in how the principles of Christianity affect all of society. He has authored and co-authored several books and videos, including *America's Providential History, Liberating the Nations,* and *The Story of America's Liberty*. I thank Stephen for his generosity in permitting the Foundation for American Christian Education to publish his article in its entirety.

The Influence of the Bible in the History of America

On June 8, 1845, President Andrew Jackson said that "the Bible is the rock on which our Republic rests." Early Americans would almost universally agree that the religious, social, educational, and political life of America was primarily shaped by the Bible.

Our states were colonized by people who desired to freely worship the God of the Bible; our schools were begun so that everyone would be able to read and understand the Bible for themselves; our universities were founded to train ministers who were knowledgeable of the Scriptures; our laws and constitutions were written based on Biblical ideas; and our founding fathers overwhelmingly had a Biblical worldview.

Most Americans today have not been taught this important truth, even though many still recognize it. Even Newsweek magazine, on December 26, 1982, acknowledged that: "Now historians are discovering that the Bible, perhaps even more than the Constitution is our Founding document." It used to be common knowledge that America's Biblical foundation produced America's freedom, justice, and prosperity. In recent generations America has been shifting from a Biblical foundation to a humanistic foundation, where the God of the Bible is being replaced by man as god. The result has been the decay of society and loss of liberty. Noah Webster wrote:

> The moral principles and precepts contained in the Scriptures ought to form the basis of all our civil constitutions and laws. All the miseries and evils which men suffer from vice, crime, ambition, injustice, oppression, slavery, and war; proceed from their despising or neglecting the precepts contained in the Bible.

For the good of America we must once again restore the Bible to the central role it played in shaping this nation. To do this we must first understand that role. Following is a brief outline examining the influence of the Bible in our history.

I. The Bible was the single most important influence in the lives of colonial Americans.

Lawrence A. Cremin writes:

> Above all, the colonists were acquainted with the Bible itself, principally in the Geneva Version but increasingly in the King James Version. The Bible was read and recited, quoted and consulted, early committed to memory and constantly searched for meaning. Deemed universally relevant, it remained throughout the century the single most important cultural influence in the lives of Anglo-Americans. . . . Though the Bible had been richly valued for generations, it was not until the seventeenth century that it was widely read and studied. The message of Protestantism was that men could find in Scripture the means to salvation, the keys to good and evil, the rules by which to live, and the standards against which to measure the conduct of prince and pastor.[1]

New England of the 1700s was described by historian George Bancroft in this way:

> In the settlements which grew up in the interior, on the margin of the greenwood, the plain meeting-house of the congregation for public worship was everywhere the central point; near it stood the public school. The snug farmhouses, owned as freehold, without quitrents, were dotted along the way. In every hand was the Bible; every home was a house of prayer; all had been taught, many had comprehended, a methodical theory of the divine purpose in creation, and of the destiny of man.[2]

The Aitken Bible

Prior to America's independence almost every house in the colonies possessed and cherished the English Bible, yet, no English Bibles had ever been printed in the colonies (some had been printed in German and native Indian languages). It would have been piracy to do so. Only after independence were English Bibles printed. When the war cut off the supply of English Bibles, the Congress, in September 1777, resolved to import 20,000 Bibles from Scotland, Holland, or elsewhere because "the use of the Bible is so universal and its importance so great." In 1782, Congress acted the role of a Bible society by officially approving the printing and distribution of the "Bible of the Revolution," an American translation prepared by Robert Aitken.

Oath of Office taken on the Bible

At the first presidential inauguration George Washington laid his hand on the Bible and took the oath of office as prescribed by the Constitution, adding the words "so help me God," after which he leaned over and reverently kissed the Bible. Washington then went to the Senate and read his inaugural address. After this they all walked to St. Paul's Chapel for prayers and a service.[3] All the presidents have taken the oath of office on the Bible.

II. The People who settled America were people of the Book. *Sola Scriptura* was their motto.

A majority of the settlers of America were a product of the Protestant Reformation. The major impetus of this reform was the Bible being translated into the common languages of the people. Throughout Europe the people read the Scriptures and began looking to them as the standard by which they judged not only their own actions but also that of priest and king. The Bible became the source of their ideas and principles. This brought many trials and persecutions and forced many to flee their native countries to America.

Many of those who had paved the way for settlement were inspired by the Scriptures as well. Composed in 1502 after his third voyage, Columbus's *Book of Prophecies* reveals he felt he was fulfilling a divine mission through his voyages. This work contains hundreds of prophetic passages of Scripture that Columbus related to his great enterprise. The man most responsible for the English colonization of America was a minister, Richard Hakluyt. He said he was first inspired by the Scriptures to promote colonization. His chief motive was to extend God's Kingdom throughout the earth.

Some of the early settlers

Pilgrims

They were enlightened by the Word of God and sought to live according to its precepts. Pastor to the Pilgrims John Robinson, wrote in his farewell letter:

> I charge you, before God and his blessed angels, that you follow me no farther than you have seen me follow the Lord Jesus Christ. The Lord has more truth yet to break forth out of his holy word. I cannot sufficiently bewail the condition of the reformed churches, who are come to a period in religion, and will go at present no farther than the instruments of their reformation. Luther and Calvin were great and shining lights in their times, yet they penetrated not into the whole counsel of God. I beseech you, remember it—'tis an article of your church covenant—that you be ready to receive whatever truth shall be made known to you from the written word of God.[4]

Puritans

The early settlers of Salem, Massachusetts, were typical of the many Puritans who came to America. One reason they came was to "wynne the natives to the Christian faith." During their voyage from England they "constantly served God, morning and evening, by reading and expounding a chapter in the Bible, singing and prayer."[5]

The First Charter of Massachusetts (1629) states the desire that all the inhabitants would "be so religiously, peaceably, and civilly governed, as their good life and orderly conversation may win and incite the natives of country to the knowledge and obedience of the only true God and Savior of mankind, and the Christian faith, which in Our royal intention and the adventurers' free profession, is the principal end of this plantation."[6]

The center of the seal of the colony of Massachusetts Bay shows an Indian speaking the words, "Come Over and Help Us." The work of John Eliot, "Apostle to the Indians," and Daniel Gookin, a civil magistrate and superintendent to the Indians, shows how many of the early settlers desired to bring the gospel to the native Americans—how they did come over to help them. These two men worked for over forty years to evangelize and civilize the Algonquin Indians of Massachusetts.

Eliot constantly traveled to various Indian villages and taught them the gospel. When many began to be converted he set up "Praying Towns" where these Christian Indians could live out their new life in Christ and learn how to separate themselves from their pagan way of life. In these towns, which came to number fourteen, the Indians were self-governed and self-supporting. Twenty-four of these Christian Indians became ministers in order to carry on the work of the gospel among their own people. Hundreds attended schools and some attended Harvard College.

Eliot believed that the Indians needed the Bible in their own language in order to truly grow in the complete liberty of the gospel, both internally and externally, both personally and civilly. Therefore, after learning the native Indian language, he developed a written language for the Algonquin tongue, as none existed. He then worked for twelve years on translating the Bible, while continuing his pastoral duties in the church in Roxbury and regularly traveling to minister to the Indians. He completed the work in 1658. The Algonquin Bible was first published in 1661–1663 with funds primarily contributed by Englishmen. This was the first Bible printed in America.

Scotch-Irish Presbyterians

Many settled on the western frontiers of Pennsylvania, Maryland, Virginia, and North Carolina. At every place they "had their pastor, and trained their children in Bible truth, in the catechism, obedience to parents—a wholesome doctrine practically enforced by all the colonists—and reverence for the Sabbath and its sacred duties."[7]

Georgia colonists

Some of the earliest settlers to Georgia were German Lutherans who were driven out of their country when they refused to renounce their Protestant faith, and were invited by the Society in England for Propagating the Gospel to emigrate to Savannah. George Bancroft writes: "On the last day of October 1733, 'the evangelical community,' well supplied with Bibles and hymn-books, catechisms and books of devotion . . . after a discourse and prayer and benedictions, cheerfully, and in the name of God, began their pilgrimage." They arrived at Charleston on March 18, 1734 and were welcomed by Oglethorpe.[8]

III.   The Bible formed the basis of America's civil laws.

Jamestown

Between 1609 and 1612 a set of laws was drawn up for the colony of Virginia. In these *Lawes Divine, Morall and Martiall*, the colonists were required to serve God, to attend divine services, to not speak against God or blaspheme God's holy name, and to not speak or act in any way that would "tend to the derision, or despight [open defiance] of God's holy word upon paine of death."[9] While this may seem extreme to us today, it nonetheless reveals their desire to live according to God's commands.

In 1619 the first Representative Assembly of the new world met in the Church in Jamestown. It was begun by prayer. One of the resolves of this body was to encourage the farmers and plantation owners to open their homes to Indian youth with the purpose of converting them to Christianity and teaching them the precepts of God's Word.

The Laws of the Pilgrims

The Pilgrims believed that God and His word were the supreme source of all authority. Their compilation of laws during the 1600s clearly revealed this. Their *Book of General Laws* (1671) begins by stating the "Laws . . . are so far good and wholesome, as by how much they are derived from, and agreeable to the ancient Platform of God's Law."[10] As one reads through these laws it is obvious they looked to the Bible to assist them in formulating good and wholesome laws. They even gave Scriptural references to support their capital laws.

Fundamental Orders of Connecticut

This first American constitution was written by Rev. Thomas Hooker in 1638. The oath imposed on the magistrates bound them "to administer justice according to the laws here established, and for want thereof according to the rule of the word of God." The oath of the governor (and similarly the Magistrate) ended with these words: "I . . . will further the execution of Justice according to the rule of Gods word; so helpe me God, in the name of the Lo[rd] Jesus Christ."[12]

New Haven Colony

Established in 1638 under the guidance of Rev. John Davenport, this colony rested its frame of government on a covenant providing that "all of them would be ordered by the rules which the scriptures held forth to them." God's word was established as the only rule in public affairs. Bancroft wrote that "New Haven made the Bible its statute book."[13]

Massachusetts Body of Liberties

Written in 1641 by Rev. Nathaniel Ward, the Pentateuch (the first five books of the Bible) was the basis for its criminal code, and "in case of the defect of a law in any particular case" the standard was "the word of God."[14] Article 65 states: "No custome or prescription shall ever prevalle amongst us in any morall cause, our meaneing is maintaine anything that can be proved to bee morrallie sinfull by the word of god."[15] The capital laws in the Body of Liberties give numerous scriptures as justification for carrying out the death penalty."[16]

Arbitrary Government Described, 1644

In explaining how the government of Massachusetts was to work, Governor John Winthrop wrote: "By these it appears, that the officers of this body politic have a rule to walk by in all their administrations, which rule is the Word of God, and such conclusions and deductions as are, or shall be regularly drawn from thence."[17]

Code of the Connecticut General Court, 1650

No man's life, liberty, or property was to be taken except by specific law established and suficiently published by the General Court (the legislature), "or in case of the defect of a law, in any particular case, by the Word of God."[18]

The Connecticut Code of Law lists several crimes receiving the death penalty. Specific Scriptures are listed as justification for these capital laws. For example:

> 4. If any person shall commit any willful murder, which is manslaughter, commited upon malice, hatred, or cruelty, not in a man's necessary and just defense, nor by mere casualty against his will, he shall be put to death. Ex. 21:12–14; Num. 35:30, 31.

> 10. If any man steals a man or mankind he shall be put to death. Ex. 21:16[19]

The Code also states that "the open contempt of God's Word, and messengers thereof, is the desolating sin of civil states and churches."[20]

Many other early constitutions, compacts, charters, and laws could be examined that reveal the central role of the Bible in shaping America's civil documents, such as the Charter of Rhode Island, the Frame of Government of Pennsylvania, the Declaration of Independence, various state constitutions, and the U.S. Constitution and Bill of Rights.

IV. Education was rooted in the Bible.

The First Schools Were Christian.

The first schools in America were started by the church to teach people to be able to read the Bible (for example, the Boston Latin School in 1636).

Massachusetts School Laws of 1642 and 1647

In 1642 the General Court enacted legislation requiring each town to see that children were taught, especially "to read and understand the principles of religion and the capital laws of this country."[21]

The laws of 1647 begin: "It being one chief project of that old deluder, Satan, to keep men from the knowledge of the Scriptures. . . ." The General Court went on to order any town with fifty families to hire a teacher, and those that increased to one hundred families to set up a school to prepare youth for the university.[22]

Grammar School at Dorchester, Massachusetts

Rules adopted by town meeting in 1645 required the schoolmaster "to commend his scholars and his labors amongst them unto God by prayer morning and evening, taking care that his scholars do reverently attend during the same." The schoolmaster examined each student at noon on Monday to see what he had learned from the Sabbath sermon. On Friday afternoon at 2:00, he was to catechize them "in the principles of Christian religion."[23]

Connecticut School Laws, 1650

The laws of 1650 required localities to provide for the education of the youth. They began like that of Massachusetts: "It being one chief project of that old deluder, Satan, to keep men from the knowledge of the Scriptures."[24]

A 1690 law declared: "This [legislature] observing that . . . there are many persons unable to read the English tongue and thereby incapable to read the holy Word of God or the good laws of this colony . . . it is ordered that all parents and masters shall cause their respective children and servants, as they are capable, to be taught to read distinctly the English tongue."[26]

Colleges started to train ministers in knowledge of Scriptures.

Harvard College, 1636

Rules, and precepts that are observed in the college:

> 2. Let every student be plainly instructed, and earnestly pressed to consider well, the main end of his life and studies is, to know God and Jesus Christ which is eternal life, John 17:3, and therefore to lay Christ in the bottom, as the only foundation of all sound knowledge and learning.

> And seeing the Lord only giveth wisdom, let every one seriously set himself by prayer in secret to seek it of him, Prov. 2:3.

> 3. Every one shall so exercise himself in reading the Scriptures twice a day, that he shall be ready to give such an account of his proficiency therein, both in theoretical observations of the language, and logic, and in practical and spiritual truths, as his tutor shall require, according to his ability; seeing the entrance of the word giveth light, it giveth understanding to the simple, Psalm 119:130.[26]

Regulations at Yale college, 1745

1. All scholars shall live religious, godly, and blameless lives according to the rules of God's Word, diligently reading the Holy Scriptures, the fountain of light and truth; and constantly attend upon all the duties of religion, both in public and secret.[27]

We could examine scores of others colleges and see the Biblical foundations. In fact 106 of the first 108 colleges were founded on the Christian faith.

Bookstores in early America had many Bibles and religious works.

De Tocqueville observed that bookseller shops in the United States contained "an enormous quantity of religious works, Bibles, sermons, editing anecdotes, controversial divinity, and reports of charitable societies."[28] They were providing what the American people wanted to read.

V. Textbooks were Christian. Bible was central text

In 1690, John Locke said that children learned to read by following "the ordinary road of Hornbook, Primer, Psalter, Testament and Bible."[29]

The New Haven Code of 1655 required that children be made "able duly to read the Scriptures . . . and in some competent measure to understand the main grounds and principles of Christian Religion necessary to salvation."[30]

Catechisms

There were over 500 different catechisms used in colonial times. Most commonly used one was *The Foundation of Christian Religion gathered into six Principles*. Later, the Westminster Catechism became the most prominent one.

New England Primer

The New England Primer (first published in 1690) was the most widely used text for one hundred years. It taught the alphabet with Biblical examples:

A: In Adam's fall, we sinned all.

B: Heaven to find the Bible mind.

C: Christ crucify'd for sinners dy'd.

D: The Deluge drown'd the earth around.

The most prominent textbooks in the 1800s were Webster's, "Blue-Backed Speller" and McGuffey's Readers. Both were thoroughly Christian. Webster's dictionary, first published in 1828, gave Biblical definitions and quoted often from Scripture.

VI. Founders' words:

John Adams

Suppose a nation in some distant Region, should take the Bible for their only law Book, and every member should regulate his conduct by the precepts there exhibited. . . What a Eutopia, what a Paradise would this region be.[31]

Benjamin Rush

The great enemy of the salvation of man, in my opinion, never invented a more effectual means of extirpating Christianity from the world than by persuading mankind that it was improper to read the Bible at schools.[32]

In contemplating the political institutions of the United States, I lament that we waste so much time and money in punishing crimes and take so little pains to prevent them. We profess to be republicans, and yet we neglect the only means of establishing and perpetuating our republican forms of government, that is, the universal education of our youth in the principles of christianity by the means of the Bible. For this Divine book, above all other, favors that equality among mankind, that respect for just laws, and those sober and frugal virtues, which constitute the soul of republicanism.[33]

Fisher Ames

[T]he Bible [should] regain the place it once held as a school book[.] Its morals are pure, its examples captivating and noble. The reverence for the sacred book that is thus early impressed lasts long; and probably, if not impressed in infancy, never takes firm hold of the mind. One consideration more is important. In no book is there so good English, so pure and so elegant; and by teaching all the same book, they will speak alike, and the Bible will justly remain the standard of language as well as of faith.[34]

Sam Adams

To our founders, the Bible was more than a good book with good principles. It contains the message and words of life. Sam Adams wrote to his daughter Hannah on Aug. 17, 1780:

you cannot gratify me so much, as by seeking most earnestly, the Favor of Him who made & supports you—who will supply you with whatever his infinite Wisdom see best for you in this World, and above all, who has given us his Son to purchase for us the Reward of Eternal Life—Adieu, and believe that I have.

Patrick Henry

The Bible is worth all the books that ever were printed, and it has been my misfortune that I have never found time to read it with the proper attention and feeling till lately. I trust in the mercy of heaven that it is not yet too late.[36]

Noah Webster

The brief exposition of the constitution of the United States, will unfold to young persons the principles of republican government; and it is the sincere desire of the writer that our citizens should early understand that the genuine source of correct republican principles is the Bible, particularly the New Testament or the Christian religion.[37]

The Bible must be considered as the great source of all the truths by which men are to be guided in government, as well as in all social transactions. . . . [T]he Bible [is] the instrument of all reformation in morals and religion.[38]

John Jay, First Chief-Justice of the U.S. Supreme Court

The Bible is the best of all books, for it is the word of God and teaches us the way to be happy in this world and in the next. Continue therefore to read it and to regulate your life by its precepts.[39]

John Quincy Adams

[S]o great is my veneration for the Bible, and so strong my belief, that when duly read and meditated on, it is of all books in the world, that which contributes most to make men good, wise, and happy.

I advise you, my son, in whatever you do and most of all in reading the Bible, to remember that it is for the purpose of making you wiser and more virtuous. I have myself, for many years, made it a practice to read through the Bible once every year.

My custom is, to read four or five chapters every morning, immediately after rising from my bed. It employs about an hour of my time, and seems to me the most suitable manner of beginning the day.

It is essential, my son, in order that you may go through life with comfort to yourself, and usefulness to your fellow-creatures, that you should form and adopt certain rules or principles, for the government of your own conduct and temper.

It is in the Bible, you must learn them, and from the Bible how to practice them. Those duties are to God, to your fellow-creatures, and to yourself. "Thou shalt love the Lord thy God, with all thy heart, and with all thy soul, and with all thy mind, and all thy strength, and thy neighbor as thyself". . . . They [our duties] are all to be learned in equal perfection by our searching the Scriptures.

Let us, then, search the Scriptures: . . . The Bible contains the revelation of the will of God. It contains the history of the creation of the world, and of mankind.[40]

Thomas Jefferson

The Bible is the cornerstone of liberty. A student's perusal of the sacred volume will make him a better citizen, a better father, a better husband.[41]

Benjamin Franklin

When members of the Constitutional Convention were discussing property qualifications for federal officials, Franklin used the Scriptures to speak against any such qualification. Madison records how Franklin said: "We should remember the character which the Scripture requires in Rulers, that they should be men hating covetousness."[42] When Franklin was presented at the Court of Versailles he tells us that a scripture verse, that his father used to quote to him when he was a boy, passed through his mind. That verse was: "Seest thou a man diligent in his business? He shall stand before kings."[43]

William Samuel Johnson, Signer of the Constitution

As President of Columbia College in New York, William Johnson gave a commencement speech where he reminded the graduates that the purpose of their education was

to qualify you the better to serve your Creator and your country. . . . Your first great duties, you are sensible, are those you owe to Heaven, to your Creator and Redeemer. . . . Remember, too, that you are the redeemed of the Lord, that you are bought with a price, even the inestimable price of the precious blood of the Son of God. . . . Love, fear, and serve Him as your Creator, Redeemer, and Sanctifier. Acquaint yourselves with Him in His Word and holy ordinances. Make Him your friend and protector and your felicity is secured both here and hereafter.[44]

James McHenry, Signer of the Constitution

The Holy Scriptures. . . can alone secure to society, order and peace, and to our courts of justice and constitutions of government, purity, stability, and usefulness. In vain, without the Bible, we increase penal laws and draw entrenchments around our institutions.[45]

Robert C. Winthrop, Speaker of the House of Representatives, 1847–1849

Men, in a word, must necessarily be controlled either by a power within them or by a power without them; either by the Word of God or by the strong arm of man; either by the Bible or by the bayonet.

VII. Founders started numerous Bible societies.

Following our independence scores of local societies were started to circulate the Bible. Many of our founding fathers were greatly involved in these. In 1816 sixty delegates representing thirty-five of these local societies gathered in New York City and formed the American Bible Society. During the first year 85 local societies joined with it. Elias Boudinot became the first President. Boudinot had been a member of the Continental Congress, chosen as President in 1782 and in that capacity a signer of the Treaty of Peace officially ending the war, a member of the first House of Representatives (1789–1796), and the Director of the National Mint (1796–1805).

In accepting the office of President of the American Bible Society, Boudinot wrote: "I am not ashamed to confess that I accept the appointment of President of the American Bible Society as the greatest honor that could have been conferred on me this side of the grave."[47] He continued as president of the society until his death in 1821.

The first Supreme Court Chief Justice, John Jay, served as President of the American Bible Society as well. General Rufus Putnam founded the first Bible society west of the Alleghenies.

VIII. The Bible was foremost in shaping the founders' worldview.

Source of Political Ideas

Dr. Donald Lutz conducted an exhaustive ten-year research of about 15,000 political documents of the Founders' Era (1760–1805), and recorded every reference our founders made to other sources. This list of 3154 citations reveals those writings and men that most shaped the political ideas of our founders. By far, the most quoted source of their political ideas was the Bible, 34% of citations. The next most quoted sources were from men who largely derived their ideas from the Bible (Montesquieu, 8.3%, Blackstone, 7.9%, and Locke, 2.9%). In fact 85% or more of all the citations were from the Bible or Biblical thinkers.[48]

Source of support in War of Independence

Churches and ministers were a great support in the cause of American liberty. The Bible provided the major source of ammunition for the clergy. Ministers had for years preached political sermons. Many of these were printed and read by the people. George Bancroft writes how the pastors were heard

> with reverence by their congregations in their meeting-houses on every Lord's day, and on special occasions of fasts, thanksgivings, lectures, and military musters. Elijah's mantle being caught up was a happy token that the Lord would be with this generation, as he had been with their fathers. Their exhaustless armory was the Bible, whose scriptures furnished sharp words to point their appeals, apt examples of resistance, prophetic denunciations of the enemies of God's people, and promises of the divine blessing on the defenders of his law.[49]

The Bible shaped their social ideas

One social evil that confronted America's founders was slavery. Most of the founders opposed slavery because it was inconsistent with the Bible. They saw it as a social evil that needed to be eradicated. In 1773, Patrick Henry wrote:

> Is it not amazing that, at a time when the rights of humanity are defined and understood with precision, in a country above all others fond of liberty, in such an age, we find men professing a religion the most humane, mild, meek, gentle, and generous, adopting a principle as repugnant to humanity as it is inconsistent with the Bible and destructive to liberty?. . . I believe a time will come when an opportunity will be offered to abolish this lamentable evil; everything we can do is to improve it, if it happens in our day; if not, let us transmit to our descendants, together with our slaves, a pity for their unhappy lot and an abhorrence of slavery. We owe to the purity of our religion to show that it is at variance with that law which warrants slavery.[50]

In the mid-1800s the leader of the Underground Railroad, Levi Coffin, was motivated by the precepts of the Bible to aid fugitive slaves to escape to Canada. After listening to friends warn him of dangers to his life and property, Coffin responded:

> I told them that I felt no condemnation for anything that I had ever done for the fugitive slaves. If by doing my duty and endeavoring to fulfill the injunctions of the Bible, I injured my business, then let my business go. As to my safety, my life was in the hands of my Divine Master, and I felt that I had his approval.[51]

The Biblical faith of many slaves in America caused them to look to God for their deliverance:

> [T]he slaves of the South. . . longed for liberty, but they looked for it through the intervention of others [rather than through violent insurrections]; they drew their hopes from the case of the Israelites led from Egypt by the hand of Moses; they trusted God would come to their aid in a similar way—raise up for them a Moses; and in this trust in Providence their faith was marvelous. The gospel of forgiveness had been preached to them by preachers both of white race and their own, and the truths of the Bible, thus orally presented, had a wonderful influence in preparing them for the events about to follow.[52]

Christians in the North and the South led the anti-slavery movement of the mid-nineteenth century.

IX. Numerous Bibles were available in early America.

The first book printed in America was the Bible. As mentioned earlier this was in the Algonquin language and was the work of John Eliot (1604–1690) who began evangelizing the Massachusetts Indians in the 1640s. Eliot organized the Indians who became Christians into communities. He wrote: "The Bible, and the Catechism drawn out of the Bible . . . are the groundwork of Community amongst all our Indian-Churches and Christians."[53]

There were hundreds of different Bibles in numerous languages in use in colonial America. The Evans microprint collection has over 500 different Bibles listed.

X. Sabbath Observance

The Christian sabbath has been observed and recognized by law from the beginning of America. Sabbath laws could be found in all the early colonies and states.

Alexis de Tocqueville described the sabbath observance of the 1830s in Democracy in America:

> In the United States, on the seventh day of every week, the trading and working life of the nation seems suspended; all noises cease; a deep tranquility, say rather the solemn calm of meditation, succeeds the turmoil of the week, and the soul resumes possession and contemplation of itself. Upon this day the marts of traffic are deserted; every member of the community, accompanied by his children, goes to church, where he listens to strange language which would seem unsuited to his ear. He is told of the countless evils caused by pride and covetousness: he is reminded of the necessity of checking his desires, of the finer pleasures which belong to virtue alone, and of the true happiness which attends it. On his return home, he does not turn to the ledgers of his calling, but he opens the book of Holy Scripture; there he meets with sublime or affecting descriptions of the greatness and goodness of the Creator, of the infinite magnificence of the handiwork of God, of the lofty destinies of man, of his duties, and of his immortal privileges. Thus it is that the American at times steals an hour from himself; and laying aside for a while the petty passions which agitate his life, and the ephemeral interests which engross it, he strays at once into an ideal world, where all is great, eternal, and pure.[54]

XI. Pioneers and the Bible

As early Americans went west to settle new lands they carried the Bible and its truths with them. De Tocqueville wrote of the contrast of the physical homes of western pioneers and their personal characteristics:

> Everything about him is primitive and unformed, but he is himself the result of the labor and the experience of eighteen centuries. He wears the dress, and he speaks the language of cities; he is acquainted with the past, curious of the future, and ready for argument upon the present; he is, in short, a highly civilized being, who consents, for a time, to inhabit the backwoods, and who penetrates into the wilds of the New World with the Bible, an axe, and a file of newspapers.[55]

The Bible was the great civilizing and educational influence for these pioneers. De Tocqueville wrote of visiting log cabins in the wilderness that had a Bible if no other book.[56]

The Bible spurred numerous awakenings and revivals which had great effect in America's history. It also inspired much missionary work to the American Indians in the west. The states of Washington and Oregon were founded by missionaries, Marcus and Narcissa Whitman and Jason Lee. Johnny Appleseed not only planted orchards throughout the frontier, but he also planted the Word of God, carrying a Bible and sowing its truth wherever he went. One of the first explorers of the west, Jedidiah Smith, always packed his Bible.

We have just touched on the great impact that the Bible has had on America. We could examine much more, including the records of the U.S. Congress, the words and laws of the state legislatures, and federal and state court rulings. The more you look, the more convinced you will become that there would be no America, the land of liberty, without God and the Bible.

As the Bible and its principles have been removed from our schools, missing from our leaders' ideas and actions, extirpated from the marketplace of ideas, and not adhered to by enough of our citizens, America has declined and will continue to decline.

America must once again restore the Bible to its place of influence. We must consider the Bible, in the words of Noah Webster, "as the great source of all the truths by which men are to be guided in government, as well as in all social transactions . . . the Bible [is] the instrument of all reformation in morals and religion."[57]

End Notes

1 Lawrence A. Cremin. *American Education, the Colonial Experience 1607–1683*. New York: Harper and Row, Publishers, 1970, 40.

2 George Bancroft. *History of the United States*, Vol. 2, 402. In CD Sourcebook of American History produced by Infobases, 1995.

3 *Historical Almanac of the U.S. Senate*, 30. In CD Sourcebook of American History.

4 Bancroft, Vol. 1, 205.

5 Ibid, 226–27.

6 *Annals of America*, Vol. I. Chicago: Encyclopedia Britannica, Inc., 1976. 103.

7 William J. Jackman, *History of the American Nation*, Vol. 2, 390, in CD Sourcebook of American History.

8 Bancroft, Vol. 2, 284–85.

9 *For the Colony in Virginea Britannia, Lawes Divine, Morall and Martiall, etc.,* compiled by William Strachey, edited by David H. Raherty. Charlottesville, VA: The University Press of Virginia, 1969, 10–11.

10 *The Laws of the Pilgrims*, A facsimile edition of *The book of the General Laws of the Inhabitants of the Jurisdiction of New Plimouth, 1672 & 1685*. Michael Glazier, Inc. and Pilgrim Society, 1977.

11 *Sources of Our Liberties*, edited by Richard Perry. American Bar Foundation, 1959, 120.

12 *American Historical Documents*, The Harvard Classics. Danbury, CT: Grolier Enterprises, 1987, 65.

13 Bancroft, Vol. 1, 271–72.

14 *Sources of Our Liberties*, 148.

15 Ibid., 155.

16 Ibid., 158–59.

17 *American Historical Documents*, 90.

18 *The Annals of America*, Vol. 1, 199.

19 Ibid., 200.

20 Ibid., 201.

21 *Significant Documents in U.S. History*, Vol. 1, Richard B. Morris, editor. New York: Van Nostrand Reinhold Co., 1969, 19.

22 Ibid., 20.

23 *The Pageant of America*, Ralph Henry Gabriel, editor. New Haven: Yale University Press, Vol. 10, 1928, 258.

24 *Annals of America*, Vol. 1, 203.

25 Edward Kendall, *Kendall's Travels*. New York: I. Riley, Vol. 1, 1809, 299–305.

26 "New England's First Fruits in Respect to the Progress of Learning in the College at Cambridge, in Massachusetts Bay," *America*, Vol. 2, 155–56.

27 *Annals of America*, Vol. 1, 464.

28 Alexis de Tocqueville, *Democracy in America*, Vol. 2, 58, in CD Sourcebook of American History.

29 *The Pageant of America*, 10:258.

30 Ibid.

31 *The Earliest Diary of John Adams*, ed. L. H. Butterfield. Cambridge, MA: The Belknap Press of Harvard Univ. Press, 1966, 1:9.

32 Benjamin Rush, *Letters of Benjamin Rush*. L H. Butterfield, ed. Princeton, New Jersey: American Philosophical Society, Vol. 1, 1951, 521.

33 Benjamin Rush. *Essays, literary, Moral and Philosophical*. Philadelphia: printed by Thomas and William Bradford, 1806, 113.

34 *Works of Fisher Ames*, as published by Seth Ames (1854), edited and enlarged by W. B. Allen. Indianapolis: Liberty Classics, 1983, vol. I, 12.

35 *Writings of Samuel Adams*, edited by Henry Alonzo Cushing, Vol. 4, New York, 1908. In *The Christian History of the American Revolution: Consider and Ponder*, Verna M. Hall, compiler. San Francisco: Foundation for American Christian Education, 1975, 82.

36 William Wirt. *Sketches of the Life and Character of Patrick Henry*. Philadelphia: James Webster, publisher, 1818, 402.

37 Noah Webster, *History of the United States*. New Haven: Durrie & Peck, 1833, v.

38 Noah Webster. *Value of the Bible and Excellence of the Christian Religion*, 1834. Republished, San Francisco: Foundation for American Christian Education, 1988, 78.

39 John Jay, *John Jay: The Winning of the Peace*, Unpublished Papers 1780–1784, p. v. Richard B. Moms, ed. New York: Harper and Row Publishers, vol. 2, 1980, 709.

40 *Letters of John Quincy Adams to His Son on the Bible and Its Teachings*, 1850, 6–21. In *The Christian History of the American Revolution*, 615–16.

41 Cited in *A Christian History of the American Republic* by Walker Whitman, 1939.

42 James Madison, *Notes of Debates in the Federal Convention of 1787*. New York: W. W. Norton & Co., 1987, 426.

43 Jackman, Vol. 9, 2690–91.

44 Edward Beardsley. *Life and Times of William Samuel Johnson*. Boston: Houghton, Muffin and Company, 1886, 141–42.

45 Bernard C. Steiner. *One Hundred and Ten Years of Bible Society Work in Maryland*. Baltimore: Maryland Bible Society, 1921, 14.

46 *Addresses and Speeches on Various Occasions*. Boston: Little, Brown & Co., 1852, 172.

47 *Eloquence: A Collection of Speeches and Addresses, by the Most Eminent Orators of America*, Frank Moore, editor. New York: D. Appleton and Co., 1858, Vol. 2, 263.

48 Donald Lutz, "The Relative Influence of European Writers on Late 18th Century American Political Thought." *American Political Science Review*, LXXVIII, 1984, 189–97.

49 Bancroft, Vol. 4, 95.

50 Bancroft, Vol. 3, 412–13.

51 "The Underground Railroad," Levi Coffin, *America*, Vol. 7, 157, in CD Sourcebook of American History.

52 Jackman, Vol. 4, 1097–98.

53 "Eliot's Brief Narrative (1670),"*American Historical Documents*, 141.

54 De Tocqueville, Vol. 2, 152.

55 De Tocqueville, Vol. I, 322.

56 De Tocqueville, Vol. 2, 374.

57 Noah Webster. *Value of the Bible and Excellence of the Christian Religion*, 1834. Republished, San Francisco: Foundation for American Christian Education, 1988, 78.

Christian History of Reading Timeline

by Elizabeth Youmans

Seek ye out of the book of the Lord, and read.
(Isaiah 34:16)

Eternity Past

Creation Link

God spoke Creation into existence. Man was created in the image of God with the gift of language.   (Genesis 1:2)

"In the beginning was the Word and the Word was with God and the Word was God."   (John 1:1)

Children were educated through apprenticeship, imitation, and rituals. Before writing, learning was done orally. Students could only learn what the teacher had memorized!

Earliest writing was *pictographs* which directly represented actions or ideas. The first reader was a clay tablet carved with signs representing animals.

4000 B.C.

Hieroglyphics, or priestly carvings, were ancient Egyptian picture writing, which led to an *alphabet*.

3000 B.C.

Egyptians used *papyrus and ink* for writing and built the first *libraries*.

2500 B.C.

Sumerians established schools for the sons of the wealthy, which became centers of culture and scholarship. Boys used copybooks. Education was for a select few.

Cuneiform, a complex system of five hundred characters, was developed by the Sumerians.

2000 B.C.

Education continued for the few.

A simple alphabet of twenty-two characters came from the Syria-Palestine region.

1600 B.C.

A written language enabled wisespread literacy.

Moses and the Law Link

1450 B.C.

"And it [a copy of the Law in a book] shall be with him [the king] and he shall read it all the days of his life: that he may learn the fear the LORD his God, to keep all the words of this law, . . . and to do them."   (Deuteronomy 17:19)

"The LORD said to Moses, Write this for a memorial in a book."   (Exodus 17:14)

Old Covenant Canon, written ca. 1450–425 B.C. In God's providence, Moses received the best education as an Egyptian prince which he used to record God's commands and write the Pentateuch.

The family was the context in which most Hebrew children learned to read. Each father was responsible for teaching his children the Torah. Education was for everyone.

Scribes laboriously copied words onto scrolls.

| 1100 B.C. |

Samuel's schools of the prophets re-established a Biblical education. Biblical reasoning restored literacy and the character of the people.

Jews became known as the "people of the Book."

| 1000 B.C. |

Hebrew schools established by scribes. Great emphasis placed on scholarship through the study of the Scriptures.

Etruscans borrowed the Greek alphabet.

| 700 B.C. |

Romans took the Greek letters from the Etruscan alphabet for their alphabet.

| 600 B.C. |

Greek education aimed to develop good citizens. Few learned to read or write.

Roman education taught reading and writing in both Greek and Latin. Roman masters, when teaching students to read, began with the memorization of the alphabet, then simple syllables (The name of the letter does not necessarily represent the sound the letter makes). This A-B-C method was still used in colonial America.

Ezra, the Jewish high priest and educational reformer, compiled the Jewish canon—books with "divine authority."

| 425 B.C. |

Socrates fought against reading. He saw books as useless tools, because they could not explain what they said, but only repeated the same words over and over again.

| 300 B.C. |

Septuagint (LXX) Old Testament translated into Greek. It was the version from which writers of the New Testament quoted.

| 285 B.C. |

| 85 B.C. |

Julius Caesar created one of the earliest codices—pages folded into booklet—and invented the "book."

| 75 B.C. |

Jews were taxed to support education. Attendance was compulsory. Elementary school was in the synagogue, called "the House of the Book." The purpose was to teach God's Word.

Jesus Christ
The Focal Point of History

| A.D. 33 |

"And the Word was made flesh and dwelt among us."

(John 1:14)

Paul and the Christian Church

| 50 |

The Gospel was written down and traveled westward to Europe. The New Testament was written ca. A.D. 50–96 in "common" Greek, the language of the people.

"Study to show thyself approved unto God, a workman who needeth not to be ashamed, rightly dividing the Word of God."

(2 Timothy 2:15)

Jerome translated the Latin Vulgate, the Bible of Europe for one thousand years.

410 — The Bible, defined as "The Book," was canonized.

540 — Among his rules for the monastery, St. Benedict of Nursia included reading aloud during mealtimes to nourish the spirit.

English acquired the Latin language from the Roman alphabet, and the people learned to read Latin literature.

600s — In the Christian missionary schools, English was first written using Roman alphabet.

The Lindesfarne Gospels were written. The Word stuggled to emerge into the Anglo-Saxon language.

700s

850 — England's Alfred the Great established schools and had civil laws written based upon the Scriptures.

1200s — Relatively few people could read and books were scarce. Learning was accomplished by memorizing what professors read aloud.

The Bible in English

1380 — "Scriptures be the property of the people." (John Wycliffe)

The Hornbook, Primer and "ABC" book now used to teach reading.

Wycliffe, "Morningstar of the Reformation," translated the Bible from Latin into English. It was called "The People's Bible."

1455 — The printing press was invented by Gutenberg. Books became more available and cheaper. People now wanted to learn to read.

Columbus

"Christ-Bearer" to the New World

1492

The Scriptures in the hands of the individual gave rise to the Protestant Reformation and a spirit of invention, creativity, and exploration.

1500s — Elementary schools established to teach the children of common citizens to read the Bible in their native language.

Tyndale translated the Bible into English from the original languages. The Bible became the "first book of instruction."

"I will cause a boy that driveth the plow to know more of Scripture than the Pope." Smaller Bibles now printed.

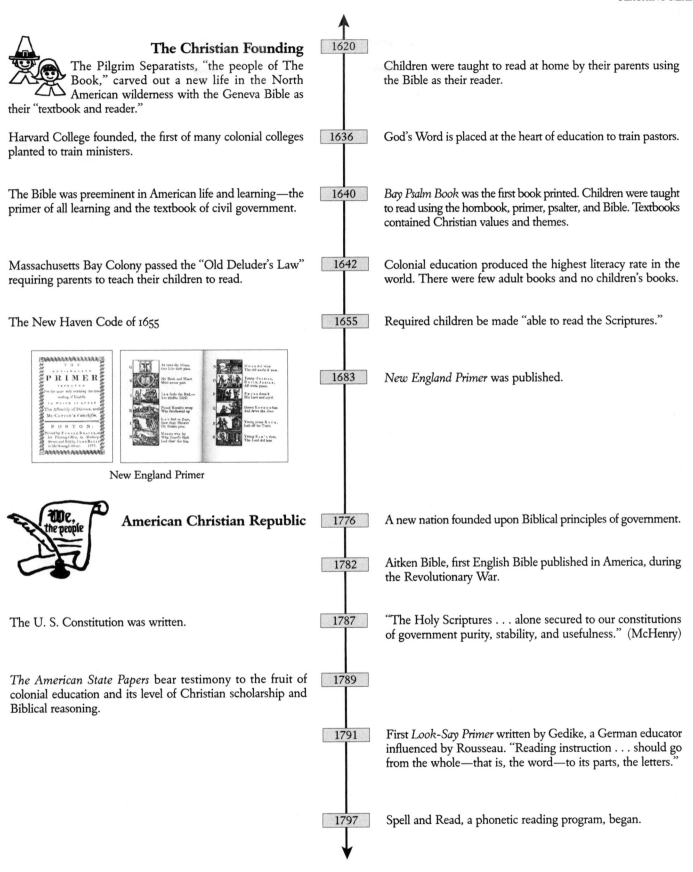

The Christian Founding

1620

The Pilgrim Separatists, "the people of The Book," carved out a new life in the North American wilderness with the Geneva Bible as their "textbook and reader."

Children were taught to read at home by their parents using the Bible as their reader.

Harvard College founded, the first of many colonial colleges planted to train ministers.

1636

God's Word is placed at the heart of education to train pastors.

The Bible was preeminent in American life and learning—the primer of all learning and the textbook of civil government.

1640

Bay Psalm Book was the first book printed. Children were taught to read using the hornbook, primer, psalter, and Bible. Textbooks contained Christian values and themes.

Massachusetts Bay Colony passed the "Old Deluder's Law" requiring parents to teach their children to read.

1642

Colonial education produced the highest literacy rate in the world. There were few adult books and no children's books.

The New Haven Code of 1655

1655

Required children be made "able to read the Scriptures."

1683

New England Primer was published.

New England Primer

American Christian Republic

1776

A new nation founded upon Biblical principles of government.

1782

Aitken Bible, first English Bible published in America, during the Revolutionary War.

The U. S. Constitution was written.

1787

"The Holy Scriptures . . . alone secured to our constitutions of government purity, stability, and usefulness." (McHenry)

The American State Papers bear testimony to the fruit of colonial education and its level of Christian scholarship and Biblical reasoning.

1789

1791

First *Look-Say Primer* written by Gedike, a German educator influenced by Rousseau. "Reading instruction . . . should go from the whole—that is, the word—to its parts, the letters."

1797

Spell and Read, a phonetic reading program, began.

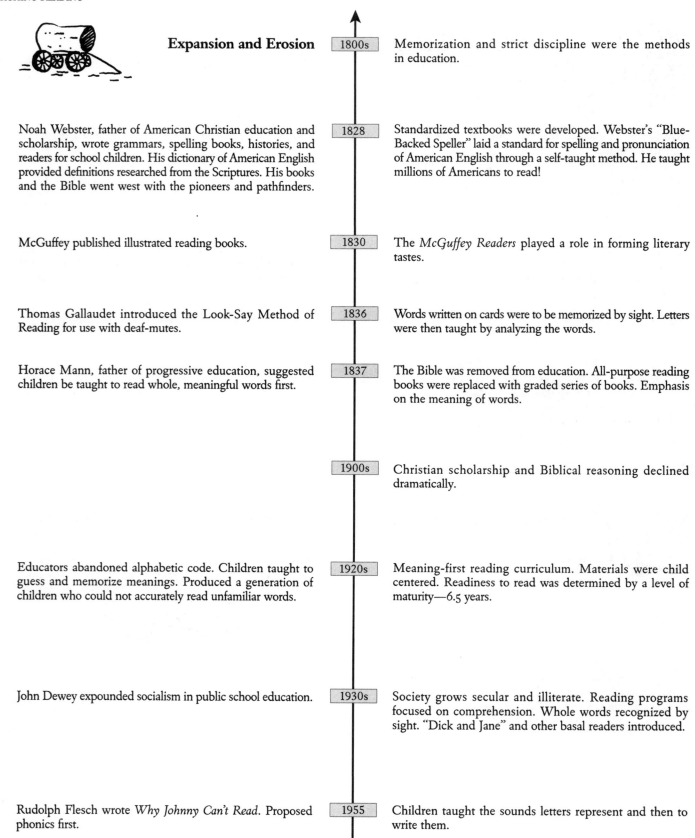

Expansion and Erosion

	1800s — Memorization and strict discipline were the methods in education.
Noah Webster, father of American Christian education and scholarship, wrote grammars, spelling books, histories, and readers for school children. His dictionary of American English provided definitions researched from the Scriptures. His books and the Bible went west with the pioneers and pathfinders.	**1828** — Standardized textbooks were developed. Webster's "Blue-Backed Speller" laid a standard for spelling and pronunciation of American English through a self-taught method. He taught millions of Americans to read!
McGuffey published illustrated reading books.	**1830** — The *McGuffey Readers* played a role in forming literary tastes.
Thomas Gallaudet introduced the Look-Say Method of Reading for use with deaf-mutes.	**1836** — Words written on cards were to be memorized by sight. Letters were then taught by analyzing the words.
Horace Mann, father of progressive education, suggested children be taught to read whole, meaningful words first.	**1837** — The Bible was removed from education. All-purpose reading books were replaced with graded series of books. Emphasis on the meaning of words.
	1900s — Christian scholarship and Biblical reasoning declined dramatically.
Educators abandoned alphabetic code. Children taught to guess and memorize meanings. Produced a generation of children who could not accurately read unfamiliar words.	**1920s** — Meaning-first reading curriculum. Materials were child centered. Readiness to read was determined by a level of maturity—6.5 years.
John Dewey expounded socialism in public school education.	**1930s** — Society grows secular and illiterate. Reading programs focused on comprehension. Whole words recognized by sight. "Dick and Jane" and other basal readers introduced.
Rudolph Flesch wrote *Why Johnny Can't Read*. Proposed phonics first.	**1955** — Children taught the sounds letters represent and then to write them.

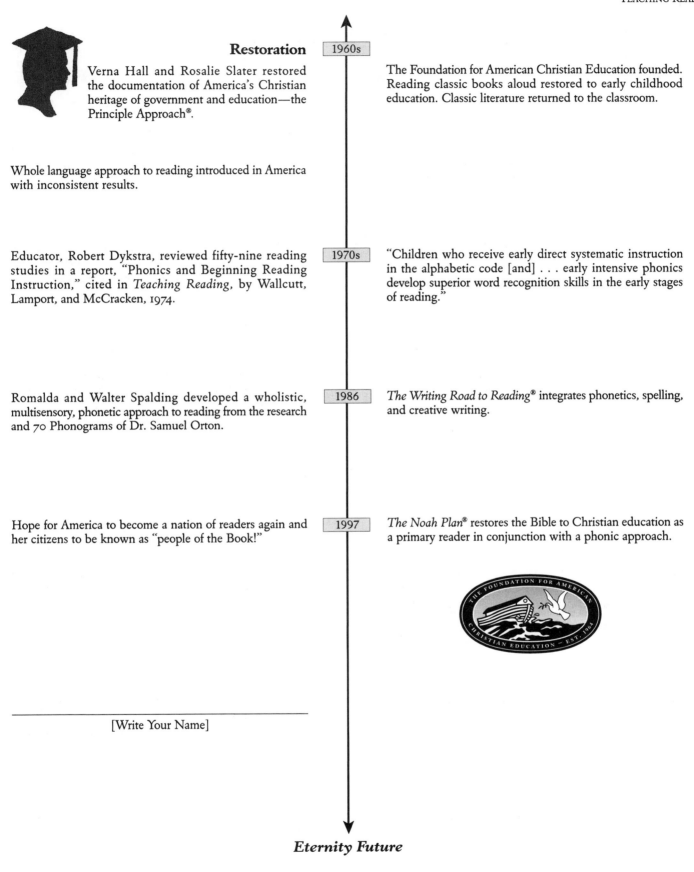

Restoration | 1960s

Verna Hall and Rosalie Slater restored the documentation of America's Christian heritage of government and education—the Principle Approach®.

The Foundation for American Christian Education founded. Reading classic books aloud restored to early childhood education. Classic literature returned to the classroom.

Whole language approach to reading introduced in America with inconsistent results.

Educator, Robert Dykstra, reviewed fifty-nine reading studies in a report, "Phonics and Beginning Reading Instruction," cited in *Teaching Reading*, by Wallcutt, Lamport, and McCracken, 1974. | 1970s

"Children who receive early direct systematic instruction in the alphabetic code [and] . . . early intensive phonics develop superior word recognition skills in the early stages of reading."

Romalda and Walter Spalding developed a wholistic, multisensory, phonetic approach to reading from the research and 70 Phonograms of Dr. Samuel Orton. | 1986

The Writing Road to Reading® integrates phonetics, spelling, and creative writing.

Hope for America to become a nation of readers again and her citizens to be known as "people of the Book!" | 1997

The Noah Plan® restores the Bible to Christian education as a primary reader in conjunction with a phonic approach.

[Write Your Name]

Eternity Future

Why Use the Bible as a Primary Reader?

The Bible as a Reader:

1. Teaches the child to fear the Lord

   "[A]nd he shall read therein all the days of his life: that he may learn to fear the LORD his God."

2. Is the highest model of the English language

   "In no book is there so good English, so pure and so elegant; and by teaching all the same book, they will speak alike, and the Bible will justly remain the standard of language as well as of faith." (Fisher Ames, 1801)

3. Imparts the knowledge of God to the reader

   a) "And it shall be, when he sitteth upon the throne of his kingdom, that he shall write him a copy of this law in a book out of that which is before the priests the Levites: and it shall be with him, and he shall read therein all the days of his life: that he may learn to fear the LORD his God, to keep all the words of this law and these statutes, to do them: That his heart be not lifted up above his brethren, and that he turn not aside from the commandment, to the right hand, or to the left: to the end that he may prolong his days in his kingdom, he, and his children, in the midst of Israel." (Deuteronomy 17:18—20)

   b) "There is a spirit in man and the inspiration of the Almighty giveth knowledge." (Job 32:8)

4. Early impresses truth on a child's mind

   a) "I believe no man was ever early instructed in the truths of the Bible without having been made wiser or better by the early operation of these impressions upon his mind." (Benjamin Rush)

   b) "[The Bible] contributes most to make men good, wise, and happy—that the earlier children begin to read it, the more steadily they pursue the practice of reading it throughout their lives, the more lively and confident will be my hopes that they will prove useful citizens to their country, respectable members of society, and a real blessing to their parents." (John Adams)

5. Enlivens the reader

   a) "[F]or thy word hath quickened me." (Psalm 119:50)

   b) "For the word of God is quick and powerful, and sharper than any two-edged sword, piercing even to dividing asunder of soul and spirit, and of the joints and marrow, and is a discerner of the thoughts and intents of the heart." (Hebrews 4:12)

6. Builds a moral, noble, and elevated vocabulary

7. Provides models and lessons of godly character

   "Rules and Principles for the Government of Conduct and Temper." (John Adams)

8. Inculcates a lifelong habit of reading the Bible

9. Consecrates the child's mind

   a) "Be ye transformed by the renewing of your mind." (Romans 12:2)

   b) "[W]e have the mind of Christ." (1 Corinthians 2:16)

10. Reveals God's promises of longevity and prosperity

    "[T]hat he may prolong his days . . . he, and his children." (Deuteronomy 17:20)

11. Develops Christian scholarship, thinking and reasoning, and writing with the Word of God and its principles

12. Encourages the reader to practice the Word

    "[B]e doers of the word." (James 1:22)

13. Cultivates an enlightened learner through reading the Word of God

    a) To be enlightened is to be illuminated with divine knowledge, or a knowledge of the truth. God's word is truth and the study thereof makes one to know wisdom. The Bible contains the revelations of God, the principles of Christian faith, and the rules of practice. (Webster's 1828 *Dictionary*)

    b) The psalmist declares, "O send out thy light and thy truth." (Psalm 43:3)

    c) "For You will light my lamp; The LORD my God will enlighten my darkness." (Psalm 18:28)

    d) "That he may be enlightened with the light of life." (Job 33:30)

    e) "[A]nd Your law is truth." (Psalm 119:142)

14. Builds a Biblical Christian worldview

    "The great source of all the truths by which men are to be guided in government, as well as in all social transactions . . . the Bible [is] the instrument of all reformation in morals and religion." (Noah Webster)

Chapter Three

The Whole Program for Teaching Reading in the Principle Approach®

The technique of reading, though always subordinate and secondary to the mastery of thought, nevertheless claims constant and careful attention. Good reading requires clear enunciation, correct pronunciation, and these can be secured only when the teacher steadily insists upon them. . . . Special drill exercises should be given and the habit of using the dictionary freely should be firmly established in pupils.

(Elson Grammar School Reader, 1911)

The Whole Program for Teaching Reading
in the Principle Approach®

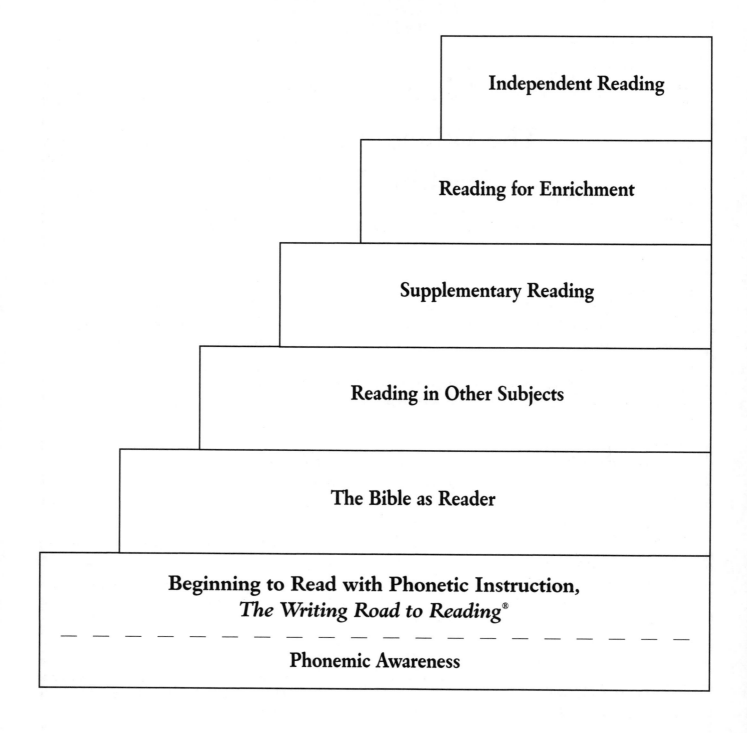

Independent Reading

Reading for Enrichment

Supplementary Reading

Reading in Other Subjects

The Bible as Reader

Beginning to Read with Phonetic Instruction,
The Writing Road to Reading®

Phonemic Awareness

Beginning to Read with Phonetic Instruction
The Writing Road to Reading®
The Reasons for Using *WRTR* in Principle Approach® Education

Goals for Teaching Reading in the Principle Approach

1. To teach wholistically, employing all the language skills in the teaching of reading—listening, speaking, penmanship, spelling, syllabication, composition, comprehension, vocabulary, grammar.

2. Learning is based on reasoning, on logical thinking processes, not solely on drill, recognition, or memorization.

3. Knowledge is not thoroughly mastered until a child can reason from it and express what he has learned—until he can think information through to its explanation to others.

How *The Writing Road to Reading*® Fits the Goals

1. Reading is taught wholistically along with writing, spelling, speaking, and thinking; and the phonogram system forms the basis of the teaching of spelling throughout the grades.

2. Language is a system of sounds. *The Writing Road to Reading*® reduces sounds to written symbols and teaches spelling in connection with the sounds of the language, arranging the correct spelling of sounds in a logical sequence.

3. Learning to read must be a reasoning, thinking experience, not just memory work. In *The Writing Road to Reading*® the writing of words is the skill most fully requiring the mind to think and direct the hand to express thoughts in logical sequence.

The Writing Road to Reading® integrates the four elements of language—speech, writing, spelling, and reading—to teach phonetics. The great advantage of this is:

1. Spelling is taught from the beginning to reveal the logic of the language.

2. Training is first in written spelling, enabling the child to begin to read with well-written books which interest, educate, and develop a love for reading and a taste for literature.

3. Handwriting and accurate pronunciation are taught from the very start, teaching the saying with the writing of the sounds used in spoken English.

4. Logic and reasoning are developed in applying the knowledge of phonograms.

5. The writing of words is the skill most fully requiring the mind to think and direct the hand to express thoughts in a logical sequence.

6. The sequence of first teaching the writing of phonograms while saying the common sounds before combining them into written and spoken words and before starting to read books, is reasonable and logical; the proper foundation and pattern for learning.

The Writing Road to Reading® Method:

The purpose of reading is to learn what the author has to say, not to learn phonics.

1. Seventy common phonograms are used to write English on paper. Forty-five basic sounds are used in speaking English.

2. The class learns phonograms by seeing, hearing, saying, and writing them.

3. Then they write from dictation the most used words as they say the phonogram sounds heard in each.

4. They write and read original sentences to show their meanings.

5. Within two months they read books.

6. The 1700 most commonly used words are taught in the order of their frequency of use.

7. Twenty-nine rules of spelling determine which phonogram is used.

8. The method is direct and so organized that children use only paper, pencil, and their minds.

9. By November the first 150 most used words have been studied in the written spelling lessons, the beginning classes are ready to start reading books—the children's Bible and well-written story books. The students are not dependent on basal readers with a controlled vocabulary.

The Spelling Connection:

The failure of most phonics programs is that they do not teach spelling, and they do not teach the saying and writing of the 45 basic sounds before trying to read.

1. The key to good writing and reading of language is the ability to spell from the spoken word.

2. Spalding's method in *The Writing Road to Reading*® always indicates the direct relationship of each sound in any spoken word to the written symbol or phonogram which represents it.

3. Words are taught in spelling lessons in the order of their frequency of use in language.

4. The important rules of spelling are taught by example when met in writing of words being studied in twenty-nine rules. Students see and correct areas before they become fixed in their mind.

5. The learning of spelling words from dictation connects at once the written symbols to their spoken sounds.

6. By fifth or sixth grade, students who have mastered the 1700 most commonly used words make twelfth grade spelling scores.

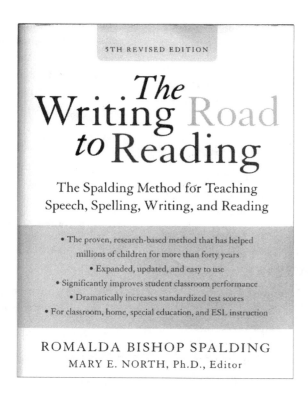

The revised fifth edition of *The Writing Road to Reading* explains more fully and in clearer detail the fundamentals of The Spalding Method®. The new text edited by Mary E. North has been reorganized in accordance with the intent, methodology, and vision of Romalda Spalding.

The book is divided into two parts:

- "Lessons, Procedures, and Why This Method Works" describes the content and methodology of the program

- "Instructional Materials," for use in lesson planning and instruction

New features in the text are instructional procedures with examples of teacher interactions—sample spelling, writing, and reading lesson dialogues designed to help teachers and parents implement the lessons.

"Instructional Materials" includes an updated list of recommended children's literature, the seventy phonograms, the language rules, and a revised Extended Ayres Word List. New features include a section on syllable division, the Extended Ayres Word List given alphabetically and by parts of speech, a recommended language arts scope and sequence, and a framework for planning integrated language arts lessons.

The Bible as Reader (BAR)

The Bible was read and recited, quoted and consulted,
early committed to memory, and constantly searched for meaning.
Deemed universally relevant, it remained throughout the [eighteenth] century
the single most important cultural influence in the lives of Anglo-Americans.
(Lawrence A. Cremin 1970, 40)

The Bible as Reader Program (BAR) schedule for reading the books of the Bible has been amended from the first edition of *The Noah Plan® Reading Curriculum Guide*. In the new edition, the BAR program has been coordinated with *The Noah Plan* Bible overview topics. It was felt that a student would benefit from the reinforcement and expansion of the Bible topics and the Biblical Principles and Leading Ideas introduced during the morning Bible class. Bible is taught daily to provide inspiration and changed hearts, while the BAR class focuses on direct instruction of reading and higher-order thinking skills using a Biblical text.

Compare/Contrast Bible Class with Bible as Reader (BAR)

Bible Class
Application

Inspirational

To know God better
To apply lessons to individual life
To grow in internal aspects

Teacher guides, inspires

**To learn to communicate
and apply God's Word**
Changed hearts
Interpretive questions
Cause-to-effect

SPIRITUALLY TRAINED
Standard of faith

Bible as inspired Word of God

Heart

BIBLE

Biblical
Christian
Worldview

Bible as Reader (BAR)
Cognitive Process

Instructional

To learn to read
Individual reading levels
To develop written word mastery &
monitor comprehension
Teacher mediates, emphasizes methods
& directed reading activity

To read from specific reading instruction:
phonemic awareness, phonics, fluency,
vocabulary, comprehension
Use Strategic Reading Process
Higher-order thinking
Application and analysis
Synthesis and evaluation

ENLIGHTENED LEARNER
Standard of language

Bible as literature: setting,
theme, characters, plot

Brain

Kindergarten

In kindergarten, we plant the seeds as the children hear the Word of God daily. There is an openness and receptive attitude to God's truths and principles. Memory work is assigned using the King James Version to build an appreciation for the vocabulary, rhythm, and patterns of the English language found in this translation of the Bible. This policy continues through the grades. *The Early Reader's Bible* with its easy-to-read Bible stories, colorful illustrations, fact and reasoning questions, and real-life applications helps increase children's understanding of God's Word. By the end of the year, the more able readers can read the Bible stories for themselves. This follows in the tradition of the kings of Israel who each wrote his own copy of the law and "[read] it all the days of his life so that he may learn to revere the LORD his God and follow carefully all the words of this law and these decrees and not . . . turn from the law to the right or to the left." (Deuteronomy 17:18–20) According to Rick Warren, "Daily Bible reading will keep you in range of God's voice." (Warren 2002, 188)

The coordination of *The Noah Plan* Bible curriculum and Bible as Reader (BAR) begins in kindergarten and continues until fourth grade with the following quarterly content:

Cremin, Lawrence A. 1970. *American Education: The Colonial Experience, 1607–1783*. New York: Harper and Row Publishers.

Warren, Rick. 2002. *The Purpose Driven Life*. Grand Rapids, MI: Zondervan.

- First Quarter—*The Immediacy of Jesus Christ*: Nine weeks are spent on chosen aspects from the Gospels revealing Christ's ministry among men from the prophecy of His coming to His ascension to the right hand of God.

- Second Quarter—*The Old Testament History:* This nine-week period starts with beginnings—the beginnings of creation, of man, of sin, of the promise of a Savior, of a people. It reveals to us a God who is merciful and forgiving, who seeks to convict His children of the necessity of obeying His law in order to maintain righteous lives. This study covers the history of Israel from its formation, through the captivity, until the return to rebuild Jerusalem.

- Third Quarter—*The Literature and Wisdom of the Bible:* This nine-week period covers the words of the prophets and the glorious knowledge of God's Wisdom Books. The prophets are taught as civil and religious reformers, as well as foretellers of some future events in His Story.

- Fourth Quarter—*The New Testament History:* This quarter focuses on the New Testament study of the church and the first-century Christian in the epistles and the book of Revelation. These faithful servants of Christ endeavored to forward His Story by taking the outreach of the Gospel to all nations.

Primary and Elementary Grades

Three days are given to whole class instruction using a Bible text or Bible stories at the instructional grade level in grades one through four. The BAR lesson provides directed instruction for teaching and learning activities that vary according to the age and ability of the group, length of the Bible selection, and the number and difficulty of the reading skills or accomplishments selected for teaching or reinforcement. The remainder of the week, the teacher organizes activities to teach reading to individuals or small groups using supplementary readers, skill builders, McCall-Crabbs lessons, SRA reading labs, and teacher-generated materials. (See Teaching Reading by Grade Levels charts, *NPRG*, 85–89.)

The coordination of *The Noah Plan* Bible curriculum and Bible as Reader (BAR) program that began in kindergarten continues with the same quarterly content through fourth grade. The seeds planted in kindergarten now grow into seedlings with the purpose to master the basic skills of reading and thinking and writing.

Middle School Grades

The middle school instruction provides for refinement and independence in reading the Bible. The Bible as Reader lessons and Bible study are merged into a daily Bible/reading class as the growing plant is transplanted and matures. Memorization of larger passages of Scripture and independent projects are assigned. The expanding reasoning abilities of middle school scholars enable them to understand cause-to-effect and logic and to demonstrate critical thinking skills. Questions that require application, analysis, synthesis, and evaluation are developed. Students mature from identifying Biblical principles to reflecting upon the truth of God's Word in every subject. This abiding in the Word will begin a transformation. God's Word says, "[W]e, who with unveiled faces all reflect the Lord's glory, are being transformed into his likeness with ever-increasing glory." (2 Corinthians 3:18):

- Fifth Grade—*Old Testament Survey*

- Sixth Grade—*New Testament Survey*

- Seventh Grade—*Christian Youth Leadership*

- Eighth Grade—*Christian Doctrine and Creeds*

THE BIBLE AS READER (BAR) COORDINATION WITH BIBLE OVERVIEW				
Grade _____ Grade Level Principle _____				
Teacher_____ Date _____				
Bible Reader _____				
Notebook Tabs _____				
Week	**Quarter I**	**Quarter II**	**Quarter III**	**Quarter IV**
1				
2				
3				
4				
5				
6				
7				
8				
9				

(See form to use, *NPRG*, 125.)

Overview of Quarterly Topics
for Kindergarten through Eighth Grade

	First Quarter	Second Quarter	Third Quarter	Fourth Quarter
Grades K–4th	The Immediacy of Christ	Old Testament History	The Wisdom Literature & Prophets	New Testament History
Grade 5	Old Testament Survey: Foundations	Old Testament Survey: Taking the Land	Old Testament Survey: Establishing the Kingdom	Old Testament Survey: Destruction, Exile, and Return
Grade 6	New Testament Survey: The Gospels	New Testament Survey: The Acts of the Holy Spirit	New Testament Survey: The Epistles	New Testament Survey: The Apocalypse
Grade 7	Christian Youth Leadership: Youth in Scripture	Christian Youth Leadership: Christian Leadership	Christian Youth Leadership: Old Testament Portraits	Christian Youth Leadership: New Testament Portraits
Grade 8	Christian Doctrine and Creeds: God & Creation	Christian Doctrine and Creeds: Person & Work of Christ, Apostles' Creed	Christian Doctrine and Creeds: Holy Spirit	Christian Doctrine and Creeds: The Church & Last Things Nicene Creed

Bible Reading Schedule

Abide in the Word
*I am the vine, ye are the branches: He that abideth in me, and I in him,
the same bringeth forth much fruit: for without me ye can do nothing.*
(John 15:5)

The Bible reading schedule is coordinated with *The Noah Plan®* Bible Curriculum topics.

Expanded Quarterly Topics
for Kindergarten through Fourth Grade

	First Quarter	Second Quarter	Third Quarter	Fourth Quarter
Grade Level Principle & Bible Reader	*The Immediacy of Christ*	*The Old Testament History*	*The Wisdom Literature & Prophets*	*The New Testament History*

Kindergarten God's Principle of Individuality **Bible Reader:** *The Early Reader's Bible*	• Jesus' birth
	• Jesus' childhood
	• Jesus' baptism
	• Parables—
	  1. Talents
	  2. The good Samaritan
	  3. The lost sheep
	• Death & resurrection
	• Map: Holy Land at the time of Christ
		• Creation
		• Adam & Eve
		• Noah & the Flood
		• Abraham & the Hebrew nation
		• Jacob & Esau
		• Joseph
		• David & Goliath
		• Daniel
			• Psalm 100*
			• Psalm 23
			• Proverbs
			• Solomon
			• The Temple
			• Elijah
			• Elisha
			• Jonah
			• Map: Temple diagram
				• The Last Supper
				• Apostles preach the Gospel
				• Philip
				• Saul
				• Paul & Silas in prison
				• Paul's shipwreck
				• Paul & Onesimus
				• Jesus, the Lamb of God
				• John; Revelation

* Memory work

Expanded Quarterly Topics
for Kindergarten through Fourth Grade (continued)

Grade Level Principle & Bible Reader	First Quarter	Second Quarter	Third Quarter	Fourth Quarter
	The Immediacy of Christ	The Old Testament History	The Wisdom Literature & Prophets	The New Testament History
First Grade "Conscience Is the Most Sacred of All Property." **Bible Reader:** *The Young Reader's Bible*	• Prophecies of Jesus' birth • Jesus at twelve • Hebrew home • Parables— 1. Sower 2. Kingdom of heaven— childlikeness • Resurrection • Map of the Holy Land at the time of Christ	• Creation • Adam & Eve • Fall of man • Tower of Babel • Isaac & Jacob • Moses & Hebrew nation • Samson • Samuel • Solomon	• Prophets & reformers • David • Psalm 1* • Proverbs • Elijah • Elisha • Daniel • Nehemiah • Flora of the Holy Land	• Acts 1, early church • Acts 2 • Acts 3 • Acts 9 • Acts 15–16 • Acts 16 • Philippians 4:8–9 • John • Revelation
Second Grade The Christian Principle of Self-Government **Bible Reader:** Kids' Study Bible, NIrV	• Baptism • Temptation & triumph • Sermon on the Mount • Jesus is Lord • Great Commandment • Crucifixion • Ascension • Map of the Holy Land at the time of Christ	• Creation • Stewardship • Joseph • Moses & the Law • Gideon • Samuel & Saul • Josiah • Ezra • Map—Exodus	• Psalm 23* • Wisdom, Job • Proverbs • Ecclesiastes • Isaiah • Jeremiah • Ezekiel • Daniel • Fauna of the Holy Land	• Pentecost • Peter • Peter after Pentecost • Jesus for all mankind • 1 Peter • 2 Peter • Revelation
Third Grade America's Heritage of Christian Character **Bible Reader:** Kids' Study Bible, NIrV	• Jesus' parents • John the Baptist • Jesus' character • Obedience & compassion • Honoring parents • Prayer life • John's miracles • Passion Week • Map: Holy Land at the time of Christ; Jerusalem	• Creation, character of God • Noah's sons & races • Patriarchs & twelve tribes • Joshua & promised land • Elijah • Elisha • OT miracles, Jonah • OT map	• Psalm 24 • Psalm 119 • Proverbs • Prophets • Isaiah • Jeremiah • Ezekiel • Daniel • Map: physical geography, mountains	• First-century Christians • Stephen • Philip • Paul • Peter • Timothy • Spiritual armor, Ephesians 6:1–18* • Map: Paul's journeys
Fourth Grade How the Seed of Local Self-Government Is Planted **Bible Reader:** The Adventure Bible, NIV	• "I Am" • Disciples' call • Disciples' training • Sermon on the Mount • Jesus: Advocate • Jesus: Intercessor • Map: Holy Land in New Testament times	• Dominion mandate • Abraham • Judges • Deborah • Gideon • Samson • Prophets, Samuel • Kings, David • Temple • Captivity & exile • Ezra • Nehemiah • Map: ancient Middle East	• Psalm 91* • Proverbs • Prophets 1. Isaiah 2. Jeremiah 3. Ezekiel • Minor prophets 1. Hosea 2. Micah 3. Habakkuk 4. Zephaniah • Map: Holy Land	• Acts: Paul's four journeys • Map of journeys • 1 Corinthians 13* • 1 Corinthians • 2 Corinthians

*Memory work

Expanded Quarterly Topics
for Fifth through Eighth Grade

Grade, Principle, & Bible Reader	*First Quarter*	*Second Quarter*	*Third Quarter*	*Fourth Quarter*
Fifth Grade The Christian Form of Our Government	*Old Testament Survey: Foundations*	*Old Testament Survey: Taking the Land*	*Old Testament Survey: Establishing the Kingdom*	*Old Testament Survey: Destruction, Exile, and Return*
Bible Reader: The Student Bible, NIV	• Introduction 　1. Bible 　2. Old Testament • Setting the stage 　1. Genesis 　2. Job 　3. Exodus 　4. Leviticus	• Preparing to enter the promised land 　1. Numbers 　2. Deuteronomy • Entering the promised land—Joshua • Possessing the promised land • Map: Palestine—Israel & Judah	• Age of judges 　1. Judges 　2. Ruth (literature class) 　3. Samuel • Age of kings 　1. Saul 　2. David 　3. Psalms 　4. 1 Chronicles 　5. Solomon 　6. Proverbs 　7. Ecclesiastes 　9. Song of Solomon 　10. 2 Chronicles	• Age of the prophets • Divided kingdom 　Northern 　1. 2 Kings—Elisha 　2. Jonah 　3. Amos 　4. Map of divided kingdom 　Southern 　1. 2 Kings—Isaiah 　2. Micah 　3. Nahum 　4. Map of divided kingdom • Destruction—2 Chronicles 36 • Exile of Judah—Daniel • Return to Zion & restoration 　1. Ezra 　2. Nehemiah 　3. Malachi • Map: Jerusalem
Sixth Grade Jesus Christ Is the Way, the Truth, the Life.	*New Testament Survey: The Gospels*	*New Testament Survey: The Acts of the Holy Spirit*	*New Testament Survey: The Epistles*	*New Testament Survey: The Apocalypse*
Bible Reader: The Student Bible, NIV	• Introduction 　1. Bible 　2. The Gospels • Map of the Holy Land at the time of Christ • Matthew • Mark • Luke • John • "I Am" Passages	• Introduction to Acts • Pentecost • Peter & the birth of the Church • Stephen, martyr • Paul's conversion & ministry—Gospel goes Westward • New Testament Church 　1. Government 　2. Growth 　3. Persecution • Key individuals • Miracles of apostles • Life in NT times • Christian symbols	• Introduction • Letters of Paul 　1. 1 & 2 Thessalonians 　2. Romans 　3. 1 & 2 Corinthians 　4. Galatians 　5. Ephesians 　6. Philippians 　7. Colossians 　8. Philemon 　9. 1 & 2 Timothy 　10. Titus • Remaining letters 　1. 1 & 2 Peter 　2. James 　3. 1, 2, & 3 John 　4. Jude 　5. Hebrews	• Introduction to Revelation • Themes of Revelation 　1. God's sovereignty 　2. Christ's return to earth 　3. God's faithful people 　4. God's final judgment 　5. Hope • Outline of Revelation 　1. Letters to churches 　2. Message for the Church

Expanded Quarterly Topics
for Fifth through Eighth Grade (continued)

Grade, Principle, & Bible Reader	First Quarter	Second Quarter	Third Quarter	Fourth Quarter
Seventh Grade Christian Leadership Is Servanthood. **Bible Reader:** Life Application Bible, KJV	*Christian Youth Leadership: Youth in Scripture*	*Christian Youth Leadership: Christian Leadership*	*Christian Youth Leadership: Old Testament Portraits*	*Christian Youth Leadership: New Testament Portraits*

	• Introduction
	  1. Biblical view of child-hood
	  2. Hebrew education in day of Christ
	  3. God's instruction for teenage years
	• Biblical portraits
	  1. Samuel
	  2. Josiah
	  3. Jeremiah
	  4. Jesus
	• Character qualities of Christian youth
	• Personal application
		• Introduction
		  1. Pagan vs. Christian
		  2. Principles of serving
		• Biblical portrait: Jesus Christ
		• Character qualities of Christian leadership
		• Personal application
			• OT Biblical portraits
			  1. Joseph
			  2. David
			  3. Daniel & three Hebrew youths
			  4. Esther
			• Shared qualities of OT teenage leaders
			• Application for twenty-first century
			• Personal application
				• Tools needed for Christian leadership
				• NT Biblical portraits:
				  1. John Mark
				  2. Timothy
				• Study of 1 & 2 Timothy
				• Personal application
				
				Expanded quarter outlines in *The Noah Plan*® Bible Overview

Eighth Grade The Word of Our God Shall Stand Forever. **Bible Reader:** Life Application Bible, KJV	*Christian Doctrines & Creeds*	*Christian Doctrines & Creeds*	*Christian Doctrines & Creeds*	*Christian Doctrines & Creeds*
	• Introduction to course • Introduction to Bible doctrine • Doctrine of God & creation • Personal application	• Doctrine of God & creation (continued) • Doctrine of man • Doctrine of the Person & work of Christ • Study Apostles' Creed* • Personal application	• Doctrine of Holy Spirit • Doctrine of work of Holy Spirit (redemption) • Personal application	• Doctrine of Church • Doctrine of last things • Study Nicene Creed • Personal application Expanded quarter outlines in *The Noah Plan* Bible Overview

*Memory work

THE NOAH PLAN® © 2005 • FOUNDATION FOR AMERICAN CHRISTIAN EDUCATION

Description of Bibles Selected for Readers

	The Early Reader's Bible	Young Reader's Bible 70 Bible Stories	Kids' Study Bible, NIrV	The Adventure Bible, NIV	The Student Bible, NIV	Life Application Bible, KJV
Publisher	Multnomah © 1995	Standard © 1994	Zondervan © 1996	Zondervan © 2000	Zondervan © 1992	Tyndale © 1989
Instructional Level [Fry Readability Graph]	Kindergarten	First grade	Second and third grades	Fourth grade	Fifth & sixth grades	Seventh & eighth grades
Notes	"Story List" "Basic & New Words List"		"Look at This"	✓	✓	✓
History of Bible		✓				
Book Introductions	Words to know for each story	Introductions to Old & New Testaments	Introduction plus "Good Verses to Read" & "Life in New Testament"	Clear and excellent; Includes: Writer, Title, Location, & Main People	✓	✓
Formatting and Illustrations	Full page and colorful	Clear, beautiful & colorful	Childlike and colorful	Illustrated; clear and instructional	More advanced format appeals to older students	
Book Outlines						✓
Timelines		✓		✓		✓
Harmony of the Gospels						✓
Profiles		Simple format; limited to the stories chosen		✓	✓	Excellent
Maps		✓		✓		✓
Charts and Diagrams		"Can You Find"	✓	✓	Three reading track charts	✓
Cross References	Story with related Scripture text			✓		✓
Textual Notes				✓		✓
Reason and Relate	"Something to Ask" "Something to Do"		"Think about This"	"Activities"	"Insights"; directions on "How to read" in each book	Relates to reader's life
Index				✓	"Where to Find It"	✓
Glossary		15 Words Defined	"Dictionary of Hard Words"	"Dictionary—Concordance"	"Subject Guide" "Non-Biblical People/Places"	✓

Reading in Other Subjects

Reading instruction is not only taught as a distinct subject but also continues through the grades in all other subjects. Students should be taught reading skills as they learn content. The subject area teachers help students to make the transition from reading for story to reading for content. Two strategies that can be used across the curriculum to help students read and comprehend content materials are word mapping and vocabulary analysis study. Word mapping is demonstrated below using "Teaching and Learning Reading" as the key phrase. See a sample vocabulary word analysis study, *NPRG*, 97, and a form to use, *NPRG*, 133.

Word Map

This strategy is similar to an outline but presents the information by visually mapping ideas rather than presenting in a linear form. A key phrase or target word is centered on the page and related notes are arranged around the center. Mapping and webbing are visual organizers of information and can be used as a prewriting strategy. See word map form, *NPRG*, 132.

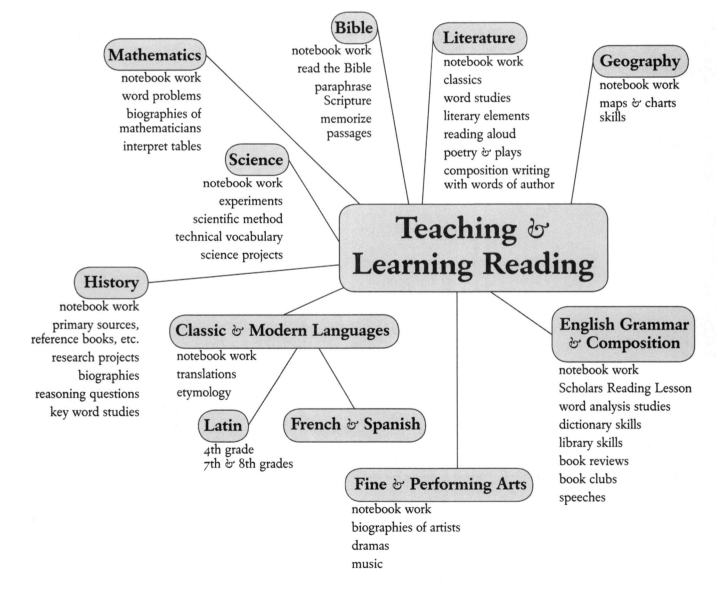

Mathematics
notebook work
word problems
biographies of mathematicians
interpret tables

Bible
notebook work
read the Bible
paraphrase Scripture
memorize passages

Literature
notebook work
classics
word studies
literary elements
reading aloud
poetry & plays
composition writing with words of author

Geography
notebook work
maps & charts
skills

Science
notebook work
experiments
scientific method
technical vocabulary
science projects

History
notebook work
primary sources, reference books, etc.
research projects
biographies
reasoning questions
key word studies

Teaching & Learning Reading

Classic & Modern Languages
notebook work
translations
etymology

Latin
4th grade
7th & 8th grades

French & Spanish

Fine & Performing Arts
notebook work
biographies of artists
dramas
music

English Grammar & Composition
notebook work
Scholars Reading Lesson
word analysis studies
dictionary skills
library skills
book reviews
book clubs
speeches

Supplementary Reading

Reading Assignment		
_____ Name			
Date	Assignment	Parent's Initials

Supplementary Reading Books

Reading materials and books are sent home with the students to provide oral reading practice with parents and to encourage independent reading for a lifetime. The level of difficulty is the free or independent reading level. At this level the student's interest is high; he has no difficulty in reading, and he uses good phrasing. His approximate accuracy is 95–98%. Practice at the independent level promotes fluency, speed, and expression. Comprehension is usually 90%. The supplementary readers provide for individualizing reading materials to give needed practice to the below-grade-level readers and to provide challenge to above-grade-level readers.

The **Supplementary Reading Bookmarker** is used by the teacher to record supplemental book reading for each student on an individual basis. The teacher records the assignment and due date and sends it home in the supplementary reader with the student. The parent listens to the child read orally and initials the bookmarker. The book is returned by the child for the next assignment.

There is a bookmarker template for your use, *NPRG*, 137.

Dear Parents,

Home reading assignments are for you to insure that your child will develop the ability to read accurately and quickly. This is called fluency. Fluency is important because it frees your child's mind to understand what he or she reads. It can be developed by you modeling fluent reading and by having your child engage in repeated oral reading.

I will be sending home weekly reading assignments for you to model fluent reading, monitor your child's repeated reading, and engage your child in a conversation about what he has read. Use the five W's—who, what, why, when, where—and how as a starting point. Short, frequent periods are better than trying to do all the reading at one time. Make sure the reading text is not too difficult to be read accurately with expression and comprehension. Thank you for committing to this partnership for reading.

Sincerely,

Your Child's Teacher

Reading for Enrichment
Choral Reading

The student's ear for language, an enriched vocabulary, and refined reading tastes are cultivated through choral reading and the Scholars Reading Lesson.

Choral reading is group reading aloud which helps to develop oral fluency and presentation manners before an audience. Choral reading may also be used by two people, one of whom usually is a better reader and serves as a model during the reading.

"Before proceeding with the choral reading of any selection, pupils should understand it—its meaning, mood, and movement. To this end, each . . . [selection] to be used should first be read aloud to the boys and girls by the teacher with the best interpretation he can bring to it. Frequently he can get some very good aids to his own reading if he will ask his pupils what particular words, phrases, or lines mean to them.

"The selected piece does not necessarily have to be a designated choral reading. The teacher may find an original way to assign parts, or draw suggestions from the children which will suit his class. The solo designation is used to call attention to each of several factors:

(1) The meaning of a particular line,

(2) the abrupt introduction of a new thought,

(3) the expression of a subdued word,

(4) phrase,

(5) or sentence,

(6) deep feeling,

(7) mock-seriousness.

In addition to all these, it offers

(8) the best possible means to give a number of different individual pupils an opportunity to participate in an important function of the reading.

Occasionally the whole reading may be enhanced when

(9) the teacher participates as a solo voice."

(Helen Ada Brown, *Let's Read Together: Books for Family Enjoyment.* Chicago, IL: Association for Library Service to Children, 1956, 5)

Procedure:

- Choose the material; use Psalms, poems, oratories from history, etc.
- Make a copy of the selection.
- Read the selection aloud.
- Discuss the meaning, mood, movement, etc.
- Assign the parts: solo or groups or chorus.
- Practice
- Present

Choral Reading Example
The Twenty-third Psalm

Voice One: The Lord to me a shepherd is,
want therefore shall not I.

Voice Two: He in the folds of tender grass,
doth cause me down to lie:

Voice One: To waters calm he gently leads
Restore my soul doth he:

Voice Two: He doth in paths of righteousness
for his name's sake lead me.

Voice One: Yea, though in valley of death's shade
I walk, none ill I'll fear:

Voice Two: Because thou art with me, thy rod,
and staff my comfort are.

Voice One: For me a table thou hast spread,
in presence of my foes:

Voice Two: Thou dost anoint my head with oil,
my cup it overflows.

All Voices: Goodness and mercy surely shall
all my days follow me:

Solo Voice: And in the Lord's house I shall dwell
so long as days shall be.

(The Bay Psalm Book
First book published in America)

Reading for Enrichment
Scholars Reading Lesson

The Scholars Reading Lesson is derived from a French method that integrates all language skills. It promotes growth in vocabulary with the goal of sharpening the quality of thinking.

The Scholars Reading Lesson is a whole approach that unifies and teaches all the language skills: seeing, listening, speaking, reading, comprehension, grammar, spelling, and composition. It should be used regularly beginning in the third grade.

Objectives:

- Challenge and build listening and memory skills.

- Increase comprehension skills. Build paraphrasing skills.

- Enrich and enlarge vocabulary to be available for thinking, speaking, and writing.

- Refine composition, grammar, and spelling skills.

- Sharpen reflective thinking and reasoning skills.

Teacher Preparation:

1. Choose an elevated passage of text from classic literature, history books, or the Bible. Anthologies of classic literature are excellent resources. Duplicate for use with the students on a sheet of lined paper or type for use.

2. Review for new words, meanings, apt expressions, author's style. Note synonyms, homonyms, alliteration, etc., that the author may have employed. Write out definitions, if necessary.

3. Select words to define with the students. Choose words that have value in building vocabulary and write out a simple definition. (The number of words selected depends upon the grade level.)

4. Formulate and write out questions to guide the students' reflective thinking and reasoning toward an important idea.

Method of Instruction:

1. List words on board for discussion of pronunciation and definition. *vocabulary*

2. Ask leading questions to help students find an important idea. *comprehension*

3. Have students read the paragraph silently to find the answer. Answer is then read orally by one child. *reflective thinking*

4. Lead the students to explain meaning of the passage and relate it to their own experience, or compare it with other selections they have read. *reasoning & relating*

5. Point out specific apt words, shades of meaning, and synonyms. Take time to write synonyms for selected words on the board.

6. Select several students to reproduce orally the heart of the passage using their own phrasing and as many of the author's key words and phrases as possible. *paraphrasing (See Method, NPRG, 109, III.)*

7. Teacher mentions specifically which new words are noted and commends the students for using them.

8. Students file the page in their reading notebooks and close.

9. Students make a written reproduction of the passage in their composition notebooks, paying attention to grammar, syntax, spelling, capitalization, and punctuation. *reflective thinking*

10. Students' reproductions are corrected quickly and returned. Students rewrite, making all corrections to produce a "fair copy." *editing*

Model Scholars Reading Lesson

Teacher _Mrs. Youmans_   Grade _4_   Date _April 12_

TITLE AND AUTHOR:

"Scrooge" from _A Christmas Carol_ by Charles Dickens

SOURCE:

Huber's _Story and Verse for Children_, 581

SELECTION:

Oh! but he was a tight-fisted hand at the grindstone. Scrooge! a squeezing, wrenching, grasping, scraping, clutching, covetous, old sinner! Hard and sharp as flint, from which no steel had ever struck out generous fire; secret, and self-contained, solitary as an oyster. The cold within him froze his old features, nipped his pointed nose, shriveled his cheek, stiffened his gait; made his eyes and his thin lips blue; and spoke out shrewdly in his grating voice. A frosty rime was on his head, and on his eyebrows, and his wiry chin. He carried his own low temperature always about with him; he iced his office in the dog-days, and didn't thaw it one degree at Christmas.

IMPORTANT IDEA:

"Scrooge . . . was a covetous old sinner!"
Being cold, hard, and miserly is not Godly.

LEADING QUESTIONS:

1. What are the characteristics of a "scrooge" or a miser?
2. How did Scrooge's heart attitude manifest itself in his physical appearance?
3. What are some opposite character qualities of a scrooge?
4. What best describes the nature and character of a scrooge?

APT EXPRESSIONS:

"tight-fisted"—showing extreme economy or frugality

"self-contained"—complete in oneself; uncommunicative

"solitary as an oyster"—alone; a "close-mouthed" person

"dog-days"—a sultry part of summer that occurs at the time of the rising of one of the Dog Stars (July 3–August 11)

VOCABULARY AND DEFINITIONS:

1. wrenching—a sudden or painful violent twisting
2. covetous—excessively desirous or eager to obtain and possess
3. flint—a hard kind of stone; used for striking fire
4. solitary—living alone; remote from society; lonely; a recluse or hermit
5. gait—manner of walking or stepping (homonym: gate)
6. shrewdly—slyly; cunning; mischievously
7. grating—rubbing; irritating; harsh; offensive (homonym: grate-great)
8. rime—a rough white icy covering; frost from fog or vapor (homonym: rhyme)

EVALUATION OF LESSON EFFECTIVENESS

Children enjoyed this lesson and grasped the vocabulary. Written reproductions were excellent!

Independent Reading

Reading is a basic life skill. It is a cornerstone for a child's success in school and, indeed, throughout life.
(Richard C. Anderson 1985, 1)

"Independent reading is sustained reading for information or for pleasure. . . . [It] is one of the most important activities for the reading development of students of all ages. Research shows that students who do a lot of reading 'on their own' become better readers because of independent reading.

- enhances their reading comprehension;
- provides them with a wide range of background knowledge;
- accounts for one-third or more of their vocabulary growth; and
- promotes reading as a lifelong activity."

(Anderson, 1985, 1)

Independent reading is encouraged in kindergarten through second grade and is required in third through twelfth grades. Reading begins with the Bookworms Club in the primary school and continues in the elementary school and throughout high school in English class using library book reading with assigned book reviews.

Bookworms Club

- Reading Club for first through third grades
- Exceptional kindergarten students are allowed to participate upon the recommendation of their teacher
- Members must read and report on a minimum number of books monthly
- The books may come from various sources but must be approved by the homeroom teacher
- The reading is on an independent level
- A monthly party recognizes the participants

Procedure for Students:

1. Declare your reading goals for the month on classroom sign-up sheet

Explorers: Five books

Adventurers: One biography or autobiography

Chroniclers: One full-length classic

2. Choose your books and have the titles approved by your teacher

3. Read the entire book

4. Write the report(s) using the "Bookworms Club Report" form, *NPRG*, 138

5. Give the completed reports to your homeroom teacher who will file them in the Bookworms folder

6. Meet the deadline for reports—the last school day of each month

How Parents Should Select a Book

1. You can be guided in helping a child select his books using the criteria from Miss Slater's "Seven Loves Encouraged by the Literature Program." (*NPLG* 1997, 85–86) Choose books that promote

- A love for God
- A love for God's written word—the Holy Bible
- A love for home and family
- A love for appreciation of the individual
- A love for the Chain of Christianity® moving westward
- A love for our own country, the United States of America
- A love of Christian scholarship and learning

2. Make sure that the book is on your child's independent reading level

- Select a passage of one hundred words
- Have him read orally
- Does he miss five words or less?
- Six or more words missed indicates the book is too difficult unless he is particularly interested in the topic, the format is age-appropriate, and/or comprehension is high
- Select another book

(See sample teacher letter to parents, *NPRG*, 72)

References:

Anderson, Richard C., Elfrieda H. Hiebert, Judith A. Scott, and Ian A. G. Wilkinson. 1985. *Becoming a Nation of Readers: The Report of the Commission on Reading.* Champaign, IL: Center for the Study of Reading, University of Illinois at Urbana-Champaign, National Institute of Education, U.S. Department of Education.

Slater, Rosalie J. 1997. *The Noah Plan Literature Curriculum Guide.* San Francisco, California: Foundation for American Christian Education.

Dear Parents,

The Bookworms Club will officially begin October 1. Your child is invited and encouraged to take part in this yearlong independent reading activity. Membership and participation are optional and are not to be considered a part of regular classroom assignments or grading.

Parents, you may need to assist your child with the first couple of written reports but withdraw as quickly as possible to encourage independence. You are inspiring future editors and writers. Please do check that your child's first and last name are on his/her report and that the reports are given to the homeroom teacher.

The reports must be turned in on time to receive an invitation to the monthly party. The first party will be held the first week of November. Your child will be excused from class to attend the party here at school. A special award will be presented at the end of the year to recognize the children who participate each month October through May.

We appreciate and invite parents who will assist at the parties with refreshments, games, and prizes. Donations are welcome! Please call the school office or send a note in care of your child's classroom teacher to indicate your preference.

Becoming a skilled reader is a matter of continuous practice, development, and refinement. Bookworms is one avenue to encourage your readers and also have some fun. Thank you for your support.

Sincerely,

Your Child's Reading Teacher

Library Reading

Book Review Format

Third through Eighth Grades

(See sample student book review on page following.)

1. Choose a book from the booklist or from the library if your teacher has approved it. Read the book carefully and enjoyably at regular times during the week.

2. Make a reading schedule after calculating how many chapters you must read a week to complete the book on time.

3. As you read notice the plot, new words, interesting facts, exciting parts, new knowledge gained, and the principles of lessons demonstrated in the book.

4. When you have completed the book, think carefully about how you would describe it for other readers. Write a book review in three paragraphs including the following information.

   • Paragraph One: Tell what the book is about, who the author is, what type of book it is (fiction, biography, non-fiction, poetry).

   • Paragraph Two: What new things did you learn from reading this book? Did you learn new words, history, science, geography? Did you learn about how people lived in a different place or time? What Christian principles or character did you observe? How will reading this book help your life?

   • Paragraph Three: Do you recommend this book to other readers? Why or why not?

   • Paragraph Four: At the end of your review, skip several lines and write the author, title, publisher, and date of your book.

5. When you have completed your book and have written your book review, proofread your review and return the book to the school or the library.

6. Make a record of book reviews and due dates:

Title	Author	Due Date

CHARLOTTE'S WEB

BY E.B. WHITE

Charlotte's Web

The name of the book that I chose was Charlotte's Web. It is a fiction book written by E. B. White. Charlotte's Web was about a pig whose name was Wilbur. He had a friend, a spider whose name was Charlotte. Charlotte saved Wilbur's life by weaving words in her web.

I learned several new words. One word is radiant, which means glowing with love, confidence and joy. I also learned what salutations means. It means an act or an action of greeting. I also learned that brutal means being cruel and thats what Wilbur thought of Charlotte.

The christian character that Fern showed was being very kind and loving because when her father was going to kill Wilbur she stopped him. The character trait that I saw in Charlotte was a very caring character, because she also saved him from being killed. In many ways she put Wilbur first. She was always a friend to Wilbur. I saw from reading this book that it always pays to be kind by helping others.

I do recommend this book to other readers because it showed kindness and loving character traits. I enjoyed reading this book.

Charlotte's Web
By E.B. White
1952
Harper & Row Publishers

Kara J.
3rd grade

Summer Reading

Summer is a great time for weekly library visits and daily quiet time for independent reading.

Requirements:

- Three high quality books are read independently at all grade levels.

- Bookmarks placed in the final report cards are used to record titles.

- Special commendations are awarded in September to those who read beyond the minimum of three books.

- Kindergarten parents are asked to read books aloud.

- Recommended book lists by grade level are in the school office.

Summer Reading Program Grades K–12

"Children and books go together in a special way . . . children don't stumble onto good books by themselves," says Gladys Hunt. (Hunt 1989, 14) They must be introduced to them and encouraged to read them by their parents and teachers.

In late spring the school announces its schoolwide summer reading program for all students. It recommends a variety of classics, biographies, poetry, and nonfiction be read for the child's summer enjoyment in order to continue building vocabulary, enhancing writing skills, and interacting with the world's greatest minds.

Gladys Hunt continues, "Any good book can be used by God in a child's development, for a good book has genuine spiritual substance, not just intellectual enjoyment. Books help children know what to look for in life. It is like developing the taste buds of his mind as a child learns to savor what he sees, hears, and experiences, and fits these into some kind of worthwhile framework." (Ibid., 18)

"A book is good if it permits, invites or evens impels a good reading . . . . While good books can be read badly, bad books cannot be read well. The question is not whether it is a good book, but whether the book compelled a good reading." (C. S. Lewis quoted in Hunt 1992, 42)

Required Reading. Each student should read a minimum of three (3) quality books during the summer. Bookmarks placed in the report card should be used to record the titles. The bookmarks are returned to the homeroom teacher the first week of school. Certificates are awarded to those students who go beyond the minimum requirement. Parents of kindergarten students may read aloud to their child and record the titles.

Reading Aloud. Summer memories can be created through establishing a "Family Reading Circle" as described in Rosalie Slater's publication, *A Family Program for Reading Aloud*. This book is highly recommended for parents who want to "recapture your family's opportunities for learning."

Book Lists and Recommendations. To guide the child's selections, the following books contain age-appropriate lists of quality classic literature and practical suggestions for parents and teachers who are "concerned with the whole person needs of children." These resources provide "information on a broad range of reading matter, making use of the many fine secular books available, along with well-written Christian titles." The books are available in local bookstores. Examination copies will be made available in the school office during the summer.

Primary School:

- Hunt, Gladys. *Honey for Child's Heart*. Grand Rapids, MI: Zondervan Publishing House, 1989.

- Wilson, Elizabeth. *Books Children Love: A Guide to the Best Children's Literature*. Wheaton, IL: Good News Publishers, 1987.

Middle School:

- Hunt, Gladys and Barbara Hampton. *Read for Your Life: Turning Teens into Readers*. Grand Rapids, MI: Zondervan Publishing House, 1992.

- Wilson, Elizabeth. *Books Children Love: A Guide to the Best Children's Literature*. Wheaton, IL: Good News Publishers, 1987.

High School:

- Estell, Doug, Michele L. Satchwell, and Patricia S. Wright. *Reading Lists for College-Bound Students*. Upper Saddle River, NJ: Pearson Education, 1993.

> See bookmark style template for
> ### Summer Reading Record,
> *NPRG,* 139.

In Praise of The Bible

The greater the intellectual progress of the ages, the more fully will it be possible to employ the Bible not only as the Foundation, but as the instrument of education.

(Johann Wolfgang von Goethe)

I believe it would startle and move anyone if they could make a certain effort of imagination and read it freshly like a Book, not droningly and chillily like a portion of the Bible.

(Robert Louis Stevenson)

The period of the Reformation was a judgment day for Europe, when all the nations were presented with an open Bible and all the emancipation of heart and intellect which an open Bible involves.

(Thomas Carlyle)

Peruse the books of philosophers with all their pomp of diction. How meager, how contemptible are they when compared with the Scriptures!

(Jean Jacques Rousseau)

How many ages and generations have brooded and wept and agonized over this book! What untellable joys and ecstasies, what support to martyrs at the stake, from it! To what myriads has it been the shore and rock of safety—the refuge from driving tempest and wreck! Translated in all languages, how it has united this diverse world! Of its thousands there is not a verse, not a word, but is thick-studded with human emotion.

(Walt Whitman)

Everything that I have written, every greatness that has been in any thought of mine, whatever I have done in my life has been simply due to the fact that when I was a child my mother daily read with me a part of the Bible and daily made me learn a part of it by heart.

(John Ruskin)

Apart from all questions of religious and historical import, the Bible is the epic of the world. It unrolls a vast panorama in which the ages move before us in a long train of solemn imagery from the creation of the world onward. Against this gorgeous background we see mankind strutting, playing their little part on the stage of history. We see them taken from the dust and returning to the dust. We see the rise and fall of empires, we see great cities, now the hive of busy industry, now silent and desolate—a den of wild beasts. All life's fever is there, its hopes and joys, its suffering and sin and sorrow.

(J. G. Frazer)

The Bible, what a book! Large and wise as the world based on the abysses of creation, and towering aloft into the blue secrets of heaven. Sunrise and sunset, promise and fulfilment, birth and death—the whole drama of humanity—are contained in this one book. It is a Book of Books. The Jews may readily be consoled at the loss of Jerusalem, and the Temple, and Ark of the Covenant, and all the crown jewels of King Solomon. Such forfeiture is as naught when weighed against the Bible, the imperishable treasure that they have saved. If I do not err, it was Mahomet who named the Jews the "People of the Book," a name which in Eastern countries has remained theirs to the present day, and is deeply significant. That one book is to the Jews their country. Within the well-fenced boundaries of that book they live and have their being; they enjoy their inalienable citizenship, are strong to admiration; thence none can dislodge them. Absorbed in the perusals of their sacred book, they little heeded the changes that were wrought in the real world around them. Nations rose and vanished, states flourished and decayed, revolutions raged throughout the earth—but they, the Jews, sat poring over this book, unconscious of the wild chase of time that rushed on above their heads.

(Heinrich Heine)

(From Ernest Sutherland Bates, ed. *The Bible: Designed to Be Read as Living Literature* . . . New York: Simon & Schuster, Inc., 1936, 1965.)

Chapter Four

Methods for

Teaching Reading

A wise teacher makes learning a joy.

(Proverbs 15:2a)

The Art and Love of Learning

Learning to Teach by Principles and Leading Ideas

by Carole G. Adams

Principle: A *principle* is a bedrock truth—when you trace a fact or idea to its most elemental origin, you will identify a truth that is general and broadly applicable—the principle of the thing.

"**Principle**, *n.* defined: [L. *principium*, beginning]

a) In a general sense, the cause, source or origin of any thing; that from which a thing proceeds; as the principle of motion; the principles of action.

b) Element, constituent part; primordial substance.

c) Being that produces anything; operative cause.

d) In science, a truth admitted either without proof, or considered as having been before proved.

e) Ground, foundation; that which supports an assertion, an action, or reasoning." (Webster's 1828 *Dictionary*)

Reasoning from principles to their application in life and learning cultivates a responsible and independent character. The ability to reason from the Word of God and to relate its principles to every area of life equips the student to walk out his

relationship with Christ with wisdom and knowledge. This was characteristic of the American clergy prior to the American Revolution and it is the mark of a mature Biblical worldview.

It is valuable to contrast the definition of *principle* to the definition of *precept*.

"**Precept**, *n.* defined: [L. *praeceptum*, to command]

• Any commandment or order intended as an authoritative rule of action; particularly commands respecting moral conduct." (Webster's 1828 *Dictionary*)

The Seven Principles of Education and Government:

God's Principle of Individuality (GPI) is the primary principle of American Christian history, education, and government. The other six principles are extensions of GPI. Each principle is expounded Biblically, educationally, historically, and governmentally in *Teaching and Learning America's Christian History: The Principle Approach®*, by Rosalie J. Slater. These seven principles are expressed within the context and vocabulary of education and government. However, the bedrock truths these principles identify can be expressed in many ways. For example:

God's Principle of Individuality	➤	"God is the sovereign Creator"
The Principle of Christian Self-Government	➤	"We are properly self-governed when we are governed by Christ."
How the Seed of Local Self-government Is Planted	➤	"Sowing and reaping."

The Principles of Each Subject:

Additionally, each subject contains bedrock truths because God is the Author of every subject in the curriculum. Principles of each subject can be identified. For instance, in the Bible as Reader curriculum, a principle is "God revealed His character and will to man in the Bible." Identifying the principles of the subject equips the student to reason Biblically. The Scripture teaches that the internal gives rise to the external—that the internal is causative, primary, invisible, unseen—while the external is the effect, secondary, visible, seen. Reasoning from internal to external, from cause to effect, is Biblical reasoning.

Principle Approach methodology is based upon the model of teaching and learning that is observed in the Scripture: the use of recurring principles to establish truth. When facts are presented in the framework of basic principles that form a structure of truth, the student builds a true model of the subject; facts are relative to the whole and fit the worldview that reflects the knowledge of God. Without this emphasis on reasoning from principles, information has no base meaning and therefore has not absolute value. The secular method can be contrasted to the Principle Approach in the following way:

Secular Methodology	Principle Approach®
1. Creates a causative environment to which the student must become responsive.	1. From the position of God's Word, the student subdues the environment rather than submits to it.
2. The student is conditioned to look to the external environment—social, economic, religious, and political—before he determines how he will act.	2. Use of the environment emphasizes the internal demands of conscience as causative of behavior and action and the external environment as effect.
3. Results in an individual who can "discern the face of the sky" but cannot "discern the signs of the times."	3. Results in the student learning to subdue the earth for God's purpose and according to His will.

Leading Idea:

The leading idea is a tool of reasoning that guides the student's thinking along a pathway of truth that helps organize the student's thinking. A leading idea can lead the reasoner to identify a principle. A principle can be reasoned from a leading idea. *Leading* is defined as "guiding; conducting; preceding; drawing; alluring" or "showing the way by going first."

For example, in teaching the Bible as Reader, one of the principles is "Reading the Bible equips man with truth for the practice of Christian liberty." This principle gives rise to the many leading ideas such as, "Using the Bible to learn to read has more value than using a basal reader."

The following chart shows the relationship of principles to leading ideas to facts representing a strong foundation that should be built into the minds of students using the Principle Approach:

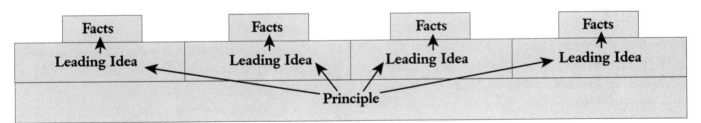

Example from the Bible as Reader Program:

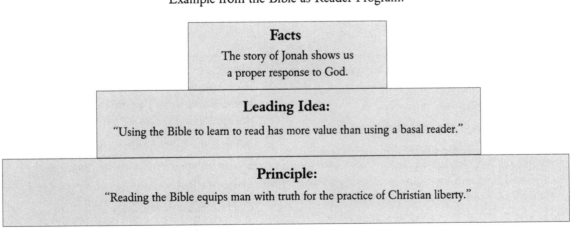

Facts
The story of Jonah shows us
a proper response to God.

Leading Idea:
"Using the Bible to learn to read has more value than using a basal reader."

Principle:
"Reading the Bible equips man with truth for the practice of Christian liberty."

Distinctives of the Principle Approach® Lesson
The Principle Approach lesson creates a specific effect in the student.

1. The lesson appears in a subject taught in the context of America's Christian history and government.

   Result: Students

   a) Learn the chronology of His Story and can identify every subject by it

   b) Understand God's purpose for each subject as it is used to further the Gospel and liberty for the individual

2. The philosophy affirms the full value of each student.

   Result: Affirmation

   a) Satisfies students' intellectual needs

   b) Appeals to their hearts and consciences for a self-government-under-God response

   c) Presents appropriate challenges to build character

3. The lesson is governed by a Christian teacher who has himself mastered the subject and the Biblical philosophy of education.

   Result: Students are engaged in producing a product—their own education. Therefore, they are able to:

   a) Research Biblically

   b) Think reflectively

   c) Develop a student notebook, leaving a record of scholarship

   d) Use the tools and practice the habits of Christian scholarship

   e) Develop a love of lifetime learning

4. Each lesson is guided by Biblical principles.

   Result: Biblical Principles

   a) Maintain the integrity of the subject, consecrating it

   b) Provide truths in the lesson, which fit into the whole revelation of God's purposes in history

   c) Enliven the subject and inspire students

5. The teacher guides the students' thinking with leading questions, calling upon reflective learning.

   Result: Students

   a) Observe

   b) Identify

   c) Discover

   d) Articulate for themselves

6. The vocabulary of the subject is defined and taught.

   Result: Students

   a) Master preciseness of language

   b) Masterfully articulate ideas and thoughts and inculcate perspicuity

   c) Study logic and rhetoric

7. Notes are recorded in an organized way in the students' notebooks

   Result: Notebooks

   a) Make the lesson productive and reflective rather than just another reading or writing assignment

   b) Provide students with permanent records of their learning

8. The teacher is a living textbook.

   Result:

   Every classroom is a reflection of a unique individual responding to the high calling of American Christian education

9. Principle Approach education produces a gentle, inquiring, dignified spirit within the school.

   Result: This spirit in turn produces

   a) A readiness for learning

   b) An honoring, Godly, wholesome character

   c) A dynamic that envelops and warms the student, cultivating, inspiring, and consecrating them for God's call and purposes for their lives

10. The end product of the American Christian Principle Approach is self-governing, Christ-reflecting character, which is enterprising and productive. It produces the kind of future leader we as parents and educators pray for daily—the kind that will change the world for the glory of God.

11. What is the fruit? Students who

    a) Are independent Christian scholars

    b) Have a lifelong love for learning and reflection

    c) Have Biblical worldviews

    d) Have Christian characters

    e) Have hearts to serve Christ and community

The Reading Paradigm

"Dr. Jeanne Chall, head of Harvard's reading department for many years, helped educators understand that learning to read is a long-term process and requires passages through stages each of which needs mastery before moving to the next stage. This understanding helps guide educators about what to teach, when to teach it, and what methods to use in reading instruction." (Hall & Moats 1999, 152)

The model used in this guide for teaching is based in part on Dr. Chall's research in her 1983 book entitled *Stages of Reading Development*. The stages are (1) Readiness to Read, (2) Learning to Read, (3) Reading to Learn, (4) Reading towards Independence, and (5) Reading with Reason.

STAGE 1. Readiness to Read
Newborn–Kindergarten

Beginning reading represents the oral tradition. The focus for the kindergarten teacher is on developing a rich oral vocabulary and understanding.

- Perceptual skills, visual and auditory discrimination
- Phonemic awareness
- The Writing Road to Reading® phonics program
- Alphabet skills, moveable ABC
- Preparation for reading
- Writing (copying letters)
- Basic vocabulary
- Classification
- Study skills
- Oral questioning
- Listening skills
- Thinking skills
- Memory verses
- Appreciation and enjoyment of literature
- The Bible as Reader program

STAGE 2. Learning to Read
Grades 1–3, Decoding and Fluency

The focus is on word recognition and phonics. Teacher assigns reading aloud to parents (home reading).

- Alphabet skills
- Writing (copying letters)
- Decoding
- Basic vocabulary
- Comprehension
- Study skills and strategies
- Oral language
- Listening skills

- Thinking skills
- Composition
- Appreciation and enjoyment of literature
- Independent reading
- Memorize Scripture and poetry
- The Bible as Reader program

STAGE 3. Reading to Learn
Grades 4–6, Refinement and Improvement

- Vocabulary
- Scholars Reading Lesson
- Comprehension (oral & written)
- Composition
- Listening
- Thinking skills
- Study and research skills
- Rate and fluency
- Appreciation and enjoyment of literature
- Recreational reading
- Independent reading
- The Bible as Reader program

STAGE 4. Reading towards Independence
Grades 7–8, Analysis and Synthesis and Vocabulary Enrichment

- Direct teaching of comprehension strategies and vocabulary meaning leading to better achievement
- Focus on more complicated texts, literary, abstract, and technical. Develop more world knowledge and current events with periodicals
- Study strategies and ways to organize information in preparation for the independent studies needed at the high school level
- Independent reading of the Bible directed by teacher
- Cooperative learning to allow for social interactions and communication skills

STAGE 5. Reading with Reason
Grades 9–12, Cultural Analysis Program

- Discussion and debate of books selected for their value in giving breadth and depth to the high school curriculum
- Incorporates classics, writing, theatre, dance, art, & music
- Recording of observations and reviews
- Mentoring by faculty members

Hall, Susan L. and Louisa C. Moats. 1999. *Straight Talk about Reading*. Chicago, IL: Contemporary Books.

Preparing to Teach Reading

Record: (1) to write or enter in a book, for the purpose of preserving authentic or correct evidence of a thing;
(2) to imprint deeply on the mind or memory; (3) to cause to be remembered. (Webster's 1828 *Dictionary*)

Step One:
- Prepare quarterly overviews
- Use the charts coordinating the BAR program and *The Noah Plan®* Bible Curriculum quarterly topics for kindergarten through eighth grade (*NPRG*, 59–64)
- Use the overview chart for your grade (*NPRG*, 61–64)

Step Two:
- Set up your reading notebooks (see outlines below)—The teacher's notebooks are a collection of resources and a record of his curriculum development: the research, the reasoning and relating, and weekly lesson plans
- Purchase two high quality three-inch, three-ring binders
- Create title pages and label divider tabs

Step Three:
- Plan the Bible as Reader lessons
- Use the Governing Steps for Writing Lessons (*NPRG*, 22–23)

Step Four:
- Assemble the tools for developing your reading curriculum
- Use a study Bible and Bible reference books to organize your curriculum. Suggestions:

  Dickson New Analytical Study Bible—An excellent resource for background study. It gives a clear overview of the books, authors, time period, etc.

  Life Application Bible—A resource that helps the teacher in choosing the Biblical principles and determining the leading ideas. A background study of characters and places is presented

  The Children's Illustrated Bible—A wonderful Bible picture book. Contains historical data explained on a level children can understand

  Matthew Henry's Commentary—Should be used when preparing to teach a new book of the Bible to give further insight into the author, setting, and main characters

  The Book of Life—A series of volumes that are a resource of art, literature, and history to enrich the teaching of the Bible. The best sets are ones from 1923, the 1952 Silver Anniversary Edition, up to 1972

  Nelson's Complete Book of Bible Maps & Charts—A compilation of Biblical maps and study charts, offering a summary of events or themes in the Bible, many on individual pages for easy copying

Notebook 1	Notebook 2

Reading Resource. This is a collection of the tools and strategies, methods and research, workshop notes, and articles that support teaching reading. As material is assembled and collected, file under the following tabs [suggested list]:
1. Foundations
  • Define *reading* using the Bible and key word studies using Webster's 1828 *Dictionary*
  • Establish the Biblical foundation
  • Determine principles and leading ideas for teaching reading and the Bible as Reader
  • Examine/copy Christian History Reading Timeline in chapter two (*NPRG*, 48–53)
2. Phonetic Instruction
  • Phonemic Awareness
3. Vocabulary
4. Comprehension
5. Reasoning and Writing
6. Remediation
7. Enrichment
8. Evaluation/Assessment
9. Graphic Organizers
10. Workshops/seminars
	Reading Curriculum
	This is the teacher's guide and planning book. Suggested tabs are the following:
	1. Grade-level Overview
	2. Classroom management
	  • Class constitution, notebook standards, grading policy, Bible as Reader Weekly Lesson Plan form, *NPRG*, 26
	3. Quarter 1
	  • Lesson plans and supporting research
	4. Quarter 2
	  • Lesson plans and supporting research
	5. Quarter 3
	  • Lesson plans and supporting research
	6. Quarter 4
	  • Lesson plans and supporting research
	7. Projects: special days, celebrations, long-range assignments, projects, student enrichment, remediation
	8. Resources: Web sites, pictures, maps, charts, graphic organizers, art, music, poetry
	9. Bibliography
	10. Sample student work

Teaching Reading by Grade Levels

What to teach, when to teach it, and what methods to use in reading instruction

Kindergarten—Learning to Read: readiness, insight about words, phonemic awareness

Component and Materials Full citations in Resource List (*NPRG*, 123–125)	Content and Methods Reference Curriculum Charts (*NPRG*, 4–21)
Phonemic Awareness • *Phonemic Awareness in Young Children*, Adams* • *NPRG*	**Select** activities for developing an awareness of the sounds (phonemes) that make up spoken words using "Suggested Kindergarten Schedule." (Adams, *Phonemic Awareness* 1998. 137–141; Phonemic Awareness Instruction, *NPRG*, xv) **Introduce**, practice, extend, and revisit the various phonemic tasks.
Phonetic Instruction/Vocabulary • *The Writing Road to Reading®* (WRTR), 2003, Spalding • Bible, literature classics, poetry	**Introduce:** • Phonograms and practice using multisensory review procedures, (*WRTR*, 39–42) • Scope and Sequence, (*WRTR*, 443–453) • Framework for Planning Lessons, (*WRTR*, 454–457) • Resources, (*WRTR*, 458) **Identify** syllables, teach precise meanings of words, enjoy words that rhyme, describe and use many new words from Bible, literature, science, history, and geography.

Oral Reading
• *McCall-Harby Test Lessons in Primary Reading*, Spalding
• Sets of storybooks
  • *Primary Phonics*, Marak
  • Grade-level readers from selected publishers: A Beka Book; Educators Publishing Service; McGraw-Hill, SRA, Open Court, etc.
• Bible, literature classics, poetry
• *WRTR*
• *The Noah Plan® Reading Curriculum Guide, 2005 (NPRG)*
	Read short passages to students to focus on comprehension rather than on decoding.
	Assign supplementary readers for home practice after mastery of single-letter phonograms is assessed.
	Check progress daily as student reads aloud to teacher.
	Read to student from literature curriculum selections.
	Ask the students to read aloud the spelling words from the board and also from their spelling notebook.
	Model fluent reading in a group through choral reading or with a partner. (For additional practice, see Fluency Instruction, *NPRG*, xvii; Choral Reading, *NPRG*, 68.)

Bible as Reader • *The Early Reader's Bible*, Beer • *NPRG* • *The Noah Plan Lessons: Kindergarten (NPLK)*, Bible Lessons	**Read** aloud stories to correspond to Bible/BAR overview topics. (*NPRG*, 59–64) **Read** aloud until student learns to read the words himself. **Direct** thinking with Biblical principles and leading ideas from weekly Bible lessons. (*NPRG*, 26–30) **Schedule** three days of Bible as Reader and two days of individual or small group work on skills or enrichment.
Comprehension • *WRTR* • *The Comprehension Connection*, Spalding • *McCall-Harby Test Lessons in Primary Reading*, Spalding	**Teach** comprehension using literary appreciation, text structure, and listening comprehension and reading comprehension. (*WRTR*, Chapter 3) **Make** the comprehension process visible by thinking aloud while reading as teacher uses each of five mental actions. • **See** *WRTR* scope and sequence for teaching sequence of mental actions for kindergarten. • **See** *The Comprehension Connection* User's Guide for an overview of teaching steps and passage analyses and answer keys. • **See** *McCall-Harby Test Lessons in Primary Reading* for short, interesting passages that are an integral part of the Spalding Method® for teaching and testing comprehension. These are read aloud to the students beginning mid-year to the end of kindergarten.
Reasoning and Writing • *The Noah Plan English Language Curriculum Guide (NPEG)* • *NPRG*	**Create** opportunities daily for student to relate, discuss, and present ideas in complete sentences and good order, preparing to write sentences by mid-year. (*NPEG*, Chapter 1, Kindergarten; Reading and Writing Connection, *NPRG*, xxiii) **Write** group paragraphs to learn form, the elements, and author's purpose by fourth quarter. **Use** the story map graphic organizer to give the students the elements of an informative-narrative. (*NPRG*, 102; blank form, *NPRG*, 130)

*Full citations in Resources (*NPRG*, 123–125)

Teaching Reading by Grade Levels

What to teach, when to teach it, and what methods to use in reading instruction

First Grade—Learning to Read—Initial Reading or Decoding

Component and Materials *Full citations in Resources (NPRG, 123–125)	Content and Methods Reference Curriculum Charts (NPRG, 4–21)
Phonemic Awareness • *Phonemic Awareness in Young Children*, Adams • *NPRG*	**Select** activities for developing an awareness of the sounds (phonemes) that make up spoken words using "Suggested First-Grade Schedule." (Adams, *Phonemic Awareness* 1998. 137–141; See Phonemic Awareness Instruction, *NPRG*, xv) **Introduce**, practice, extend, and revisit the various phonemic tasks. May need only eight weeks to establish an awareness of phonemes before formal instruction in reading and phonics.
Phonic Instruction/Vocabulary • *The Writing Road to Reading*®, 2003, Spalding, (WRTR) • *NPEG* • *NPRG*	**Introduce** phonograms and practice using multisensory review procedures of the Spalding Method®: • Chapter 1: "The Spelling Lesson" (*WRTR*, 39–42) • "Scope and Sequence" (*WRTR*, 443–453) • "Framework for Planning Integrated Arts Lessons" (*WRTR*, 454–457) • "Resources" (*WRTR*, 458) **Build** understanding of words parts, i.e., compound words, prefixes, and suffixes. (*NPEG*, Chap. 4, Etymology) **Introduce** Webster's 1828 *Dictionary*. **Define** words from reading in other subjects. **Introduce** root words and synonyms and homonyms.

Oral Reading
• *McCall-Harby Test Lessons in Primary Reading*, Spalding
• *McCall Crabbs Standard Test Lessons in Reading*, Book A, Spalding
• Sets of storybooks
  • *Primary Phonics*, Marak
  • Grade-level readers from selected publishers: A Beka Book; Educators Publishing Service; McGraw-Hill, SRA, Open Court, etc.
• Bible, literature classics, poetry
• *The Noah Plan® Literature Curriculum Guide (NPLG)*
• *NPRG*
	Read short passages to students to focus on comprehension rather than on decoding.
	Assign supplementary readers for home practice after mastery of single-letter phonograms is assessed.
	Use the "Oral Reading Assessment" chart to check progress as student reads aloud to teacher. (*NPRG*, 142)
	Read to student from literature curriculum selections.
	Ask the students to read aloud the spelling words from the board and also from their spelling notebook.
	Model fluent reading in a group through choral reading or with a partner. (For additional practice, see Fluency Instruction, *NPRG*, xvii; Choral Reading, *NPRG*, 68.)

Bible as Reader • *The Young Reader's Bible*, Bruno • *The Noah Plan Lessons: First Grade (NPLI)*	**Read** aloud stories in Bible reader to correspond to Bible/BAR overview topics. (*NPRG*, 59–64) **Read** aloud until the student learns to read the words himself. **Direct** thinking with Biblical principles and leading ideas from weekly Bible lessons. (*NPRG*, 26–30) **Schedule** three days of Bible as Reader and two days of individual or small group work on skills or enrichment.

Comprehension
• *WRTR*
• *The Comprehension Connection*, Spalding
• *McCall-Harby Test Lessons in Primary Reading*, Spalding
• *McCall Crabbs Standard Test Lessons in Reading*, Book A (1961)
• *NPRG*
	Teach comprehension using literary appreciation, text structure, and listening comprehension and reading comprehension. (*WRTR*, Chap. 3)
	Make the comprehension process visible by thinking aloud while reading as you use each of the five mental actions.
	• See *WRTR* scope and sequence for teaching sequence of mental actions for grade one.
	• See *The Comprehension Connection* User's Guide for an overview of teaching steps, passage analyses, and answer keys.
	  • *McCall-Harby* passages are read aloud to the students at the beginning of the year.
	  • *McCall Crabbs, Book A* is used after mid-year.
	Use the Strategic Teaching Method, strategies, and graphic organizers to engage the thinking of the student before, during, and after reading. (*NPRG*, 91–110)

Reasoning and Writing • *WRTR* • *NPEG* • *NPRG*	**Teach** composition of paragraphs using the three basic types of writing. (*WRTR*, Chap. 2 & *NPEG*, Chap. 7 on Composition) **Use** the story map graphic organizer to give the students the elements of a narrative and an informative-narrative. Using the organizer facilitates writing stories from the Bible text passages. (*NPRG*, 102, 110; form, 130) **Write** complete sentences for reason questions from the Bible text. **Use** the "People Who Impacted History" chart to write short descriptive paragraphs. (*NPRG*, 99; form, 129)

*Full citations in Resources (NPRG, 123–125)

Teaching Reading by Grade Levels

What to teach, when to teach it, and what methods to use in reading instruction

Second Grade—Acquires fluency, consolidates skills learned in Stage 1

Component and Materials Full citations in Resource List (*NPRG*, 123–125)	Content and Methods Reference Curriculum Charts (*NPRG*, 4–21)
Phonic Instruction/Vocabulary • *WRTR* • *How to Teach Spelling*, Rudginsky • *How to Spell 1*, Rudginsky • *NPEG* • *NPRG*	**Review** phonograms and practice using multisensory review procedures of the Spalding Method® • Chapter 1: The Spelling Lesson (*WRTR*, 39–42) • Scope and Sequence, (*WRTR*, 443–453) • Framework for Planning Integrated Arts Lessons, (*WRTR*, 454–457) • Resources, (*WRTR*, 458) **Transition** during Quarter 2 to using *How to Teach Spelling* for weekly lists and dictation and *How to Spell Workbook 1* for student practice and reinforcement. **Identify** words parts, i.e., roots, prefixes *&* suffixes, compound words, syllables. (*NPEG*, Chap. 4, Etymology) **Use** Vocabulary Development Skills list on second grade curriculum chart. (*NPRG*, 9) **Define** words from reading in other subjects and continue use of Webster's 1828 *Dictionary*. **Develop** new vocabulary *indirectly* through daily oral discussions and wide reading. **Develop** vocabulary *directly* through explicit teaching and word learning strategies. (*NPRG*, 92–95, 97) **Practice** vocabulary strategies using the Bible text passages read during the morning Bible lesson.
Oral Reading • *McCall Crabbs Standard Test Lessons in Reading*, Book A, Spalding • Grade-level readers from selected publishers: A Beka Book; Educators Publishing Service; McGraw-Hill, SRA, Open Court, etc. • Bible, literature classics, poetry	**Read** short passages to students to focus on comprehension rather than decoding. **Use** Think-Aloud technique, verbalizing specific mental steps used to perform a comprehension task. **Assign** supplementary readers for home practice to develop fluency. (*NPRG*, 67–77) **Use** "Oral Reading Assessment" chart to monitor progress weekly as student reads aloud to teacher. (*NPRG*, 142) **Read** to the students from literature curriculum selections. **Model** fluent reading in a group through choral reading or with a partner. (For additional practice, see Fluency Instruction, *NPRG*, xvii; Choral Reading, *NPRG*, 68.) **Use** the Bible text passages for oral reading.
Bible as Reader • Kids' Study Bible, NIrV, Zondervan • *The Noah Plan Lessons: Second Grade (NPL2)* • *SRA Reading Lab 1a*, SRA/McGraw-Hill • *Getting the Main Idea*, Books A–C, *Specific Skills Series*, Boning	**Teach** directed reading activities for Bible text passages from Kids' Study Bible that correspond to Bible/BAR overview topics. (*NPRG*, 59–64) **Read** aloud until student learns to read the words himself. **Direct** thinking with Biblical principles and leading ideas from weekly Bible lessons. (*NPRG*, 26–30) **Schedule** three days of Bible as Reader (BAR) instruction and two days of individual or small group work on skills or enrichment.
Comprehension • *WRTR* • *The Comprehension Connection*, Spalding • *McCall Crabbs Standard Test Lessons in Reading*, Book A (1961) • *NPRG*	**Teach** comprehension using literary appreciation, text structure, and listening comprehension and reading comprehension. (*WRTR*, Chap. 3) **Make** the comprehension process visible by thinking aloud while reading as he uses each of the five mental actions. See *WRTR* scope and sequence for teaching sequence of mental actions for second grade. • See *The Comprehension Connection* User's Guide gives an overview of teaching steps, passage analyses, and answer keys. • See *McCall Crabbs Standard Test Lessons in Reading*, Book A are short, interesting passages that are an integral part of the Spalding Method® for teaching and testing comprehension. **Use** the Strategic Teaching Method, strategies, and graphic organizers to engage the thinking of the student before, during, and after reading. (*NPRG*, 90–110) **Practice** comprehension strategies using the Bible passages read during the morning Bible lesson. Include additional Bible passages to extend thinking and/or to meet individual reading abilities.
Reasoning and Writing • *WRTR* • *NPEG* • *NPRG*	**Teach** composition of paragraphs using the three basic types of writing. (*WRTR*, Chap. 2 *&* *NPEG*, Chap. 7 on Composition) **Use** the story map graphic organizer to give the students the elements of a narrative and an informative-narrative. Using the organizer facilitates writing stories from the Bible passages. (*NPRG*, 102, 110) **Write** compositions using the graphic organizers generated from the BAR lessons. Examples: T-charts, sequence chains, picture graphs, Venn diagrams. (*NPRG*, 91–110; forms 126–132) **Write** complete sentences to answer reason questions from the Bible text. **Use** the "People Who Impacted History" chart to write short descriptive paragraphs. (*NPRG*, 99; form, 129)

*Full citations in Resources (*NPRG*, 123–125)

Teaching Reading by Grade Levels

What to teach, when to teach it, and what methods to use in reading instruction

Third Grade—Masters reading fluency and skills taught in Stage 2

Component and Materials *Full citations in Resources (*NPRG*, 123–125)	Content and Methods Reference Curriculum Charts (*NPRG*, 4–21)
Phonetic Instruction/Vocabulary • *How to Teach Spelling*, Rudginsky • *How to Spell 2*, Rudginsky • NPEG • NPRG	**Use** *How to Teach Spelling* for weekly lists and dictation exercises and *How to Spell Workbook 2* for practice and reinforcement. Read, copy, and learn rules. **Identify** words parts, i.e., roots, prefixes and suffixes, syllables. (*NPEG*, Chap. 4, Etymology) **Use** Vocabulary Development Skills list on 3rd grade curriculum chart to plan instruction. (*NPRG*, 11) **Define** and analyze words from reading in other subjects; continue use of Webster's 1828 *Dictionary*. **Develop** new vocabulary *indirectly* through daily oral discussions and wide reading. **Develop** vocabulary *directly* through explicit teaching and word learning strategies. (*NPRG*, 91–95, 97) **Practice** vocabulary strategies using unfamiliar vocabulary from the Bible passages read during the morning Bible lesson. (*NPRG*, 91–97)
Oral Reading • *McCall Crabbs Standard Test Lessons in Reading*, Book B • *The Comprehension Connection*, User's Guide for Book B, Spalding • Grade-level readers from selected publishers: A Beka Book; Educators Publishing Service; McGraw-Hill, SRA, Open Court, etc. • Bible, literature classics, poetry	**Read** short passages to students to focus on comprehension rather than on decoding. **Use** Think-Aloud technique—verbalize specific mental steps used to perform a comprehension task. **Assign** supplementary readers for home practice to develop fluency. (*NPRG*, 67–77) **Use** the "Oral Reading Assessment" to monitor progress weekly as student reads aloud to teacher. (*NPRG*, 142) **Read** to the students from literature curriculum selections. **Model** fluent reading in a group through choral reading.(For additional practice, see Fluency Instruction, *NPRG*, xvii; Choral Reading, *NPRG*, 68.) **Assign** partner reading activity—students take turns listening and reading. **Organize** Readers Theatre for fluency training and enrichment. (See Fluency Instruction, *NPRG*, xvii.) **Use** the Bible passages from the Bible lesson for oral reading.
Bible as Reader • Kid's Study Bible, NIrV, Zondervan • NPRG • *The Noah Plan Lessons: Third Grade* (NPL3) • SRA Reading Lab 1a, SRA/McGraw-Hill • *Getting the Main Idea*, Books A–C, Specific Skills Series, Boning	**Teach** directed reading activities for Bible passages from Kids' Study Bible that correspond to Bible/BAR overview topics. (*NPRG*, 59–64) • **Read** aloud until student learns to read the words himself. • **Use** six-step lesson plan format to plan BAR lessons. (*NPRG*, 24–25) **Direct** thinking with Biblical principles and leading ideas from weekly Bible lessons. (*NPRG*, 26–30) **Schedule** three days of Bible as Reader (BAR) instruction and two days of individual or small group work on skills or enrichment.
Comprehension • WRTR • *The Comprehension Connection*, User's Guide for Books B–E, Spalding • *McCall Crabbs Standard Test Lessons in Reading*, Books B or C • NPRG	**Teach** mastery of comprehension using literary appreciation, text structure, and listening comprehension and reading comprehension. (*WRTR*, Chap. 3) **Make** the comprehension process visible by thinking aloud while reading as he uses each of the five mental actions. • **See** *WRTR* scope and sequence for teaching sequence of mental actions for grade three. Review and reinforcement are the goals. • **See** *The Comprehension Connection* User's Guide for an overview of teaching steps and passage analyses and answer keys. • **See** *McCall Crabbs Standard Test Lessons in Reading*, Books B & C for short, interesting passages that are an integral part of the Spalding Method® for teaching and testing comprehension. Choose level depending on the student's reading ability. **Use** the Strategic Reading Process, strategies, and graphic organizers to engage the thinking of student before, during, and after reading. (*NPRG*, 90–110) **Practice** comprehension strategies using the Bible passages that have been read during the morning Bible lesson. • **Include** additional Bible passages to extend thinking and/or to meet individual reading abilities. • **Vary** reading rate depending on types of passages.
Reasoning and Writing • WRTR • NPEG • NPRG	**Teach** composition of paragraphs using the three basic types of writing. The students write three basic types of paragraphs. (*WRTR*, Chap. 2 & *NPEG*, Chap. 7 on Composition; *NPRG*, 134) **Use** the story map graphic organizer to give the students the elements of a narrative and an informative-narrative. Using the organizer facilitates writing stories from the Bible passages. (*NPRG*, 102, 110; form, 130) **Write** compositions using graphic organizers generated from BAR lessons. (See examples & forms: T-charts, sequence chains, picture graphs, Venn diagrams, "People Who Impacted History" chart, etc., *NPRG*, 91–110; forms 126–132) **Use** the Bible text for writing reason questions, for paraphrasing, and for models of figurative language. (See example, *NPRG*, 109–112.) **Write** book reviews. (See sample, *NPRG*, 73–75.)

*Full citations in Resources (*NPRG*, 123–125)

Teaching Reading by Grade Levels

What to teach, when to teach it, and what methods to use in reading instruction

Fourth Grade—Reading to Learn for New Information; relates print to ideas—Stage 3

Component and Materials Full citations in Resource List (*NPRG*, 123–125)	Content and Methods Reference Curriculum Charts (*NPRG*, 4–21)
Phonetic Instruction/Vocabulary • *How to Teach Spelling*, Rudginsky • *How to Spell 3*, Rudginsky • *NPEG* • *NPRG*	Use *How to Teach Spelling* for weekly lists and dictation exercises and *How to Spell Workbook 3* for student practice and reinforcement. Use the Progress Chart at end of the workbook to adjust the material to the age and ability of the students, proceeding as rapidly or as slowly as needed. **Read, copy, and learn** • Spelling rules: doubling rule, silent-e, y rule, and i-before-e generalization • The six kinds of syllables; syllabication (dividing words into syllables) practice • Words parts, i.e., roots, prefixes, and suffixes. (*NPEG*, Chap. 4, Etymology) • Plurals, contractions, endings, homonyms, possessives **Use** Vocabulary Development Skills list on fourth grade curriculum chart to plan instruction. (*NPRG*, 12–13) **Define** and analyze words from reading in other subjects; continue use of Webster's 1828 *Dictionary*. **Develop** new vocabulary *indirectly* through daily oral discussions and wide reading. **Develop** vocabulary *directly* through explicit teaching and word learning strategies. (*NPRG*, xix; 92–98) **Practice** vocabulary strategies using unfamiliar vocabulary from the Bible text passages. (*NPRG*, 92–98)
Oral Reading • *NPLG* • *NPRG*	**Model** reading aloud selections from literature curriculum and the Bible text. **Assign** supplementary readers for home practice to develop fluency. (*NPRG*, 67–77) • **Use** Oral Reading Assessment chart to monitor progress. (*NPRG*, 141) • **Assign** books at independent reading level.
Bible as Reader • *The Adventure Bible*, NIV • *NPRG*	**Teach** reading activities from The Adventure Bible for Bible passages that correspond to Bible/BAR overview topics. (*NPRG*, 59–64) • **Use** six-step lesson plan format to plan BAR lessons. (*NPRG*, 22–30) • **Pace** the steps to match the age and ability of students. • **Incorporate** vocabulary and comprehension strategies to construct meaning and new understandings. **Build** Biblical Christian worldview with principles and leading ideas from weekly Bible lessons. (*NPRG*, 26–30) **Schedule** three days for group instruction of BAR and two days of individual or small group work on skills or enrichment.

Comprehension
• *The Comprehension Connection*, User's Guide for Books B–E, Spalding
• *McCall Crabbs Standard Test Lessons in Reading*, Books C or D
• *NPRG*
	Use a reading comprehension approach in which the teacher models and demonstrates how reading strategies work until the students gain independence in applying the strategies. (*NPRG*, xxii)
	• **Develop** prereading strategies
	  • **Activate** prior knowledge
	  • **Teach** new words
	  • **Set** purposes for reading
	• **Use** Think-Aloud technique verbalizing specific mental steps during reading using five mental actions.
	  • **Monitor** comprehension • **Make** connections • **Make** predictions
	  • **Mentally** summarize • **Reformat**
	• **Apply** the Strategic Reading Method (draw inferences before, during, and after reading). Read between the lines.
	Assess which students can use strategy independently and those who require mediation. (*NPRG*, 117–119)
	Schedule small group work or individual sessions for remedial or enrichment.
	• SRA Reading Lab provides individual levels for vocabulary and comprehension.
	• *McCall Crabs Standard Test Lessons in Reading*, Books B–E used as timed reading rate builder. Choose level depending on student's reading ability.
	Practice comprehension strategies using the Bible passages. Include additional Bible passages to extend thinking and/or to meet individual reading abilities.

Reasoning and Writing • *NPRG* • *The Adventure Bible*	Use Bible text for answering reason questions, for paraphrasing, and for models of figurative language. (See samples, *NPRG*, 109, 111–112.) **Use** the story map graphic organizer to give the students the elements of a narrative and an informative-narrative. Use the organizer to facilitate writing stories from the Bible text passages. (*NPRG*, 110) **Write** compositions using graphic organizers generated from BAR lessons. (See examples & forms: T-charts, sequence chains, picture graphs, Venn diagrams, "People Who Impacted History" chart, etc., *NPRG*, 91–110; forms 126–132.) **Write** book reviews. (See sample, *NPRG*, 73–75.)

*Full citations in Resources (*NPRG*, 123–125)

The Strategic Reading Process

The reading process used in this guide has three stages: before reading, during reading, and after reading. Each stage has components.

Teaching using the strategic reading process involves students in learning before, during, and after they read. The research of the past decade on the nature of reading emphasizes, "that reading must be strategic. Skilled readers are flexible. How they read depends upon the complexity of the text, their familiarity with the topic, and their purpose for reading."

The teacher of reading models, coaches, provides support (scaffolding and fading) as needed then withdraws as the student gains mastery. A skilled reader analyzes and plans before reading to establish purpose and to recall prior knowledge. He monitors and thinks about what he is reading during reading and he evaluates and reinforces his thinking after reading. Applying the strategic reading process develops a reader who can extend his thinking, understanding, and reasoning abilities.

Please see the following checklist of components.

Before reading analyze and plan	Skilled readers respond	✓
Preview	Look over the text to be read	
Recall prior knowledge	What do I know about the subject?	
Identify goals	What am I expected to learn?	
Establish purpose	Read to answer the following question . . .	
Understand different ways of reading	Reading for enjoyment does not require detailed, close reading while reading for a test may	
Plan appropriate strategies	Does the text lend itself to analysis using a T-chart or rereading aloud using Readers Theatre activity?	
Predict	Who? What? Where? When? Why? How?	
During reading monitor and regulate comprehension	Skilled readers respond	✓
Focus on Biblical principle	What is God's truth in this text?	
Look back, reread	Read to answer the question or to clarify a response	
Read ahead to predict and clarify	Read to relate the text to your experiences	
Create mental images	What do you "see" as you read?	
Use text organization	Note the titles and subtitles	
Consult sources and/or take notes	Confirm what you are reading with another text Writing in your own words helps you to remember	
Look for relationships	How are the ideas or facts alike or different?	
Predict, revise, predict again	Continue your thinking as you read	
After reading evaluate and react	Skilled readers respond	✓
Fit new material to previous experience	Make a connection to what was read before about this particular person or event	
Summarize	The main ideas were . . .	
Organize	Fill in a graphic organizer or outline	
Reflect	Did I learn what I wanted to learn?	
Remember	What will I write about what I learned?	
Judge predictions	Was I correct? Why not?	

Anderson, Richard C., Elfrieda H. Hiebert, Judith A. Scott, and Ian A. G. Wilkinson. 1985. *Becoming a Nation of Readers: The Report of the Commission on Reading.* Champaign, IL: Center for the Study of Reading, University of Illinois at Urbana-Champaign, National Institute of Education, U.S. Department of Education, 13.

Methods & Strategies for Teaching Bible as Reader Program

For the teacher of the Bible as Reader program (BAR), the following methods and tools will guide and direct students in the process of reading, writing, and thinking. The methods and strategies are based on current reading research and traditional approaches. The goal of reading from the Bible is to increase a student's understanding of God's Word, to reflect and write using the truths of God's principles, and to reason Biblically from internal to the external, cause to effect.

The following basic methods of the Principle Approach®—the notebook method, the Four R's (research, reason, relate, record), key word studies using Webster's 1828 *Dictionary*, maps, and timelines are used in teaching the BAR program, but they have not been listed below because of their extensive explanations in other Foundation for American Christian Education publications—*The Noah Plan® Self-Directed Study*

in the Principle Approach, The Noah Plan Lessons for grades kindergarten through third grade, and the subject curriculum guides. The methods and strategies for BAR have been organized under the following five headings: vocabulary, comprehension and interpretation, reading and writing, remediation/enrichment, and evaluation.

The beginning sound/reading skills of phonemic awareness instruction are included under vocabulary and phonetic instruction using the Spalding Method® in chapter three of this guide. Additional cross-resources in this guide are the grade-level curriculum charts and the Guide for Writing Reading Lesson Plans in chapter one. At the end of the introduction, there are reviews of the latest research in reading instruction and methods for fluency, vocabulary, comprehension, and reading and writing.

1. Vocabulary

Concept/ Definition map*	Multiple meanings	Vocabulary word analysis*
Context clues	Phonemic awareness	Word map*
Dictionary	Three word parts	Word webs
Figurative language	Venn diagram*	Word wheels

2. Comprehension & Interpretation

Cause and effect organizer*	Picture graph		Sequence chain*	
Character chart—"People Who Impacted	Questioning strategies		Story circle	
History"*	• Levels of questions	• Think Aloud	Story map*	
Cyclical organizer	• QAR	• Reciprocal teaching* **	T-chart*	
Five mental actions	• Bloom's Taxonomy	• Think-Pair-Share	Timeline	
K-W-L chart*	SQ3R		Venn diagram*	

3. Reading & Writing

Paraphrasing from Scripture	Story map composition
Reason, relate, and record questions	Writing process in three types of passage structures

4. Remediation & Enrichment

Choral Reading		Oral reading*
Fluency Instruction		Readers Theatre**
• Teacher model	• Partner	Supplementary reading—home reading
• Student-adult	• Parent/home	Word wheels
• Choral		

5. Evaluation

Student profile*	Reading inventory

*Forms & **Samples in Appendix, *NPRG*, 126–139.

Vocabulary
Methods & Strategies for Teaching Bible as Reader Program

The knowledge of words is the gate of scholarship. (John Wilson)

Research tells us that most vocabulary is learned indirectly and some vocabulary must be taught directly. See "Vocabulary Instruction," (*NPRG*, xix–xx), a research article; and "The Guide for Writing Reading Lesson Plans," (*NPRG*, 24–25), an instruction chart. Some additional lessons to know are the following:

1. Key terms are introduced before reading to improve comprehension.

2. Charts or graphic organizers are used to fully explain and deepen understanding.

3. Concepts are built through elaboration over time.

4. Definitions do not teach students how to use a word or how to demonstrate a new concept. Minimize rote copying of definitions. (McKenna 2002, 36)

5. Phonics instruction helps the student to sound out a word to recognize if it is in his listening and speaking vocabulary.

6. Wide reading is encouraged as often as possible

7. "Vocabulary development is promoted by reading to students and having them read independently and silently both in and out of school." (Adams and Cerqui 1989, 13)

Vocabulary Methods and Strategies	Applications
Concept/definition maps are used to help enrich a student's understanding of a word or concept (Buehl 2001, 41). The graphic structure focuses the student's attention on key components of a definition. Steps: 1. Display blank form (*NPRG*, 128) 2. Write the concept or word to be defined in center block 3. Point out the questions. *What is it?* To what group, class or category does the word belong? 4. *What is it like?* Along the side of the paper write the properties or characteristics. 5. *What are some examples?* At the bottom give illustrations or examples. 6. *How is it defined?* Write a sentence to demonstrate understanding of the word or concept. For enrichment or to challenge the student, emphasize that his definition should include the category of the word, its properties or characteristics, and specific examples. This will require several sentences.	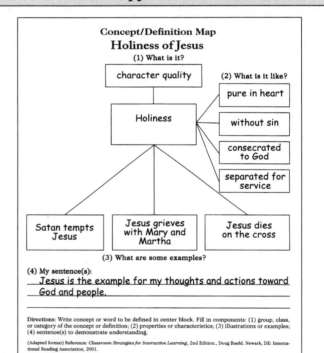
Context clues means using the information from the immediate or surrounding text to identify a word you don't know. There are six kinds of context clues (Robb 2004, 98): 1. *Synonyms* are words that mean the same as the new word. 2. *Antonyms* are words that mean the opposite of the word.	Examples of using the six kinds of context clues from Scripture: 1. Synonyms: "You have laid down precepts that are to be fully obeyed." (Psalm 119:4) "You have given me rules that I must obey." (Psalm 119:4, NIrV) 2. Antonyms: "God resists the proud but gives grace to the humble." (James 4:6)

Vocabulary Methods and Strategies	Applications
3. *Surrounding sentences* are clues in other sentences.	3. *Surrounding sentences:* Abraham was righteous. He believed God, was called God's friend and did what God asked. (James 2:23–24)
4. *Definitions* are statements of what a new word means.	4. *Definitions:* "The Word was God." (John 1:1)
5. *Examples* are specific examples of a new word.	5. *Examples:* "The wisdom that comes from heaven is first of all pure; then peace-loving, considerate, submissive." (James 3:17)
6. Repeated words are difficult words used more than once.	6. *Repeated words:* "[T]he true worshipper shall worship the Father in spirit and in truth: for the Father seeketh such to worship him. God is a spirit: and they that worship him must worship him in spirit and in truth." (John 4:23–24)
The *Dictionary* is used to help a student understand the terms. Provide more than a definition. Just copying without understanding is time wasted. Use the Vocabulary Word Analysis strategy (below in the chart) or the Webster's 1828 *Dictionary* word study method in *The Noah Plan® Self-Directed Study in the Principle Approach®*, 23–26.	The student writes a definition in his own words. Biblical principles are then deduced and recorded from the study. The written work is filed appropriately in his notebook and becomes a permanent record of learning and is available for future reference. See model, *NPSDS*, 23–26.
Figurative language is used throughout the Bible text but particularly in the Old Testament poetical books: Job, Psalms, Proverbs, Ecclesiastes, and Song of Solomon. Point out the vivid "figures of speech" the Hebrew poets used to create visual images. Figures of speech are variations of the literal or ordinary forms of expression, the intention being to make the thought more attractive or more striking (*NPEG*, Chapter 6, Prosody) For example: "My tongue is like the pen of a skillful writer." (Psalm 45)	The student's appreciation of language is enriched as he notes the writer's use of language to develop special effects. Use as a resource *The Noah Plan English Language Curriculum Guide*, Chapter 6, titled "Prosody," which includes a sample lesson plan for teaching figures of speech and gives definitions of *simile, metaphor, personification, hyperbole, onomatopoeia, rhythm,* and *alliteration*.
Multiple meanings use words in a variety of contexts. Draw two pictures to depict two different meanings for the same word or use the same word in different sentences, written or oral, depending on the age and ability of the students.	*Lie*, a falsehood. "believe a lie." (2 Thessalonians 2:11) *Lie*, be prostrate, down. "lie all night in sackcloth." (Joel 1:13) *Lie*, tell a falsehood. "lie not against the truth." (James 3:14)
Phonemic awareness is the awareness of the sounds (phonemes) that make up spoken words. It is a pre-reading skill that children need to become aware of how sounds in words work. Phonemic awareness training enhances subsequent phonics instruction or other reading instruction.	See the research article, Phonemic Awareness (*NPRG*, xv–xvi), and the Teaching and Learning Phonemic Awareness activities (*NPRG*, 96). In addition, teachers can provide experiences through literature, nursery rhymes, rhymes, and poems that focus on playing with sounds. For example use the Dr. Seuss books: *There's a Wocket in My Pocket* and *Hop on Pop*.

Vocabulary Methods and Strategies	Applications

Three types of word parts are prefixes, suffixes, and roots. Use the vocabulary from the Bible text to illustrate how prefixes and suffixes can be used to generate a large number of words or to analyze a word into its parts.

1. *Prefix*—a word part added to the beginning of a base word or word root that may change the meaning of the word

2. *Suffix*—a word part comes at the end of a base word or word root that may change the form of the word and what part of speech it is

3. *Root*—the main part of the word that carries the meaning

Introduce to illustrate how prefixes and suffixes can be used to generate a large number of words.

Word part	Meaning	Example
Prefix	*dis*=do the opposite	disobey
Suffix (nouns)	*ence*=quality or state	obedience
(verbs)	*ed*=past tense	obeyed
(adjectives)	*ent*=adjective	obedient
Roots	*obey*=to comply	obey

Lists of word parts are in the vocabulary section of *The Reading Teacher's Book of Lists*, Fry, Kress and Fountoukidis, 2000.

Venn diagram is a graphic organizer of overlapping circles that shows those features either unique or common to two or more concepts.

different **alike** **different**

Authority

Heaven **Christ is the head** **Earth**

1 Peter 3:22, Ephesians 1:20–23, Hebrews 1:3

Vocabulary word analysis is a tool for developing vocabulary and analyzing words. Use Webster's 1828 *Dictionary* to give the part of speech, etymology, definition, additional meanings, synonym and antonym (and homonym if applicable). Write a sentence using the word.

See example, (*NPRG*, 97), and use blank form (*NPRG*, 133).

Word maps give a student an opportunity to apply the definition to his own ideas and in his own words. The strategy uses the relative size of the circle to indicate the importance of ideas and lines to indicate relationships. The more important ideas have larger circle than the less important ideas. Lines from one circle to another indicate that the concepts in the connected circles are related in some way. See additional example using *blessing*, (*NPRG*, 98), and form (*NPRG*, 132).

Proverbs 1:1–7
The Purposes and Main Point

Teaches wisdom

For those who listen

Author: Solomon

Son of David

Increases discernment

Understanding between right and wrong

PROVERBS
Noun
Wise Sayings

Despised by fools

For those who fear the Lord

Requires respect for God

Vocabulary Methods and Strategies	Applications
Word webs are used to organize information, brainstorm ideas, and remember details. Make a box or circles and label the subject. Draw circles near the subject box or circle and connect with lines. Write details or words that relate to your subject in each circle. You might have two or three, or you might have many more. (Robb 2004, 425) 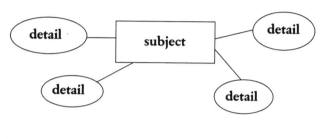	**God's Faithfulness Is Trustworthy** 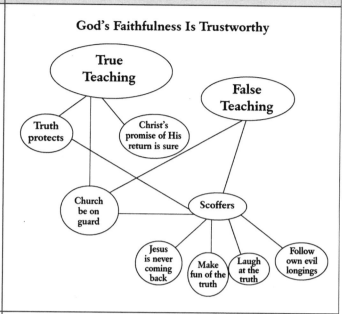
Word wheels are used to expand and enhance vocabulary. Write the word in the center of the wheel, then have the student write another word in each spoke of the wheel which is similar or opposite in meaning. Identify the synonyms and antonyms.

Iniquity

Synonyms	Antonyms
injustice	righteousness
sin	holiness
wickedness	
disobedience			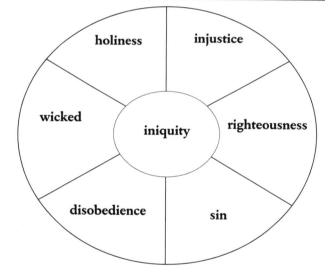

References:

Adams, Carole. 1998. *The Noah Plan English Language Curriculum Guide*. Chesapeake, VA: The Foundation for American Christian Education.

Adams, Carole and Elizabeth Youmans. 2004. *The Noah Plan® Self-Directed Study in the Principle Approach®*. Chesapeake, VA: The Foundation for American Christian Education.

Adams, Dave and Cicely Cerqui. 1989. *Effective Vocabulary Instruction*. Kirkland, WA: Reading Resources.

Buehl, Doug, 2001. *Classroom Strategies for Interactive Learning*, 2nd Ed., Newark, DE: International Reading Association.

Fry, Edward Bernard, Jacqueline E. Kress and Dona Lee Fountoukidis. 2000. The Reading Teacher's Book of Lists. 4th Ed. Upper Saddle River, NJ: Pearson Education.

McKenna, Michael C. 2002. *Help for Struggling Readers: Strategies for Grades 3–8*. New York, NY: The Guilford Press.

Robb, Laura. 2004. *Reader's Handbook*. Wilmington, MA: Houghton Mifflin Co.

Teaching & Learning Phonemic Awareness

Effective phonemic awareness instruction teaches a student to notice, think about, and work with (manipulate) the individual sounds in spoken language. The broad term *phonological awareness* refers to a general appreciation of the sounds of speech as distinct from their meaning and includes phonemic awareness. In addition to phonemes, phonological awareness activities can involve work with rhymes, words, syllables, and onsets (beginning) and rimes (ending).

Kindergarten and first grade schedules of activities are available in *Phonemic Awareness in Young Children* by Adams, Foorman, Lundberg, and Beeler (Adams 1998).

1. Develop the student's phonological awareness—the sounds of language. He needs to understand how speech is represented by print.

   • Model and demonstrate how to break short sentences into individual words—use manipulatives (chips, cards, etc.) to represent words and importance of order to meaning.

   • Develop awareness of individual sounds in words by clapping out syllables.

   • Listen for and generate rhymes.

2. Develop phonemic awareness—words and syllables are comprised of a sequence of elementary speech sounds.

   • Focus on sounds of words, not letters or spellings.

     T: How many sounds in the word *sun*?

     T: Let's try it together: /s/ /u/ /n/. How many? Good, three.

   • Focus attention and perception of isolated sounds.

     T: What is the first sound in *ham*?

     S: The first sound in *ham* is /h/.

   • Identify initial sounds and ending sounds

     T: What sound is the same sound in *sun, seal,* and *sat*?

     S: The first sound, /s/ is the same.

     T: What is the ending sound in *see, bee,* and *me*?

     S: The ending sound is /e/.

   • Blend phonemes into words.

     • Say initial sound, /m/ *ilk*, /s/ *at*.

     • Sound separate phonemes within words, /s/ /a/ /t/.

     • Say last sound, *k*/ /it/.

     • Break up words into component sounds, *e.g.,* /m/ oo/ /s/ =moose

3. Use blending and segmenting activities to develop the relationship between sounds in words. Use the letters of the alphabet to demonstrate to the student the connection between the sound and the letter. Use foam shaped letters for more tactile awareness.

   a. Blending

     T: What word is /p/ /i/ /g/? (Say the sound only.)

     S: /p/ /i/ /g/ is *pig*.

     T: Now let's use our letters to "write" the sounds in *pig*.

     T: (Spells *pig* with the letters.)

     T Now we will read the word *pig*.

   b. Segmentation

     T: How many sounds are in *sun*?

     S: /s/ /u/ /n/. Three sounds.

     T: Let's "write" the sounds in *sun* using the letters.

     T: Runs hand under the whole word. "Now we're going to read *sun*."

   • Provide frequent, brief practice.

References:

Adams, Marilyn Jager, Barbara R. Foorman, Ingvar Lundberg and Terri Beeler. 1998. *Phonemic Awareness in Young Children*. Baltimore, MD: Paul H. Brookes Publishing Co.

Vocabulary Word Analysis

The *vocabulary word analysis* is a tool used for developing the middle school student's vocabulary from the content of all subjects in the curriculum. It teaches students helpful ways to analyze words. Three to five words (depending upon the grade level) are assigned weekly as homework to be completed using Webster's 1828 *Dictionary*. The word analyses are checked and returned to students and the words are included on the weekly spelling test. Students must be able to spell the words, define them, and use them in a sentence. The student receives a Vocabulary Word Analysis form and a sample vocabulary word analysis and places them in his English notebook. The assignments are completed on notebook paper, one word analysis per sheet of paper. Returned work is filed in the vocabulary section of the English notebook as a record.

See blank form to use, *NPRG*, 133.

Sample Vocabulary Word Analysis

principle

1. **Part of Speech:**	Noun
2. **Etymology:** **root meanings and original languages**	Latin: principium—beginning
3. **Definition:**	The cause, source, or origin of any thing: That from which a thing proceeds
4. **It also means:**	Element Ground, foundation A general truth Tenet; that which is believed
5. **Synonym:**	Tenet
6. **Antonym:**	
7. **Homonym:**	Principal—a chief or head; one who takes the lead
8. **Write a sentence using the word:**	God's Principle of Individuality reveals the nature and character of God in His creation and creatures.

Word Map

Use *word mapping* to give students opportunity to apply the definition to their own ideas and in their own words.

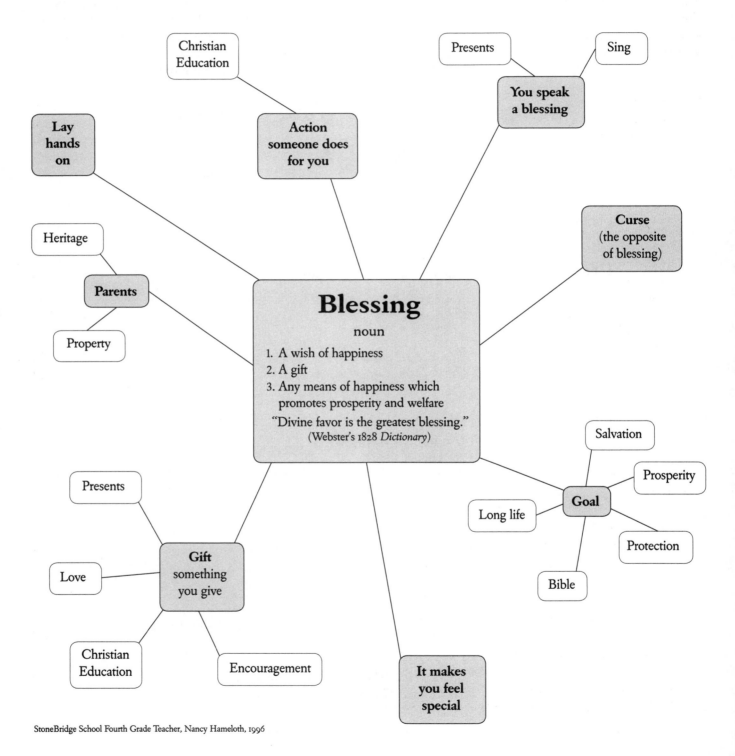

StoneBridge School Fourth Grade Teacher, Nancy Hameloth, 1996

Comprehension
Methods & Strategies for Teaching Bible as Reader Program

The virtue of books is the perfection of reason, which is indeed the happiness of man. (Richard de Bury)

Some important guidelines when teaching comprehension:

1. Preteach key terms to improve comprehension. This is repeated from the vocabulary section because of the importance of the principle. McKenna says, "Even if some of the terms are already familiar to the students, introducing them serves to activate prior knowledge." (McKenna 2002, 85)

2. Set the stage by building background for the story or passage for the reader. (See the Guide for Writing Lesson Plans for specific suggestions, *NPRG*, 24–25.)

3. Engage your student's attention and focus as he reads by providing specific purposes for reading. Enlist his help in the formulation of the purpose-setting activities.

4. After reading, have the student engage in reformatting the information. Direct him to use what he has read by writing a summary, filling in a chart or graphic organizer, or answering reason questions. As the student processes and uses the information, he increases his understanding. See Five Mental Actions Strategy below.

5. Challenge your student's level of thinking by the variety and level of questioning you use. McKenna's advice is to aim for higher levels of comprehension. "[U]nless inferences and critical judgments are included in classroom activities, comprehension may be superficial and inadequate." (McKenna 2002, 86) Questioning strategies are listed below.

Comprehension Methods and Strategies	Applications
Cause and effect organizer is helpful when you are organizing and synthesizing information. The organizer helps you to focus on two important elements of comprehension: what happens in the story and why it happened. The causes can be listed first, followed by effects. Or the effects can be listed first followed by causes. (See the form to use, *NPRG*, 127.)	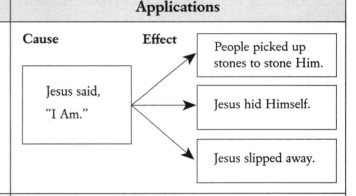
Character chart—"People Who Impacted History" chart is a tool for ordering and recording one's research and study of an individual to identify the hand of God in his life and his response. 1. Procedure: Use statements or quotes, which identify and describe each area. 2. Four areas of significance: •*Providential Setting* is when and where God placed this person. •*Spheres of Influence* are the influences responsible for his character development or training. •*Characterization* are the attributes of his personality, character, and physical appearance, which are marked or prominent. •*Contributions* are what the person did to forward or hinder the Gospel and liberty for individuals and nations.	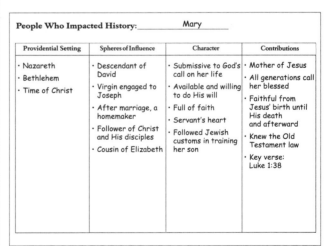 (See the blank form to use, *NPRG*, 129.)

Comprehension Methods and Strategies	**Applications**
Cyclical Organizer is used during or after reading to sequence events of a story or selection. The cyclical organizer shows the series of events in a circular formation. The student lists the events as they occur and is encouraged to go back to the story to verify his responses. After the summary statements are written, illustrations can be drawn to match the events. Number and use the drawings when retelling the story to the class. This is good practice for speaking skills. An example is the story of Noah from Genesis 6–9.	

1. God was sad that He had made humans and said, "I will destroy people and animals."

2. God was pleased with Noah.

3. God directed Noah to build an ark for his family and two of every living thing.

4. God brought the flood.

5. After the water went down, God told Noah and his family to come out of the ark.

6. God makes a covenant with Noah.

7. The rainbow is the sign that God will not destroy the world by flood ever again.

Five Mental Actions are explicitly taught thinking processes a student engages in as he listens and reads. "Children of any age learn to use the mental actions while listening, so they can apply them automatically when reading." (*WRTR*, 141)

1. Monitoring comprehension—checking for understanding words, phrases, and sentences. Student becomes active and engaged in learning.

2. Making connections—connecting prior information he has already learned to the stated information.

3. Making predictions—forecasting, supporting, and revising. Predicting the author's purpose, type of writing, topic and main idea.

4. Mentally summarizing—confirming or deriving the main idea using essential information.

5. Reformatting—categorizing (reorganizing) information into a new form such as list, outline, or graphic organizer to use or file for later use.

Teacher can write the mental actions on strips of paper and display in a pocket chart or order from the Spalding Education Foundation, 1-877-866-7451 or http://www.spalding.org.

Procedure for Teaching Five Mental Actions using Bible text Mark 14:27–31; 66–72	
Monitoring comprehension	Check understanding of new vocabulary and expressions • denial • disown • Nazarene • Galilean
Making Connections	Connect with prophecy from Zechariah 13:7. Use Psalm 23 to explore the relationship between a shepherd and his sheep.
Making predictions	When does Jesus predict Peter's denial? Where will Peter disown Christ? How is Peter affected?
Mentally summarize	When the rooster crowed, Peter remembered Jesus' words and he wept.
Reformatting using a new form	See sample using a sequence chain, *NPRG*, 103.

Comprehension Methods and Strategies	**Applications**

K-W-L chart is a method for engaging a student's thinking during the three phases of a reading lesson—preparing to read, reading, and summarizing what was read.

1. Before reading, check with the student to discover what he already knows about the topic.
   - Make connections with previously learning.
     Say, "Now we will be studying Samuel. Have we studied a person before that was dedicated to God? Yes, Samson."
   - After a brief introduction, formulate questions to focus student's attention as he reads.
2. What do I want to learn about Samuel? (see the chart.)
3. After reading, ask what was learned from the text and fill in the *L* column
   - During the discussion, pose additional questions. For example, "What was the response of the people when Samuel warned them about a king? What was in their hearts?"
   - The student can examine his thinking before, during, and after reading the text. He also links or makes a connection between new learning and old.

K **What I know**	W **What I want to learn**	L **What I learned**
Samuel was Hannah's son. He was dedicated to service for God. He heard from God. He was the last judge.	What is a judge? Why did the people want a king? Why was Samuel upset when the people wanted a king? What did God do?	One who is not faithful to God's commands can influence others to fall. God's plan was for Him to be the people's king. God wants us to choose to obey. Be careful for what you ask.

(See the blank form to use, *NPRG*, 128.)

Picture graphs are one way a student can represent his understanding of what he has read. Drawing pictures is recommended for kindergarten and first grade. A variation of a picture is the picture graph which uses symbols or symbolic pictures to generate a mental picture of the facts. The sample picture graph in column two illustrates the consequences of obeying or disobeying from Deuteronomy 11, "Love and Obey the Lord," in the NIrV Kids' Study Bible. "You will be blessed if you obey them. But you will be cursed if you don't obey them [commands]." (Deuteronomy 11:27–28) In a land of cursing the trees would be dead. In a land of blessing the trees would be growing.

Rules   Blessings / Forgiveness   Rules

Choices (Power)

Field of CURSES   Field of BLESSINGS

Jasmine T.

Questioning strategies extend thinking and deepen the understanding of the text. "[S]tudents learn what to focus on by the type of questions they are asked. Therefore, teachers must consciously ask questions that go beyond the literal level and lead students into higher level thinking." (Hinson 2003, 22) In addition to teacher-generated questions are those developed by the student. Hinson continues, "When students are in charge of the questions, they take control of information and become active learners. Students must be taught to question themselves about their learning. They must learn about the levels of questions and practice asking questions from all levels." (Hinson 2003, 22)*

Classroom methods that promote independent learning include the following: (See discussion and examples, *NPRG*, 102, 104–107)
- SQ3R
- Levels of Questions
- Question-Answer Relationships (QAR)
- Bloom's Taxonomy
- Think Aloud

Strategies that improve comprehension of students working with partners or small groups:
- Reciprocal Teaching (*NPRG*, 107; sample & form, 135)
- Think-pair-share (*NPRG*, 108)

Comprehension Methods and Strategies	Applications
SQ3R is a strategy that takes time but is very effective in improving comprehension because students are allowed to break the reading text into manageable parts. (Sadler 2001, 62)	Steps: S–Survey, Q–Question, R–Read, R–Recite, R–Review. For the procedure, see *NPRG*, 104.
Sequence chain is used to organize information in a chronological or sequential order. They are useful for organizing events that have a specific beginning and end. Sequential patterns are usually linear. The form in the Appendix can be adapted for the student who can write or one who draws his events. (See sample, *NPRG*, 103; blank form to use, *NPRG*, 132.)	Title: Jonah learns to obey God sent a big storm. → The big fish swallowed Jonah. → Jonah asked God for forgiveness. He obeyed God. → He went to Nineveh. → Jonah told the people about God. Sean B.
Story circle is a strategy that helps a student's comprehension, discussion, and summarizing skills. Procedure: The teacher models the technique by drawing a circle on the board or on an overhead transparency. The circle is divided into the number of parts necessary to tell the story. The number will vary based on the age of the child and the complexity of the story. Number the sections to read clockwise. After reading, discuss the events, recalling the sequence and record on lines outside the circle. The student illustrates each event inside the circle segments. After the student has mastered the strategy, let him draw his own circle or provide a form.	Joshua The Last Supper They met in Jerusalem / The friends ate together Jesus began to sing / the friends were sad
Story map identifies the central structure and content of a story in order to recall the important parts and thus be able to think critically about the story. Being aware of the explicit structure of a story is an aid to summarizing information. The story map asks the student to identify the following elements: • Title—the name that identifies or describes the story • Setting—the time, place, and context in which the story took place • Characters—the main individuals involved • Problem—the conflict the main character(s) tries to resolve or what goal the main character(s) sets • Events—story incidents or how the main character(s) try to accomplish the goal • Solution—the resolution, conclusion, outcome • Biblical Principle—truth demonstrated or revealed	Student: _____ Teacher: Mrs. Shirley Class: Bible as Reader Grade: 2 Date: Quarter One, Week 5 **Story Map** Title: Jesus Feeds the Five Thousand Setting: A mountainside in Bethsaida Characters: Jesus, the apostles, Philip, and Andrew, a boy with a lunch **Problem(s):** There was no food to feed the crowd who had followed Jesus to listen to his teaching about God's kingdom. **Event(s):** 1. Jesus saw a large crowd and felt deep concern. 2. He taught them until late in the day. 3. The people were hungry and there was no food. 4. The disciples found five loaves and two fish. 5. Jesus blessed the food and fed all the 5000 people. 6. Twelve baskets of leftovers were picked up by the disciples. **Solution(s):** Jesus prayed to his heavenly father and performed a miracle. **Biblical Principle(s):** Jesus is God's Son and has authority over all things. He can do a lot with the little we have to give Him. (See the blank form to use, *NPRG*, 130.)

Comprehension Methods and Strategies	Applications

T-chart makes a comparison and a contrast between two topics. When the student compares and contrasts two things, he thinks about how they are alike and how they are different. For example, when studying the Great Commandment the student looks at two kinds of love—human love vs. Godly love. When reading the beatitudes, he compares and contrasts the need and the blessing Jesus promises.

(See the blank form for your use, *NPRG*, 131.)

Matthew 5:1–11

Jesus Gives Blessings
The Sermon on the Mount

Need	Blessing
Spiritually needy	Kingdom of heaven
Sad	Comforted
Free of pride	Give the earth
Hungry and thirsty for right	Filled
Show kindness and mercy	Receive mercy
Hearts that are pure	See God
Peace	Called children of God
Suffering for doing right	Kingdom of heaven
Teased and hurt and lied about	Great reward in heaven

Timeline is a ordering of events in chronological sequence. It is useful for organizing events that have specific beginning and end like the sequence chain discussed earlier.

(See the Christian History of Reading Timeline, *NPRG*, 48–53.)

Timeline of Mark's Gospel
Jesus in Action and Power

A.D. 26	John baptizes Jesus
	Satan tempts Jesus in the desert
A.D. 26–27	Jesus preaches
A.D. 28	Jesus chooses twelve disciples
A.D. 29	Jesus feeds the five thousand
A.D. 30	Jesus is crucified, rises again, and ascends

Venn diagram is a graphic organizer of two overlapping circles used to represent information that is being compared and contrasted. The diagram provides a student with notes to refer to as he discusses the text or writes about it.

different   alike   different

COMPARE AND CONTRAST LUKE AND JOHN

LUKE
• Author: doctor, Greek, Gentile Christian
• Written for Greeks
• Christ presented as the Son of Man

GOSPELS
Tell the story of Jesus Christ

JOHN
• Author: apostle, "Son of Thunder," brother of James
• Written to new Christians
• Jesus is the Son of God, yet fully God

Sample **Sequence Chain**

Title   Peter's Denials (Mark 14:27–31; 66–72)

Peter says he will never turn away → Peter in courtyard warming himself → 1st denial, servant recognizes him

2nd denial at entrance of courtyard → 3rd denial before rooster crowed → Peter wept

(See the blank form to use, *NPRG*, 132.)

References:

Hinson, Bess, Editor. 2003. *New Directions in Reading Instruction, Revised*. Newark, DE: International Reading Association.
McKenna, Michael C. 2002. *Help for Struggling Readers: Strategies for Grades 3–8*. New York, NY: The Guilford Press.
Sadler, Charlotte Rose. 2001. *Comprehension Strategies for Middle Grade Learners*. Newark, DE: International Reading Association.
Spalding, Romalda. 2003. *The Writing Road to Reading*®. Phoenix, AZ: Spalding Education International.

Comprehension—SQ3R

The virtue of books is the perfection of reason, which is indeed the happiness of man. (Richard de Bury)

Learning from reading is facilitated more by time spent recalling what has been read than by rereading. Following the five steps of SQ3R can help a student process and remember what he reads. This technique gives you a purpose for reading. Practice regularly for these steps to become a habit.

Survey—Question—Read—Recite—Review	
Survey the text before you read	• Read the title—Focus your mind on the topic. • Read the introduction—What is the author's purpose? • Read the main headings—These are the main ideas. • Read the summary—What was the author's conclusion? • Read the questions at the end—What did the writer think was important? • Notice any pictures, charts, or tables. • This survey provides a frame of reference and gives the organization of the text.

Question
while you are
surveying
	• Turn headings from the survey step into questions.
	  1. When learning this technique, it is best to write out your questions in your own words. (See example below.)
	  2. Formulate your own questions using the 5 W's—Who, What, When, Where, Why, and How.
	  3. Questioning keeps your mind actively searching for answers. You are not simply looking at words.
	• This example is from Mark 2 in the NIrV text.
	  1. The first title in bold is "**Jesus Heals a Man Who Could Not Walk.**"
	  2. You could ask: "Who is this man? Why could he not walk? How will Jesus heal him? When will the man be healed?"
	  3. There are additional questions in a study helps section enclosed in the middle of the text. You should also read these as you survey.

Read selectively	• Read to answer your questions. • Use your own words for the answers to understand and comprehend more fully. • Adjust your speed or rate to fit the difficulty of the passage. • Stop and reread parts that are not clear. • Read a section at a time.
Recite at the end of each section	• Stop and recite the answers to the questions. • Look back at the text if you are not sure. • Listen to your answers. Are they complete? If not, don't continue until you are correct. • Write the answers if this reinforces your memory. Record key facts and phrases as needed for each question.

Review
is ongoing
	• At the end of the chapter go back over your questions from all the headings.
	• If you cannot answer the questions, look back and refresh you memory.
	• Review using a variety of tools and methods: summary paragraphs, flash cards, oral recitation, graphic organizer, or a tape recorder.
	• Tape recorder method using a question and answer format:
	  • Record the question and then pause long enough for the answer to be given.
	  • Record the answer.
	  • Play the tape; hear the question and say the answer in the pause time.
	  • Hear yourself give the previously taped answer to check your accuracy.

Comprehension Questioning Strategies

How do you know so much about everything?—was asked of a very wise and intelligent man; and the answer was, "By never being afraid or ashamed to ask questions as to anything of which I was ignorant." (Jacob Abbott)

The purpose of the questioning strategies is to extend thinking and deepen the understanding of the text and to model self-questioning for students.

The following methods are listed under "Questioning strategies" in section 2, Comprehension and Interpretation, *NPRG*, 91.

Levels of Questions

Asking questions at various levels of thinking gives the teacher an opportunity to encourage thinking from all the students and to check the depth of their understanding.	The following is one way to think of questions in terms of three fundatmental levels of comprehension. (McKenna 2002, 97)

Reading the lines	**Literal** questions require recall of facts stated in the text.
Reading between the lines	**Inferential** questions are based on facts but not directly stated in the text. The reader uses the facts in the text to infer the answer. He makes connections among the facts presented to reach a conclusion.
Reading beyond the lines	**Critical** questions require the student to form value judgments. The questions usually target whether the text was well written, whether certain topics should have been included, or if the views of the author were biased or objective. A hint is to insert the word *should* to elevate the question to the critical level. McKenna says there are other ways, but using *should* is surefire! (McKenna 2002, 98)
Examples	Mark 1 **Literal:** Who baptized Jesus? **Inferential:** What did Jesus look like after baptism? **Critical:** Should John have baptized Jesus? Why?

Question-Answer Relationships (QAR)

This strategy helps students to recognize the four possible areas in which answers can be found—right there, putting it together, on my own, and writer and me. Procedure: Teacher defines and models. • Reads a story or passage and questions the student using the four types of QARs. • Points out the information needed to answer the questions.	Classify the questions by asking: 1. Is the information "right there" plainly stated? 2. Does the answer require the reading of information in several places and putting the information together? 3. Can you draw from your own knowledge and experience to answer? 4. Can you combine your background information with information from the story to answer? Student generates. After the student understands the differences, ask him to generate his own questions. (Sadler 2002, 59) The four areas are further explained in the chart below.

Right there	The answer is found in one sentence in the text that you can point to: the student is answering literal-level questions.
Putting it together	These are inferential questions that require the student to make connections among several sentences in the text. The student must think and search the text.

On my own	The student is on his own. He must use his experience. What does he already know? This category includes critical-level questions.
Writer and me	The answer is not in the text but must come from the reader's own background.
Examples	Job 1 **Right There:** Where did Job live? **Putting It Together:** Why was Job worried about his children? **On My Own:** In what ways have you been tested? **Writer and Me:** If you were in Job's place, what would you have been thinking about yourself?

Bloom's Taxonomy

In 1956, Benjamin Bloom created a classification of levels of intellectual behavior important in learning. The taxonomy provides a structure for categorizing questions from the simplest (recall) to the most complex (evaluating information). Bloom identified six levels: knowledge, comprehension, application, analysis, synthesis, and evaluation. These levels are still useful today as you develop the critical thinking skills of your student. (Bloom, 1956)

A useful tool is a handheld 5 x 7 inch flip chart with key words and question stems. You can make your own chart from Dr. Bloom's list or order from the website or bookstore. *Quick Flip Questions for Critical Thinking*, developed by Linda G. Barton, 1977. Edupress, Inc., PO Box 883, Dana Point, CA: 92629. www.edupressinc.com.

The following are examples using Dr. Bloom's levels.

Level	Examples
1. **Knowledge**	Recall facts, terms, basic concepts and answers. Key words: define, label, list, name, relate, state
2. **Comprehension**	Understanding facts, interpret, predict consequences. Key words: compare, contrast, demonstrate, infer, explain, relate
3. **Application**	Use information, concepts, and theories in new situations. Solve problems. Key words: apply, build, choose, develop, solve, identify, plan
4. **Analysis**	Make inferences and find evidence to support generalizations. Key words: analyze, categorize, classify, examine, survey
5. **Synthesis**	Use old ideas to create new ones. Predict and draw conclusions. Create a new pattern or propose alternative solutions. Key words: compile, invent, improve, modify, construct, suppose
6. **Evaluation**	Make judgments about the value of ideas or materials. Key words: criticize, interpret, conclude, defend, prioritize, value
Examples	**Knowledge:** Name the disciples who questioned Jesus in John 15. **Comprehension:** Summarize the reaction of the disciples when Jesus predicted His betrayal in John 16. **Application:** How did Jesus demonstrate His love to the disciples? (John 15:13–14) **Analysis:** Explain what Jesus meant when He said, "I am the true vine," in John 15? **Synthesis:** Can you suggest some of the other miraculous signs Jesus performed but were not recorded in John 21:25? **Evaluation:** How would you explain the difference in Judas and Peter's response to betraying Jesus? (Matthew 27, John 21)

Think Aloud

Think aloud strategy can help a student to understand the thought process that takes place while reading. "This strategy helps students recognize that they should be thinking about various things related to the text as they read." (Sadler 2001, 65) Procedure:

"[A] teacher or student verbalizes the specific mental steps used to perform a comprehension task. Think alouds can be effective to clarify information in difficult reading materials, to create a visual image for written material, to connect background experiences to new information, and to recognize other clues that will help, such as pictures, graphics, and bold and italicized words." (Hinson 2000, 8)

Example	**On the Road to Emmaus** (Luke 24:13–35)
	• When I read verse 14 in this passage, I picture in my head the two men walking and talking and a third man joins them. I wonder at their response. How do they look? What are they saying?
	• This is a new phrase in verse 25, "slow of heart." How can I find out what it means?
	• This part in verse 27 is not clear. "[B]eginning with Moses and all the Prophets, he explained . . . the Scriptures." Should I read it again or just keep going in case it is explained later?

Reciprocal Teaching

This strategy allows students to begin to work together and to teach each other as they take over the discussion. (Sadler, 2001, 23) Students are taught four strategies: predicting, question generating, clarifying, and summarizing. Then students take charge and make the predictions, ask the questions, clarify difficult passages, and make summaries. Rich discussion and interaction that focuses on comprehension enables students to take control of their learning. (Hinson 2000, 23)

Procedure:
• Teacher models and demonstrates the four strategies.
• Students read short passages, observe, and practice.
• Students take turns being the teacher in their small group. The teacher keeps the group on task as it moves from one strategy to the next and from one page to the next.
• Teacher moves from group to group, monitoring their activity.
• Rich dialogue and discussion enhances student's comprehension. (Hinson 2003, 23)

Predict	Make an educated guess about what will happen in the passage.
Question	Ask a question about the reading. Ask questions that require inferring and evaluation.
Clarify	Define words or phrases that are hard to understand. Make sure the group understands before moving on.
Summarize	Restate what was read in a summary. The summary can be short statements or it can take the form of an outline, a word web, a T-chart, a sequence chain, timeline, or poster.
Examples	Luke 8:1–3
	Predict: Jesus did not travel alone. I predict that others were with him.
	Question: Who were the women? Why were the women helping him? What was their place in his ministry?
	Clarify: What does the phrase, "the good news of the kingdom" mean?
	In summary: This story tells us Jesus took his message that their savior had come to people in towns and villages. In addition to the disciples, Jesus traveled with women he had healed. They helped support him with their money. Jesus respected women.
	Prediction (predict the next passage): I predict that Jesus is going to teach using a parable.
	Continue with question, clarify, and summarize for the next section of text. Choose manageable portions of Scripture depending on the age and ability of the group.
	(See the Reciprocal Reading Teacher Key & Student form, *NPRG*, 135.)

Think-Pair-Share

"This is a partner activity that allows students to work together to check for comprehension." (Sadler 2001, 65) Teachers need to allow for reflection time to allow students to process information and reflect on it at each step.

Procedure:
Read a passage or selection. Select a question or topic for discussion.
1. Think silently for two minutes
2. Pair off and share thinking with a partner
3. Share thinking with the whole group

(Hinson 2000, 8)

References:

Barton, Linda G., developed from Bloom's Taxonomy. 1977. *Quick Flip Questions for Critical Thinking*. Dana Point, CA: Edupress.

Bloom, Benjamin S., Ed. 1956. *Taxonomy of educational objectives: The classification of educational goals: Handbook I, cognitive domain.* New York: Longmans, Green.

Hinson, Bess, Editor. 2000. *New Directions in Reading Instruction, Revised*. Newark, DE: International Reading Association.

McKenna, Michael C. 2002. *Help for Struggling Readers: Strategies for Grades 3–8*. New York, NY: The Guilford Press.

Sadler, Charlotte Rose. 2001. *Comprehension Strategies for Middle Grade Learners*. Newark, DE: International Reading Association.

Reading and Writing
Methods & Strategies for Teaching the Bible as Reader Program

It seems to me that in a literate culture like ours, where most of us know how to read and where books are available,
the Biblical mandate is to keep on reading what will open the Holy Scriptures to you more and more,
and to keep praying for Bible-saturated writers.
There are many great old books to read, but each generation needs its own writers to make the message fresh.
Read and pray. And then obey. (John Piper 1997, 59)

Better readers are generally better writers. The reading-writing connection needs to be emphasized in all classrooms. "'Reading and writing inform and improve each other—the more students write the better their reading will become. The more students read, the better their writing will become. As students write and begin to believe in themselves as real writers for real purposes, they will read more widely and deeply' (Silvers 1986, 39, 684–688). And, reading with the eyes of a writer helps students see what it takes to make engaging and accessible texts for a wide variety of readers." (Rasinski 2000, 2) See *NPRG*, xxiii for additional research and discussion on the reading and writing connection.

Reading & Writing Methods and Strategies	Applications
Paraphrasing from Scripture is a restatement of a text, passage, or work giving the meaning in another form. To paraphrase from Scripture is to write an original summary of the important thought of the Bible text. See *NPRG*, 111–112 for a discussion of the purpose, historic method, and principles of paraphrasing from Scripture. See also the sample form, *NPRG*, 112.	**Paraphrase Chart** **Scripture**: A soft answer turneth away wrath; but grievous words stir up anger. (Proverbs 15:1) **My Paraphrase**: "A harsh word stirs up anger," means if someone says something mean to you, don't say something mean back because it will eventually cause a fight. **Relate to My Life** I can say something nice to someone and it is hard for them to say something mean back. (Third grader)
Reason, relate, and record are three of the steps in Principle Approach® learning. The teacher guides the student to reason from Biblical truths and to apply them to people or events being studied. She asks leading questions which bridge story content with the Biblical principle and which relate to the student's life. He records his thinking and files the copy in his notebook.	Sample assignment for second grade: read Deuteronomy 11, "Love and Obey the Lord," in the NIrV Kids' Study Bible. Teacher has students focus on the blessings and the curses in the text by asking the following: • What are the conditions of the covenant between God and Israel? • What was Israel's part of the covenant? • What were the blessings and what were the curses? Lead the student to reason and relate by asking the questions: • What are some results of choosing to obey? • What are some results of choosing to rebel? • What are some choices facing you presently or in the future? The student records his answers and files the page in his notebook.

Reading & Writing Methods and Strategies	Applications

Story map composition uses the story map as a framework for composition. The student first identifies the main elements of the narrative—setting, characters, problem, events or plot, the solution or resolution and the Biblical principle. He then uses the information to write his composition.

This story map was developed in a third grade class studying the story of Noah.

(See the blank form for your use, *NPRG*, 130.)

Story Map form:

Student: _____ Teacher: _____
Class: Bible as Reader Grade: 3 Date: Quarter **2** , Week **3**

Story Map
Title: God Makes a Covenant with Noah
Setting: Earth, after creation
Characters: Noah, his children, animals

Problem(s): The flood destroyed everything

Event(s):
1. Everything is drowned.
2. God blesses Noah and his family.
3. God encourages them to have more children
4. God makes a covenant with Noah and future generations and every living thing.

Solution(s): The sign of the covenant is God's rainbow.

Biblical Principle(s): God keeps His promises.

The following composition was written from the story map.

Class composition — January 10, 2002
Informative-Narrative — Genesis 9: 1–17

God Makes a Covenant with Noah

God made a covenant with Noah and his children and the animals that lived on the earth. God said, "I will never flood the earth again." Noah was standing in front of the ark when God said, "Noah, you are going to have control over all things."
"Thank you, God," said Noah. "I will obey you. I love you."
"We do too," added Noah's sons. "Thank you," they added. God also told Noah that when he sees a rainbow it will be a sign of God's covenant with Noah and his sons and all living things.

Writing process in three types of passage structures is a method introduced using the procedures from the section titled, "The Writing Lesson." (Spalding 2003, 107–120) The teaching sequence begins with related sentences, attributes of paragraphs and the stages in the writing process. The teacher moves from paragraph construction to the composition of the three types—narratives, informative (expository) and narrative-informatives.

During the Bible as Reader lessons, the students identify the elements of the three basic types of text structure: narrative, informative (expository), and a combination—the informative-narrative. The student uses the elements of each type as a guide as he writes his compositions using the characters, events, and information in the Bible text. There are sample lessons in BAR section of *The Noah Plan® Lessons* for second and third grades. (See teacher key & student forms, *NPRG*, 134–135.)

References:

Piper, John. 1997. *A Godward Life*. Sisters, OR: Multnomah Publishers, Inc.

Rasinski, Timothy V. et al., editors. 2000. *Developing Reading-Writing Connections: Strategies from the Reading Teacher*. Newark, DE: International Reading Association. (Also quoting: Silvers, 1986.)

Silvers, P. 1986. *Process Writing and the Reading Connection: The Reading Teacher*.

Spalding, Romalda. 2003. *The Writing Road to Reading: The Spalding Method® for Teaching Speech, Spelling, Writing, and Reading*, 5th Edition. Phoenix, AZ: Spalding Education International.

Paraphrasing from Scripture

Definition:

Paraphrase is a restatement of a text, passage, or work giving the meaning in another form. To paraphrase from Scripture is to write an original summary of the important thought of the Bible text.

Purpose:

"Perspicuity is that quality of writing or language which readily presents precise ideas to the mind of another. Noah Webster, the 'man who defined America,' acknowledged it as 'the first excellence of writing or speaking.'" (*NPSDS* 2003, 27)

"**Perspicuity**, *n.* [L. *per* and *speculum*, a glass.] Clearness to mental vision; easiness to be understood; freedom from obscurity or ambiguity; that quality of writing or language which readily presents to the mind of another the precise ideas of the author." (Webster's 1828 *Dictionary*)

Historic Method:

1. The Bible:

    Also it shall be, when he sits on the throne of his kingdom, that he shall *write for himself* a *copy* of this *law* in a *book*, from the one before the priests, and it shall be with him, and he shall *read* it all the days of his life, that he may *learn* to fear the LORD his God and be careful to *observe* all the *words* of this law and these statutes, that his *heart* may not be lifted above his brethren, that he may not *turn aside from commandment* to the right or to the left, and that he may *prolong* his *days* in his kingdom, he and his *children* in the midst of Israel.
    (Deuteronomy 17:18–20, NKJV; emphasis added)

    Matthew Henry's *Commentary on the Whole Bible*, 1706:

    Though the king might be presumed to have very fair copies by him from his ancestors . . . Though he had secretaries about him whom he might employ to write this copy, and could write in a better hand must write his own copy for himself, . . . to labor and study, that he might thereby be obliged to take particular notice of every part of the law and by writing it might imprint it in his mind.

    Note, it is of great use for each of us to write down what we observe as most affecting and edifying to us, out of the Scriptures and good books, and out of the sermons we hear.

A prudent pen may go far towards making up the deficiencies of the memory, and the furnishing of the treasures of the good householder with things new and old. . . .

And we must persevere in the use of the written word of God as long as we live. Christ's scholars never learn above their Bibles. . . .

His writing and reading were all nothing if he did not reduce to practice what he wrote and read. The word of God is not designed merely to be an entertaining subject of speculation, but to be a commanding rule of conversation.
(Henry 1706, 797)

2. American colonial scholarship:

    In the copybooks of James Madison, the architect of the United States constitution, one finds the paraphrase method familiar to colonial American students. Passages from Scripture, literature classics, and philosophers such as John Locke are found in Madison's notebooks.

    Wishing to master the art of writing with clarity and conciseness, Madison sometimes rewrote the authors' sentences in an effort to make them clearer and more precise. He also strove to summarize clearly the main ideas of the writer when they appeared in a particularly involved passage.
    (Swanson 1992, 57)

Principles Gleaned from Writing or Paraphrasing Scripture:

1. Over time, many portions of Scripture will be noted.

2. Students will learn to fear the Lord (Deuteronomy 17:19).

3. Students will learn to follow and obey God's Word (v. 19–20).

4. A spirit of humility will be imparted (v. 20).

5. God promises prolonged life for the writer and his family and his children (v. 20).

6. By paraphrasing verses or passages of Scripture, students are called to a standard of composition by imitating the beauty, meter, vocabulary, and literary value of the Scriptures, our highest model of language.

7. Paraphrasing clarifies the meaning of Scripture.

8. Thinking and reasoning skills are challenged and refined.

9. Paraphrasing builds perspicuity for clear, concise writing and speaking, aiding the student to be ready always to give a defense for the hope that lies within him.

Method:

1. Assign passage or verse to students in the reading class where the Bible is used as a primary reader beginning in the third grade. This is an excellent exercise for adults, as well.

2. Students should copy the assigned verse or passage from the Bible. Unknown vocabulary should be defined on the paper. The student's paraphrase then follows.

3. Have students complete as seat work while the teacher works tutorially with the individual readers; or conclude the reading lesson by paraphrasing the key Scripture verse.

4. Assign as homework. Include Vocabulary Word Analysis (*NPRG*, 97) or Word Studies (*NPSDS*, 23–26) in conjunction with the assignment.

5. Students could paraphrase a book of the Bible over the course of the year and illustrate their work. They could paint or design illuminated letters, then write in calligraphy. The book of Proverbs would make a great beginning place.

Reference:

Swanson, Mary-Elaine. 1992. *The Education of James Madison: A Model for Today*. Montgomery, AL: The Hoffman Center for the Family.

Paraphrase Chart	
Scripture	**My Paraphrase**
Relate to My Life	

(See sample, *NPRG*, 109.)

Remediation & Enrichment

The law of the LORD is perfect, converting the soul: the testimony of the LORD is sure, making wise the simple.
The statutes of the LORD are right, rejoicing the heart: the commandment of the LORD is pure, enlightening the eyes.
(Psalms 19:7–8)

Providing for the individuality of the learner is based on an understanding of the student's instructional needs—remedial or enrichment. Teachers plan for exceptions but need to keep in mind the needs of all students.

Often a deeper understanding of learning difficulties will lead to the creation of strategies and compensations that can help other children in the classroom as well, because each student is bringing his or her own unique set of strengths and weaknesses while celebrating strengths. With time and persistence, a classroom of differences can become a classroom of learners, and a rewarding experience for all those involved. (Hinson 2000, 15)

Reading appreciation enriches the mind. Supplying related readings in biographies, poetry, and plays can supply above level readers with enrichment.

Remediation & Enrichment	Applications
Choral reading is group reading aloud which helps to develop oral fluency and presentation manners before an audience. Choral reading may also by used by two students, one of who usually is a better reader and serves as a model during the reading.	Example of choral reading procedure using the Twenty-third Psalm from the *Bay Psalm Book*—first book published in America, is on *NPRG*, 68.
Fluency instruction helps students become more fluent readers. Fluency is the ability to read a text accurately and quickly. It is important because it frees students to understand what they read. A teacher can help his students by providing them with a model of his own reading and by having them repeatedly read passages as he offers guidance. Comprehension is slowed when the brain is busy recognizing the words (decoding) and understanding their meaning. The memory is overloaded and the interpretation of the text is insufficient. As the student practices he develops a broader perceptual span or word identification span, which allows taking in more information in a single fixation. (See Fluency Report, Chapter 3, 3–9. National Reading Panel. December 2000.) Additional information on fluency is in the research section, *NPRG*, xvii–xviii.	**Activities in the classroom are the following:** • Teacher models. Teacher reads and student rereads on his own. Repeated reading of text four times is sufficient to improve fluency. This number holds true for each type below. • Student-adult reading. Student reads one-on-one with an adult. • Choral reading. (See discussion above.) • Partner reading. Paired students take turns reading aloud to each other. More fluent readers can be paired with less fluent readers. The stronger reader reads first. Or two readers of equal ability can practice rereading after hearing the teacher read the text. **Parent Reading/Home Reading** • Monitor fluency practice with short passages over time. • Allow 15–30 minutes depending on child's needs • Discuss the reading selection to promote comprehension. Ask who, what, where, why, when, and how questions. • Check progress by determining if child can decode text and comprehend it at the same time. • Poor expression indicates the need for more practice.

Remediation & Enrichment	Applications
Oral reading is reading aloud and is taught in beginning reading instruction. Reading with the remedial student gives the teacher an opportunity to correct inappropriate strategies and provide correction and support. Oral reading for enrichment purposes can include dramatic reading, Scripture, speeches, and poetry.	Methods of teaching oral reading are on *NPRG*, 115. An oral reading checklist in located on *NPRG*, 141.
Readers Theatre is an activity for repeated oral reading practice. The students rehearse and perform before their peers or an audience a dialogue-rich script derived from the Bible text.	See on *NPRG*, 146, a skit, "God and Satan," written by a fifth grade student. Job is the topic of the conversation. The students had many opportunities to read and reread the story of Job in preparation for writing and delivering the skit.
Supplementary reading—home reading assignments provide oral reading practice with parents. See *NPRG*, 67 for a discussion and a bookmark template on *NPRG*, 137.	Principle Approach® methodology uses a notebook and the teacher as the lively textbook. Therefore, much practice in reading textbooks is limited. The home reading assignment is an opportunity for developing fluency in developing readers. Parents become partners in the learning experience.

References:

Hinson, Bess, editor. 2000. *New Directions in Reading Instruction, Revised.* Newark, DE: International Reading Association. Quoting Randall Fielding, interview published online, 1999.

National Reading Panel. December 2000. *Teaching Children to Read: An Evidence-Based Assessment of the Scientific Research Literature on Reading and Its Implications for Reading Instruction.* National Institute for Literacy, U. S. Deptartment of Health and Human Services. NIH Pub. No. 00-4754.

Oral Reading

Historically written or printed text was intended to be read aloud. To pronounce words, letters, and sounds is the first definition of *read* in Webster's 1828 *Dictionary*.

Read: 1. To *utter* or *pronounce* written or printed *words*, *letters* or *characters* in the proper order; to repeat the names or utter the *sounds* customarily annexed to words, letters or characters; as,

to read a written or printed discourse; to read the letters of an alphabet; to read figures; to read the notes of music, or to read music. (emphasis added)

"Today . . . oral reading is emphasized in beginning reading instruction to help link printed text to speech." (Harris 1995, 173) "The long-term objective of reading instruction is for students to read silently, accurately, and with comprehension. However, long-term objectives do not necessarily determine how to begin instruction." (Carnine 1990, 39)

Beginning Reading Instruction

1. Teach oral reading, then silent reading.

2. "During early reading instruction, oral reading enables the teacher to keep students actively practicing reading and, in addition, provides information about problems the students may be having. This feedback allows the teacher to correct inappropriate strategies, thereby helping students develop the skill necessary to become successful readers." (Ibid.)

Mid- and Late-Primary Instruction

1. Students should read silently most of the time.

2. Use oral reading for teaching specific skills such as reading with expression or in making periodic checks of students' decoding ability.

3. "While oral reading does not interfere with improvements in reading rate and comprehension during early instruction, it could interfere at later stages if ample silent reading practice is not provided." (Ibid.)

4. Reading Scripture

5. Choral reading

6. Reading parts in scripts or plays, narrative, and skits

Intermediate and Upper Grades

Reading aloud:

1. Scripture

2. Notices, instructions, announcements

3. To inform, amuse, or prove a point

4. Anecdotes or stories

5. Prepared speeches

6. Poetry, dramas, etc.

Characteristics of the Good Oral Reader

1. He prepares the reading in advance.

2. He reads in idea units, not word by word.

3. He reads with sufficient volume to be easily heard.

4. He reads distinctly, never slurring ends of words.

5. He uses his voice to transmit emotion, etc.

6. He reads at a suitable rate—neither too fast nor too slow.

7. His reading shows that he wants to hold the interest of his audience. (He exhibits vitality.)

8. He brings out the "sock" words as announcers do. (Gray 1963, 274)

Future Value in Life

1. The ability to read aloud with confidence and fluency in a group

2. To make presentations to a group

3. To give reports of information

4. To give directions for others to follow

5. To present announcements

Oral Reading Checklist

(*NPRG*, 141–142)

References:

Carnine, Douglas, Jerry Silbert and Edward J. Kameenui. 1990. *Direct Instruction Reading*. Columbus, OH: Merrill Publishing Company.

Gray, Lillian. 1963. *Teaching Children To Read*. New York, NY: The Ronald Press Company.

Harris, Theodore L. and Richard E. Hodges. 1995. *The Literary Dictionary*. Newark, DE: International Reading Association.

Assessment and Evaluation

Be diligent to present yourself approved to God,
a worker who does not need to be ashamed, rightly dividing the word of truth.
(2 Timothy 2:15)

Assessment involves determining student strengths and needs as it relates to evaluating instruction and learning. The end result of assessment is to move the student forward and determine the next steps for teaching. Decoding (identifying words) alone is not sufficient for understanding and meaning in the reading process. When reading Bible text, we need more than just a retelling of the story and who the characters are. We want to know, as Routman says, "why characters behave the way they do, what actions lead to other behavior (cause and effect), or infer character's intentions, motivations, and feelings." (Routman 2003, 107) In Principle Approach® methodology, we want to draw the Biblical principles and leading ideas from the text.

Remediation & Enrichment	Applications
Student profile forms can be teacher-generated to organize the particular information the teacher has available to help in the assessment of each student. These may be standardized scores, informal assessments, and observations notes made while working with a student.	See sample form used at StoneBridge School, *NPRG*, 143.

Reading inventory is a method usually used by the classroom teacher to quickly assess students' reading performance. The Ekwall/Shanker Reading Inventory is a set of test instruments that may be used by educators for different purposes. Teachers can group students for instruction and select reading materials for both instructional purposes and students' independent reading. Quick assessment also helps teachers identify those students who may need more thorough diagnosis or referral to a specialist.
 	
Reading specialists to conduct a thorough diagnosis of reading abilities can also use the Ekwall/Shanker. An analysis of the student's performance can provide for prescriptive instruction to remediate reading difficulties. "Pre- and post-testing of oral and silent reading will enable the examiner to measure the student's progress over time." (Ekwall/Shanker 2000, 3) The tests covers pre-primary through ninth grade.
	The Ekwall/Shanker Reading Inventory consists of thirty-eight different tests in ten different areas designed to assess the full range of students' reading abilities. These tests are:
	1. San Diego Quick Assessment or Graded Word List (GWL)
	2. Reading Passages Tests
	  a. Oral Reading
	  b. Silent Reading
	  c. Listening Comprehension
	3. Emergent Literacy Tests
	  • Phonemic Awareness
	4. Basic Sight Vocabulary Tests
	5. Phonics Tests
	6. Structural Analysis Tests
	7. Knowledge of Contractions Test
	8. El Paso Phonics Survey
	9. Quick Word List Survey
	10. Reading Interests Survey

A. Create Individual Student Folders

Prepare a manila folder for each student for the classroom files:

- Standardized tests scores
- Checklists
- Anecdotal records
- Informal reading inventory results
- Personal tape for oral reading

B. Make a Quick Class Survey

At the beginning of the year, the reading teacher needs to do a quick assessment to determine the reading levels of students in the class: all the students take part in reading it.

Combine a quick oral reading survey and a silent comprehension test to locate the students for whom a book is too difficult. The survey not only discloses the children who are not ready for the book, but also indicates if the book is suitable for the majority of the class. This will prevent much frustration as the term proceeds. Normally children are not asked to read aloud material they have not read silently but for test purposes, an exception is made.

1. Quick Oral Reading Survey

a) Each child reads two or three sentences in turn as quickly as he can. Watch for some of the following behaviors:

First, some child may refuse to read. The teacher will say, "All right. Next one, read on."

Or, a child will read with great hesitation and difficulty. To him, the teacher will instantly supply any word that stops him, say "Good," and go on.

b) Since each student reads only a few sentences, there will be little embarrassment.

c) The teacher will have the poor readers identified at once. In addition to oral reading, a comprehension check is necessary.

(Adapted from Harris 1961, 155)

2. Silent Comprehension Check

A quick test on comprehension can also be given for preliminary screening of the pupils unable to get adequate meaning from a particular book. One can choose a short selection (four or five pages) from near the beginning of the book and ask the children to read it silently. As each

pupil finishes, he closes the book and looks up; in this way the slowest readers can easily be spotted. When everyone has finished, the teacher can read a list of questions and the pupils write their answers. For this kind of brief test, short answer questions are generally preferable. The children who are unable to score at or above 70 percent are likely to have difficulty in understanding the book. (Harris 1961, 165)

C. Assess Students

Teachers and parents need to use a variety of means to determine the reading profile of a child. The result from one test at one particular time is not a complete picture of the student's achievement. Multiple indicators that look at the student over time give a more balanced view.

1. Formal Assessment

a) Written tests—may be teacher-generated tests or publisher-generated tests.

b) Standardized tests:
- The results tell how the student compares with his peers but give little information that is useful in the best way to instruct the child.
- The grade equivalent score may overrate the student's reading performance, particularly on tests requiring one word answers or a multiple-choice format. Similarly a timed test may penalize a slow reader.

2. Informal Evaluation

a) Checklists—oral reading, reading rates, skills

b) Anecdotal Records—brief comments of what a child is doing and needs to be doing

c) Reading Records—lists of books read, book reports

d) Informal reading inventory—determine reading proficiency levels: independent, instructional, frustration

e) Interviews and surveys

D. Determine Reading Proficiency Levels

The percentages of determining the three levels vary slightly with reading authorities. The following descriptions of the three levels are based on research by Dr. Harris. (Harris 1961, 59–160)

1. Independent or free—The level at which a student can read independently with good fluency, accuracy, and comprehension. This is the level for library reading or

recreational reading. Errors or miscues are no more than two or three per hundred words. The major parts of the story are easily recalled and details are given when questioned. "The child feels that the selection is easy."

2. Instructional—"Reading is mostly fairly fluent, but slows down or becomes hesitant when word recognition or comprehension difficulties are encountered, and some repetitions and omission may appear." This level is for classroom learning with the teacher giving guidance and support. Recognition and correct pronunciation are at least ninety-five percent and the student can comprehend at least seventy-five percent of the text. "The child's feeling is that the selection is not easy, but that he can handle it."

3. Frustration—The level at which the reading is too difficult. Behaviors usually demonstrated at this level:

a) Dislikes reading

b) Shows anxiety in reading situations

c) Reads orally with poor rhythm and timing

d) Points to words as he reads them

e) Makes poor contributions to classroom discussions

f) Has poor work habits (Botel 1968, 18)
    The student fails to recognize, mispronounces, or refuses to pronounce more than five percent of the running words and shows less than seventy percent comprehension of the text.

E. Grouping
Research Supports Mixed Ability Grouping

• Research supports the advantage of mixed ability grouping at the elementary and secondary levels. "Robert Slavin, who has done a comprehensive analysis of the data available on ability grouping, states that 'every means of grouping students by ability or performance level has drawbacks that may be serious enough to offset any advantages.'" (Routman 1994, 77)

• "Heterogeneous grouping provides opportunities for students of different abilities to work together. Lower-ability students benefit from the enriched vocabulary and oral discussions of quality material. While gifted students offer explanations which often are easier for students to understand than the teacher explanation. Providing for all students to work together creates a "classroom community of learners and promotes the self-esteem of all students." (Slavin 1989, 68, quoted in Routman 1994, 77)

• Types of Grouping
  • Whole-class for guided reading lesson and follow-up discussion; teach skills within the context of the story as the need arises.
  • Small groups for skills and strategies practice: vocabulary, phonics, and word-decoding.
  • Individual for oral and silent reading and writing

1. Whole-class grouping

Whole-class grouping occurs with a core book with enough copies for each student. Including all children in group instruction and discussion gives opportunity for different levels to interact and read books for meaning rather than just decoding words. Routman says discussing vocabulary in the context of the story allows students to "see the relevance of word meanings and [the students] are enabled to read the text more efficiently. That is, when the focus of reading and group time is discussing a book and reacting personally to it, most students—even if they have needed assistance with reading the words—can participate on a high level. The children also showed that when the teacher is gentle, caring, and has high expectations for all students, every student has the opportunity to become a capable reader." (Routman 1994, 73)

In first grade, the guided reading lesson is geared mostly to developing fluency confidence, early reading strategies and to promoting independence. The format may be varied.

a) The period could begin with the teacher reading aloud while the students follow visually in their own copies.

b) The teacher may demonstrate think aloud, verbally describing the thought processes and strategies. The teacher can show how to infer the meaning of a word from context and background experiences.

c) The students may read silently for a specific purpose or read to answer a specific question or to determine the author's purpose.

d) The silent or oral reading is followed by whole-class discussion. (Suggestions from Routman 1994, 40)

2. Small-group work

a) Planned for low-achieving students to teach and reinforce particular skills. Additional practice reading material at their instructional level may be needed. A student is ready to move on when less practice is needed to master a new skill and is ready to answer before the other students.

b) Independent and enrichment activities for high-achieving students can be planned during the small-group work time.

3. Individual, one-on-one

a) Oral reading checklists

b) Informal reading inventory

c) Interviews to determine reading interests, strategies, levels of confidence

d) Writing conferences

F. Year-end

1. Evaluate the progress and make recommendations for the following year.

2. Make summer reading assignments.

3. File the Reading Record Form in the Permanent Folder in the school office.

Reading Proficiency Levels

Levels	Accuracy of Oral Reading	Silent Comprehension
Independent	98%, 2 words wrong out of 100 words	7 or 8 correct out of 8, about 90%
Instructional	95%, 5 words wrong out of 100 words	5 or 6 correct out of 8, about 70%
Frustration	Below 95%	Fewer than 5 out of 8, less than 70%

References:

Botel, Morton. 1968. *How to Teach Reading.* Chicago, IL: Follett Educational Corporation.

Ekwall, Eldon E. and James L. Shanker. 2000. *Ekwall/Shanker Inventory.* Needham Heights, MA: Allyn & Bacon.

Harris, Albert J. 1961. *How To Increase Reading Ability: A Guide to Developmental and Remedial Reading.* New York, NY: David McKay Company.

Routman, Regie. 2003. *Reading Essentials: The Specifics You Need To Teach Reading Well.* Portsmouth, NH: Heinemann. Also citing Slavin, 1989.

Slavin, R. E., Ed. 1989. *School and Classroom Organization.* Hillsdale, NJ: Erlbaum. As quoted in Routman, 2003.

Appendix

Blessed is he that readeth, and they that hear the words of this prophecy,
and keep those things which are written therein: for the time is at hand.

(Revelation 1:3)

Dear Mrs. Shirley,

Thank you so much for thinking of such a program that we can use as a reader instead of using regular textbooks. It helps us to read the Bible more often and really think about it from the questions. Each day it makes me think about how great our God is.

Love,
Luke

Glossary

Ayres's word list*: A list of the most frequently used words compiled by the late Dr. Leonard P. Ayres, (in *The Writing Road to Reading*® by Romalda B. Spalding).

Context clues: The hints about the meaning of an unknown word that are provided in the words, phrases, and sentences that surround the word.

Decoding: The reader's ability to identify a word's pronunciation without always knowing the meaning.

Fluency: The ability of a reader to read a text quickly without errors and with expression.

Graphic organizer: A graphic organizer is a visual representation of knowledge. Graphic organizers facilitate prereading, postreading, writing, reasoning, and discussion of text in all subjects. The graphic organizer is a holistic visual representation of concepts and facts that benefit not only students who are visual learners but also students who are not primarily visual learners. All students need opportunities to develop their ability to learn using all their senses—visual, auditory, kinesthetic, and tactile. In developing graphic organizers there is discussion, problem solving, researching, and organizing.

Mental Actions*: The ways in which the brain processes information.

- **Monitoring comprehension** is checking understanding of words, phrases, sentences to identify unfamiliar words/concepts

- **Making connections** is linking stated information with information already learned to draw conclusions.

- **Making predictions** is forecasting, supporting, and/or revising forecasts using stated information and information already learned.

- **Mentally summarizing** is confirming or deriving the main idea using stated information and information already learned.

- **Reformatting** is reorganizing or categorizing information (oral or written) into new forms, like lists, outlines, clusters, etc. to file or use.

Passage structure*: An organization for different types of writing.

- **Narrative writing** relates an event or a story in first or third person point of view (fiction). The author's purpose is to develop understanding about people and the world. If this is done well it is engaging, absorbing, and may be entertaining.

- **Narrative elements** include character(s), setting, plot, point of view, tone, and style.

- **Informative (expository) writing** explains, informs, or instructs using a series of facts or arguments in a logical sequence (non fiction). It is written in third person point of view. The author's purpose is to inform or explain.

- **Informative elements** include topic, topic sentence, essential information, additional information, and thesis.

- **Informative-narrative writing** combines elements of both narrative and informative writing. It is written in first or third person point of view.

- **Informative-narrative elements** combine elements of both narrative and informative writing (fiction or non-fiction). It is written in first or third person point of view.

Phonemic awareness: The conscious awareness that words are composed of separate sounds and the ability to identify and manipulate those sounds.

Phonic Analysis: Identifying words by their sounds.

Phonics: Instruction in how the sounds of speech are represented by letters and spellings that stresses symbol-sound relationships.

Phonograms: A phonogram is a single letter, or a fixed combination of two, three, or four letters, that is the symbol for one sound in a given word. English has seventy common phonograms that represent the forty-five basic sounds used in speaking.

Sight word: A word that can be recognized immediately as a whole and does not need word analysis for pronunciation.

Structural Analysis: Identifying the parts of the word to better understand the meaning as a whole. Note the root, prefix or suffix, compound, endings, number of syllables. Combine with phonic analysis for pronunciation.

Syllable: The smallest sound unit comprised of a vowel sound or a vowel-consonant combination.

---

* Terms from *The Comprehension Connection: User's Guide with Passage Analyses and Answer Keys,* 1999. Phoenix, AZ: Spalding Education Foundation.

Resources

Adams, Carole G. *The Noah Plan® English Language Curriculum Guide*. Chesapeake, VA: Foundation for American Christian Education, 1997.

Adams, Carole G. and Elizabeth L. Youmans. *The Noah Plan Self-Directed Study in the Principle Approach®*. Chesapeake, VA: Foundation for American Christian Education, 2004.

Adams, Marilyn Jager. *Beginning to Read: Thinking and Learning about Print*. Cambridge, MA: The MIT Press, 2000.

Adams, Marilyn Jager, Barbara R. Foorman, Ingvar Lundberg and Terri Beeler. *Phonemic Awareness in Young Children*. Baltimore, MD: Paul H. Brookes Publishing Co., 1998.

Anderson, Richard C., Elfrieda H. Hiebert, Judith A. Scott, and Ian A. G. Wilkinson. *Becoming a Nation of Readers: The Report of the Commission on Reading*. Champaign, IL: Center for the Study of Reading, University of Illinois at Urbana-Champaign, National Institute of Education, U.S. Department of Education, 1984.

Armbruster, Bonnie B., Fran Lehr, and Jean Osborn. *Put Reading First: The Research Building Blocks for Teaching Children to Read*. Jessup, MD: National Institute for Literacy, 2001.

Barton, Linda G. *Quick Flip Questions for Critical Thinking*, based on Bloom's Taxonomy. Dana Point, CA: Edupress, 1977.

Beers, Gilbert V. *The Early Reader's Bible*. Sisters, OR: Multnomah Publishers, Inc., 1995.

Bennett, William J. *The Book of Virtues*. Riverside, NJ: Simon & Schuster, 1995.

Bennett, William J. *The Children's Book of Virtues*. Riverside, NJ: Simon & Schuster, 1995.

Bishop, Margaret M. *The Complete Reference Book of Phonics and Spelling: The ABC's and All Their Tricks*. Fenton, MI: Mott Media, 1986.

Boning, Richard A. *Getting the Main Idea, Books A–C, Specific Skills Series*. Columbus, OH: SRA/McGraw-Hill, 1997.

Brown, Helen Ada. *Let's Read Together: Books for Family Enjoyment*. Chicago, IL: Association for Library Service to Children, 1956.

Bruno, Bonnie and Carol Reinsma. *The Young Reader's Bible*. Cincinnati, OH: Standex International Corporation, 1994.

Buehl, Doug. *Classroom Strategies for Interactive Learning*. Newark, DE: International Reading Association, 2001.

Carlisle, Joanne. *Reasoning and Reading, Levels 1 & 2*. Cambridge, MA: Educators Publishing Service, 2002.

Carnine, Douglas, Jerry Silbert, and Edward J. Kameenui. *Direct Instruction Reading*. Columbus, OH: Merrill Publishing Company, 1990.

Clark-Edmonds, Sheila. *Sounds Sensible*. 2nd ed. Cambridge, MA: Educators Publishing Service, 2004.

Dickson, John A., Editor. New Analytical Study Bible. John A. Dickson Publishing Company, 1931. Reprinted 1973 Iowa Falls, IA: World Bible Publishers.

Ervin, Jane. *Reading Comprehension in Varied Subject Matter*. Cambridge, MA: Educators Publishing Service, 1980–82.

Estell, Doug, Michele L. Satchwell and Patricia S. Wright. *Reading Lists for College-Bound Students*. Upper Saddle River, NJ: Pearson Education, 1993.

Fry, Edward Bernard, Jacqueline E. Kress and Dona Lee Fountoukidis. *The Reading Teacher's Book of Lists*. 4th ed. Upper Saddle River, NJ: Pearson Education, 2000.

Gospel Light Publications. *Reproducible Maps, Charts, Time Lines and Illustrations*. Ventura, CA: Gospel Light Publications, 1989.

Hall, Susan L. and Louisa C. Moats. *Straight Talk about Reading*. Chicago, IL: Contemporary Books, 1999.

Hall, Verna M. and Rosalie J. Slater. *The Bible and the Constitution of the United States of America*. Chesapeake, VA: Foundation for American Christian Education, 1983.

Hall and Wood, ed. *The Book of Life*. 8 Vols., Chicago, IL: John Rudin & Company, 1923–1952 editions.

Harris, Albert J. *How to Increase Reading Ability: A Guide to Developmental and Remedial Reading*. New York: David McKay Company, 1961.

Hastings, Selina. *The Children's Illustrated Bible*. New York: Dorling Kindersley, Inc., 1994.

Henry, Matthew. *Matthew Henry's Commentary on the Whole Bible*. Peabody, MA: Hendrickson Publishers, Inc., 1991.

Hinson, Bess, ed. *New Directions in Reading Instruction, Revised*. Newark, DE: International Reading Association, 2003.

Hunt, Gladys. *Honey for a Child's Heart*. Grand Rapids, MI: Zondervan, 1989.

Hunt, Gladys and Barbara Hampton. *Read for Your Life: Turning Teens into Readers*. Grand Rapids, MI: Zondervan, 1992.

International Bible Society. The Adventure Bible, New International Version. Grand Rapids, MI: Zondervan Publishing House, 2000.

International Bible Society. Kids' Study Bible, New International Reader's Version. Revised. Grand Rapids, MI: Zondervan Publishing House, 1998.

International Bible Society. The Student Bible, New International Version. Grand Rapids, MI: Zondervan Publishing House, 1996.

Irvin, Judith L. *Reading and the Middle School Student: Strategies to Enhance Literacy*. Boston, MA: Allyn and Bacon, 1990.

Makar, Barbara W. *Primary Phonics*, Sets 1–5. Cambridge, MA: Educators Publishing Service, 1995.

McCall, William A. and Lelah Mae Crabbs. *Standard Test Lessons in Reading*, Books A–E. New York: Teachers College Press, 1961.

McCall, William A. and Mary Lourita Harby. *Test Lessons in Primary Reading*. New York: Teachers College Press, 1965.

McKenna, Michael C. *Help for Struggling Readers: Strategies for Grades 3–8*. New York: The Guilford Press, 2002.

Mears, Henrietta. *What the Bible Is All About*. Ventura, CA: Gospel Light, 1999.

National Reading Panel. *Teaching Children to Read: An Evidence-Based Assessment of the Scientific Research Literature on Reading and Its Implications for Reading Instruction*. National Institute for Literacy, U.S. Deptartment of Health and Human Services. NIH Pub. No. 00-4754, December 2000.

Nelson, Thomas. *Nelson's Complete Book of Bible Maps & Charts*, Nashville, TN: Thomas Nelson, 1993.

Rasinski, Timothy V. et al., ed. *Developing Reading-Writing Connections: Strategies from the Reading Teacher*. Newark, DE: International Reading Association, 2000.

Richardson, Judy S. and Raymond F. Morgan. *Reading to Learn in the Content Areas*. Belmont, CA: Wadsworth Publishing Company, 1997.

Robb, Laura. *Reader's Handbook*. Wilmington, MA: Houghton Mifflin Co., 2004.

Routman, Regie. *Invitations: Changing as Teachers and Learners K–12*. Portsmouth, NH: Heinemann, 1994.

Rudginsky, Laura Toby and Elizabeth C. Haskell. *How to Spell*, Workbooks 1–3. Cambridge, MA: Educators Publishing Service, 1997.

Rudginsky, Laura Toby and Elizabeth C. Haskell. *How to Teach Spelling*. Cambridge, MA: Educators Publishing Service, 1997.

Sadler, Charlotte Rose. *Comprehension Strategies for Middle Grade Learners*. Newark, DE: International Reading Association, 2001.

Science Research Associates. *SRA Reading Laboratory*, Labs 1a, 1b, 1c, and 2a. DeSoto, TX: SRA/McGraw-Hill, 1982.

Shanker, James L. and Eldon E. Ekwall. *Ekwall/Skanker Reading Inventory*. Boston, MA: Allyn and Bacon, 2000.

Slater, Rosalie J. *The Noah Plan® Literature Curriculum Guide*. Chesapeake, VA: Foundation for American Christian Education, 1997.

Slater, Rosalie J. *A Family Program for Reading Aloud*, 2nd Edition. Chesapeake, VA: Foundation for American Christian Education, 1991.

Slater, Rosalie J. *Teaching and Learning America's Christian History: The Principle Approach®*. Chesapeake, VA: Foundation for American Christian Education, 1965.

Spalding Education Foundation. *The Comprehension Connection*, Books A–E. Phoenix, AZ: Spalding Education Foundation, 1999.

Spalding Education International. *Spelling Assessment Manual*. Phoenix, AZ: Spalding Education International, 2003.

Spalding, Romalda. *The Writing Road to Reading: The Spalding Method® for Teaching Speech, Spelling, Writing, and Reading*, (kit or book and set of 70 Phonogram Cards). Phoenix, AZ: Spalding Education International, 2003.

Strong, James. *Strong's Exhaustive Concordance of the Bible*. Nashville, TN: Thomas Nelson Publishers, 1990.

Tyndale House Publishers. Life Application Bible, King James Version. Wheaton, IL: Tyndale House Publishers, Inc., 1989.

Tyndale House Publishers. Student's Life Application Bible, New Living Translation. Wheaton, IL: Tyndale House Publishers, 1997.

Veith, Gene Edward, Jr. *Reading Between the Lines: A Christian Guide to Literature*. Wheaton, IL: Good News Publishers, 1990.

Webster, Noah. *An American Dictionary of the English Language*, 1828 facsimile. Republished, Chesapeake, VA: Foundation for American Christian Education, 1967.

Webster, Noah. *The Value of the Bible and Excellence of the Christian Religion for the Use of Families and Schools*, 1834. Republished, Chesapeake, VA: Foundation for American Christian Education, 1988.

Wilson, Elizabeth. 1987. *Books Children Love: A Guide to the Best Children's Literature*. Wheaton, IL: Good News Publishers.

Forms
(Forms may be duplicated for classroom use.)

THE BIBLE AS READER (BAR) COORDINATION WITH BIBLE OVERVIEW

Grade _____ Grade Level Principle _____

Teacher_____ Date _____

Bible Reader _____

Notebook Tabs_____

Week	Quarter I	Quarter II	Quarter III	Quarter IV
1				
2				
3				
4				
5				
6				
7				
8				
9				

Cause & Effect Organizer

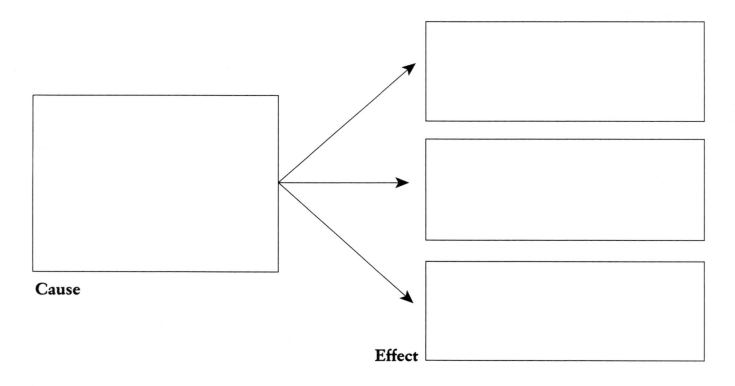

Cause

Effect

Venn Diagram

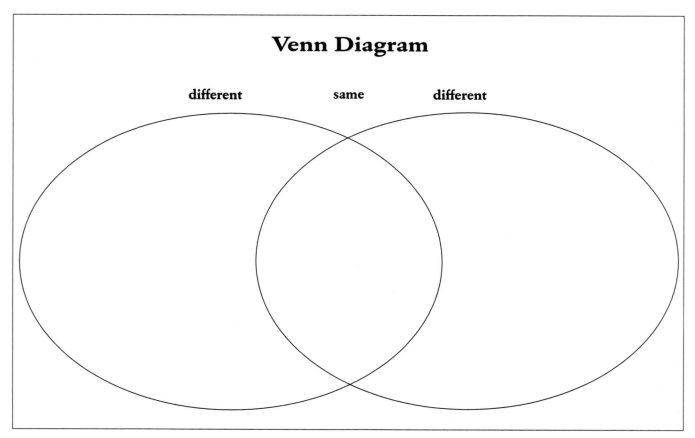

Concept/Definition Map

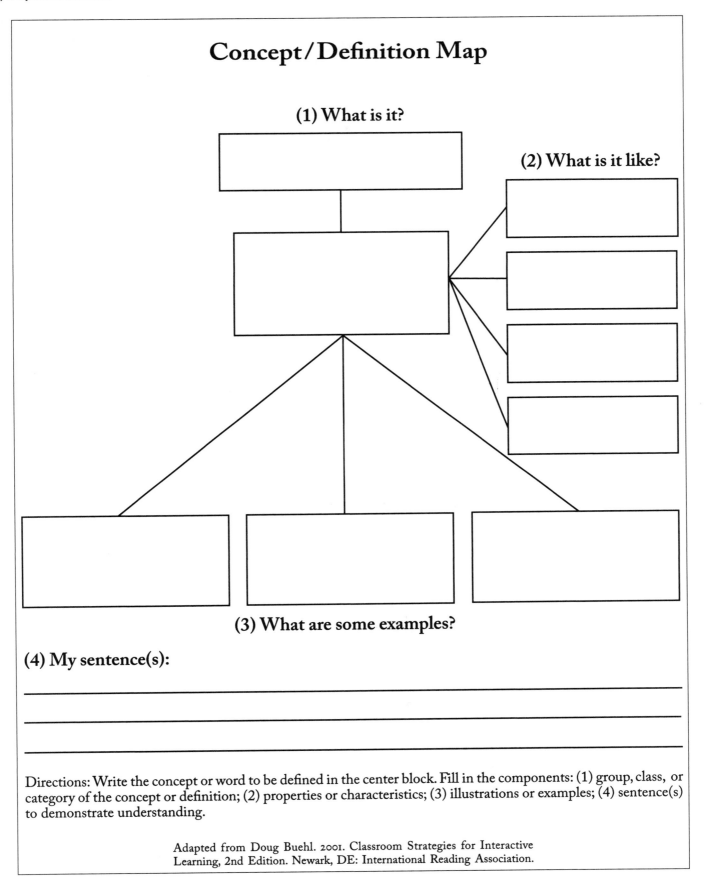

(1) What is it?

(2) What is it like?

(3) What are some examples?

(4) My sentence(s):

_____

_____

_____

Directions: Write the concept or word to be defined in the center block. Fill in the components: (1) group, class, or category of the concept or definition; (2) properties or characteristics; (3) illustrations or examples; (4) sentence(s) to demonstrate understanding.

Adapted from Doug Buehl. 2001. Classroom Strategies for Interactive Learning, 2nd Edition. Newark, DE: International Reading Association.

K What I *Know*	W What I *Want* to Learn	L What I Have *Learned*

People Who Impacted History:

Providential Setting	Spheres of Influence	Character	Contributions

Student: _____   Teacher: _____

Class: _____   Grade: _____

Date: _____

Story Map

Title: _____

Setting: _____

Characters: _____

Problem(s):

_____

_____

_____

_____

Event(s):

_____

_____

_____

_____

_____

_____

_____

Solution(s):

_____

_____

_____

Biblical Principle(s):

_____

_____

_____

T-chart

Sequence Chain

Title

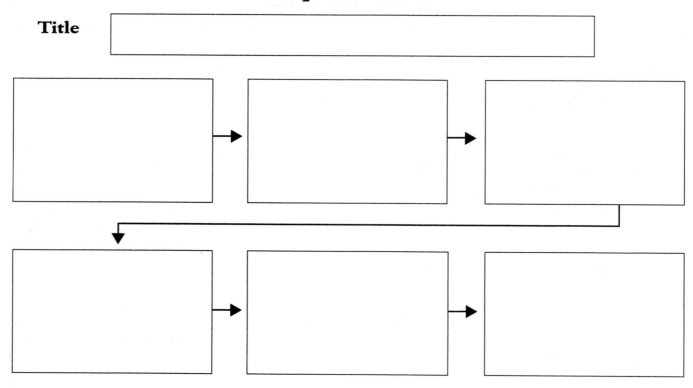

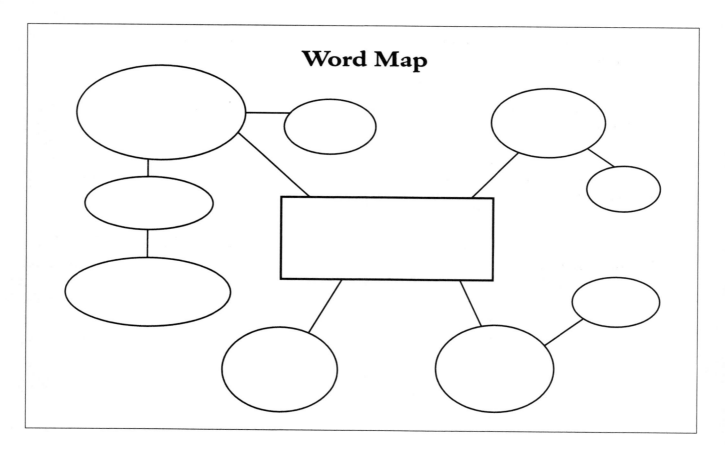

Word Map

Vocabulary Word Analysis

_ _ _ _ _ _ _ _ _ _ _ _ _

1. **Part of Speech:**	
2. **Etymology** (root meanings and original languages):	
3. **Definition:**	
4. **Other meanings:**	
5. **Synonym:**	
6. **Antonym:**	
7. **Homonym:**	
8. **Write a sentence using the word:**	

Name _____ Date _____

Three Types of Passage Structures

Elements	Narrative	Informative	Informative-Narrative
Characters			
Plot			
Setting			
Point of View			
Theme			
Tone			
Style			
Topic			
Topic Sentence			
Information			
Concluding Sentence			
Author's Purpose			

Teacher Key to the Writing Process Using
Three Types of Passage Structures

Elements	Narrative	Informative	Informative-Narrative
Characters	✓		✓
Plot	✓		✓
Setting	✓		✓
Point of View	1st & 3rd person	3rd person	1st & 3rd person
Theme	✓		
Tone	✓		
Style	✓		
Topic		✓	✓
Topic Sentence		✓	
Information		✓	✓
Concluding Sentence		✓	
Author's Purpose	To entertain / develop understanding	To inform / explain	To inform in an interesting way

Reciprocal Teaching

Name _____ Date _____

Passage:

Predict

Question

Clarify

Summarize

Sample Teacher Key

Reciprocal Teaching

Passage: Romans 12:9–21

(Read your assigned passage of Scripture.)

(Use the Bible subtitle to predict what information will be in the passage.)

Predict   What does, "behave like a Christian" mean?

(Compile some open-ended questions from your reading. Construct well-written sentences. Watch your spelling.)

Question   In these verses, how does it say we should live?

How, and in what verse, does it give an example of this way of life?

How does the widow in 1 Kings 17:10–11 obey Romans 12:20?

How are we to we to treat God's people when they're in a time of need?

(Review your Scripture verses. What thing might need some clarification? Write your answers in the form of a question.)

Clarify   What does the word "conceited" mean?

What is "God's wrath"?

(Compose a summary of your reading.)

Summarize   These verses are telling us that we need to treat people as we would ourselves. We should not take revenge on those who have done evil to us; instead we need to let God do it Himself.

(Without reading ahead, what do you predict Paul might write next.)   **Passage:** Romans 13:1–7

Predict   I think that Paul might write about how Jesus was not taking revenge on everyone who did Him wrong. He also might write about times when Jesus was comforting people when they were in times of mourning.

The Scholars Reading Lesson Plan

Teacher_____ Grade_____ Qtr_____ Week_____

TITLE AND AUTHOR:

SOURCE:

SELECTION:

IMPORTANT IDEA:

LEADING QUESTIONS:

APT EXPRESSIONS:

VOCABULARY AND DEFINITIONS:

EVALUATION OF LESSON EFFECTIVENESS:

THE NOAH PLAN® © 2005 • FOUNDATION FOR AMERICAN CHRISTIAN EDUCATION

Supplementary Reading

Reading Assignment

_____
Name

Date	Assignment	Parent's Initials

Date	Assignment	Parent's Initials

Bookworms Club

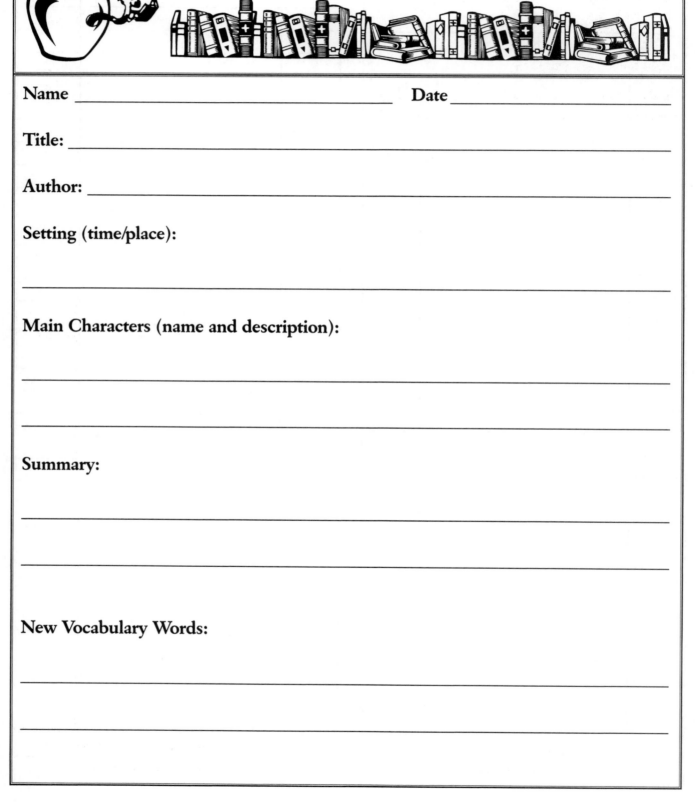

Name _____ **Date** _____

Title: _____

Author: _____

Setting (time/place):

_____

Main Characters (name and description):

_____

_____

Summary:

_____

_____

New Vocabulary Words:

_____

_____

Summer Reading

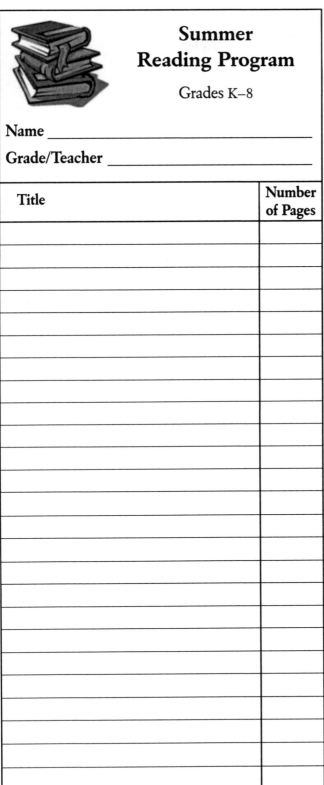

Summer Reading Program

Grades K–8

Name _____

Grade/Teacher _____

Title	Number of Pages

Return bookmark in September
(Read a minimum of three quality books.)

Title	Number of Pages

Return bookmark in September
(Read a minimum of three quality books.)

Individual Reading Progress Record of

Last Name   First Name   Birthdate

School Year	Name of Book	Publisher	Grade	Teacher	Date Given	Completed	Outside Books Read	Comments

Oral Reading Assessment

Student _____ Homeroom Teacher _____ Reading Teacher _____ Grade _____

	Date /Score	Quarter 1 Notes	✓	Quarter 2 Notes	✓	Quarter 3 Notes	✓	Quarter 4 Notes
Fluency								
Good phrasing								
Correct enunciation								
Reads without hesitations								
Maintains place								
No repetitions of words or phrases								
Notes punctuation								
Good expression								
Word Recognition								
No errors on small words								
No hesitations								
No omissions								
No substitutions								
No gross mispronunciation								
Voice								
Correct enunciation								
Correct volume and intonation								
Natural intonation/not strained								
Posture								
Follows with eyes/limited head movement								
Correct posture								
Reading Rate (100 word passage)								

Additional Comments

Rating Scale: 5–6 Mastery   3–4 Good   1–2 Fair   0 Poor   ☐ I–Independent   ☐ S–Instructional   ☐ F–Frustration   Divide totals by number of items checked to determine an overall total.

Basic Sight Word Assessment
The Dolch Basic Sight Words

The Dolch basic sight words are the 220 words prepared by Edward William Dolch, Ph.D in his book, *Problems in Reading*, the Garrard Press, Champaign, IL, 1948. The words are generally known as *Dolch Words, high-frequency words*, or *sight words*. A newer set of "instant words" determined by Fry, Kress, and Fountoukidis in *The Reading Teacher's Book of Lists*, is grouped according to frequency order.

A *sight word* is a word that is immediately recognized as a whole and does not require word analysis for recognition. The sight words are service words comprising 50 to 75% of the reading material at primary levels. These words are usually learned in first and second grade and provide a base for fluent reading and comprehension. Sight word lessons should include word recognition practice with word cards, reading booklets with controlled vocabulary, and writing and tracing exercises. Matching games or bingo-type games can be used to practice the words.

Scoring Scale: The following scale can be used to estimate a child's reading level using the 220 Dolch Basic Sight Words.

Sight Words Known	Estimated Reading Level
0–75	Pre-primer
76–120	Primer
121–170	First year
171–210	Second or above
Above 210	Third and above

Basic Sight Word Test

Test using the Dolch basic word list. The words should be known instantly without the use of word attack skills. If the student hesitates longer than one second before pronouncing a word, then count it wrong.

Marking Directions:

1. If a word is called correctly, make no mark.
2. If a word is miscalled then corrected, write C and what he called at first.
3. If a word is miscalled but not corrected, write the child's pronunciation above it.
4. If a child makes pertinent comments about a word, it is wise to write in the margin.
5. If child "spells out," mark above the word what he spells.
6. If a child tries to sound out a word, mark it as he sounds out, for example—b-b-boy.

Scoring: The child's score on the test is the number of words called correctly.

Analysis: The test errors may be analyzed for types of mistakes, although sometimes there isn't a recognizable pattern.

1. Configuration: mother/another
2. Wrong start: black/back
3. Wrong middle: may/my; pan/pin
4. Wrong ending: carry/call; back/bank
5. Reversals: stop/spot; was/saw
6. Completely wrong, guesses: always/often

The test should be carefully dated so that progress can be charted.

Resource: The list of 220 words is readily available online at www.english-zone.com/reading/dolch.html, www.literacyconnections.com/Dolch1.html or a local teacher/parent store.

Student Profile for Reading

Student _____ Birthdate _____

Parents _____ Phone (h) _____ (cell/work) _____

Address _____

OLSAT SCHOOL ABILITY

	Total	Verbal	Non-Verbal
Grade ____ Age ____ Date _____ School Ability Index	_____	_____	_____
Age/%/Stanine	_____	_____	_____
Grade ____ Age ____ Date _____ SAI	_____	_____	_____
A/PR/S	_____	_____	_____
Grade ____ Age ____ Date _____ SAI	_____	_____	_____
A/PR/S	_____	_____	_____

STANFORD SCHOOL ACHIEVEMENT

Grade _____ _____ _____ _____ _____ _____ _____

Total Reading						
Percentile Rank						
Stanine						
Grade Equivalent						
Reading Vocabulary						
PR						
S						
GE						
Reading Comprehension						
PR						
S						
GE						
Language						
PR						
S						
GE						
Spelling						
PR						
S						
GE						

Additional Scores

Informal Reading Assessments:

STRENGTHS: NEEDS:

GOALS:

Kaitlin's Psalm 23

Thank you God for being my Shepherd. It makes me feel Wonderful !!!

God takes care of me.

Thank you, Lord for restoring my soul and making me be still.

Thank You for leading me in the paths of righteousness.

Thank You, Lord for helping me to not be afraid when I am very close to You.

Thank you for turning me away from danger.

Thank you for preparing the manna from heaven.

Thank you for anointing me.

Thank you for filling me

with goodness and mercy.

23rd PSALM

The Lord is my SHEPHERD; I shall not want.

Shepherd, Jehovah-Raah
_____
GOD'S NAME

Guide, Provide, Correct, Protects
_____
GOD'S CHARACTER

We can have Confidence in our God's Grace and care.
THE PRINCIPLE

Thank you God for being my Shepherd.
It makes me feel Wonderful!!!

Kaitlin J., 2nd Grade

Readers Theatre Activity—*Original Script by a Fifth Grader*

Job   Brittany S.
Bible / Ms. Shirley   October 3, 2000

God and Satan

Scene 1: God and Satan talking

God: (yawn) "Well, Satan, how are you this fine and lovely morning?"

Satan: (in an angry voice) "Fine, just fine!"

God: "My, my, my, looks like someone woke up on the wrong side of the bed today?"

Satan: (in grumpy voice) "Okay, maybe I did wake up on the wrong side of the bed."

God: "And why might that be?"

Satan: "Well, you know that Job fella? Well, he just keeps trusting you no matter what."

God: (says it smiling) "Well, I guess you are right, not to be bragging or anything, but I do think that he trusts me a lot, well, least more than anyone would trust you."

Satan: "Yeah, well, he does trust you way too much."

God: "Well, I wouldn't say that, somebody can never trust me too much."

Satan: "Yeah, well I bet ya that there will be people that will trust me as much as they trust you."

God: "Satan, haven't you learned yet that there is nothing to trust about you, and a lot of people know it?"

Satan: "Well, no you don't know that because you have never done something to 'one of my followers' like I did to Job."

God: "I don't have to because I am God, I know everything."

Satan: (sarcastically) "Gee, thanks for rubbing it in. I can't tell you how much I appreciate it."

God: "No, I did not mean it like that."

Satan: "Well, thanks for chit chatting with me, but I gotta run and break a sweat."

God: (in a whisper) "Like you don't already."

Nancy pioneered the Bible as Reader Program at StoneBridge School, the national demonstration school for the Foundation for American Christian Education. For two years she never flagged in her commitment and enthusiasm in helping to develop the pilot program in her fourth grade class and in working with this author to make this guide user-friendly for the classroom teacher. She was amazed to see how the students began to apply what they were learning in class to their individual lives.   (Author)

Teacher Testimonies

The Bible as Reader program has been an invaluable blessing to our school. The children are learning to reason Biblically as they explore the Word of God for themselves. They have a joy and excitement each time they start a new book.

Here are a few comments from some of my students:

> The Bible is so great. If you have any problem you can just read the Bible and that problem will vanish. The Bible is like a map that guides us through life. It also has wonderful stories to fit our moods. I think we should all read the Bible and live our lives for God.   (Ian W.)

> I think that using a Bible as a reader is a great idea. When you are reading a Bible and you are in a very exciting part you can't stop reading so you learn more and more about God, Jesus, and His Holy Word. It is very fascinating how more and more people are turning into Christians. That is what I think the Bible is all about.   (Adie H.)

These are just a few comments that indicate how much the Bible as Reader program is changing the lives of our children. They are learning to think governmentally, to reason from cause to effect, to relate what they are learning to their lives, and to see firsthand the wonders of God as they read the old familiar stories for themselves. This program challenges them to new depths of comprehension and also works on enriching their vocabulary. It has been a blessing in my life and I look forward to hearing how it has affected yours as well.   (Nancy Hameloth, Fourth Grade Teacher)

Using the Bible as Reader program in the classroom is exciting. It is very rewarding to help children to become confident readers using the truth of the Bible as the standard by which they learn. The students not only develop excellent comprehension, reasoning, and writing skills, but they also develop a Biblical worldview and Christian character as they handle God's Word. I highly recommend the BAR program to anyone interested in helping his students become as God has planned for them to be.
                                                                          (Peg Ricks, Second Grade Teacher)